HOMOSEXUALITY

*Catholic Teaching
and
Pastoral Practice*

by
Gerald D. Coleman, S.S.

Paulist Press
New York/Mahwah

Cover design by Tim McKeen

Copyright © 1995 by Gerald D. Coleman, S.S.

Imprimatur: Most Reverend John R. Quinn, D.D.
          Archbishop of San Francisco

Nihil Obstat: Reverend Robert W. McElroy, S.T.D.

Library of Congress Cataloging-in-Publication Data

Coleman, Gerald D.
  Homosexuality : Catholic teaching and pastoral practice / by Gerald D. Coleman.
    p.   cm.
  Includes bibliographical references.
  ISBN 0-8091-3605-8 (alk. paper)
    1. Homosexuality—Religious aspects—Catholic Church. 2. Gays—Pastoral counseling of. 3. Catholic Church—Doctrines. 4. Gays—Religious life. I. Title
BX1795.H66C65 1996   95-45756
261.835766´08822—dc20   CIP

Published by Paulist Press
997 Macarthur Boulevard
Mahwah, NJ 07430

Printed and bound in the
United States of America

TABLE OF CONTENTS

Foreword

by
Cardinal Roger Mahony
Archbishop of Los Angeles

In 1986 I established in the Archdiocese of Los Angeles a pastoral ministry program for homosexual Catholics, expressing the concern the bishops of the United States made in 1976 that homosexuals "...like everyone else, should not suffer from prejudice against their basic human rights. They have a right to respect, friendship and justice. They should have an active role in the Christian community" (*To Live in Christ Jesus*, n 52).

In the Archdiocese of Los Angeles, as well as many other dioceses across the United States, such ministry programs are rooted in the belief that the church bears a responsibility to minister to homosexual persons with a calm and prayerful concern, remembering always the compassion of Jesus toward all those who are struggling to find the kingdom of God.

It is a core tenet of pastoral ministry programs for homosexual people that lesbian and gay persons are capable of living a full Catholic life in union with all the members of the church. The church regrets the distance and alienation experienced by many homosexual people. It is for this reason that I wrote in 1986 that pastoral ministry to homosexual persons must have as its primary goal "to foster a spirit of community and fellowship among gay Catholics so that they can offer and receive mutual support in living out their lives of faith within the Church."

I am reminded of a distinction by Gabriel Marcel between a puzzle and a mystery—a distinction cited in a 1989 article in *America* magazine about Catholic leadership. A puzzle is a problem that has one best solution that awaits only a mind keen enough to find the missing piece. When we deal with puzzles we are dispassionate and use criteria of efficiency that make a single best answer seem unarguable to all rational "puzzle-solvers."

On the other hand, a mystery involves not merely efficiency but ultimate questions about how we are to live and believe. When we deal with mysteries we are passionately concerned and seek responsible responses. For a mystery, being right means being wise. While both are difficult, it is easier to be smart than to be wise.

Pope Paul VI wrote that authentic dialogue sustains the spirit of "meekness": it is not proud, bitter or offensive; it is peaceful and avoids violent methods; it is patient and generous. He concluded: "The dialogue will make us wise."

In dealing with the complex issues surrounding homosexuality, it is very easy to give simple and at times caustic answers. It is much more difficult—but rewarding—to travel the journey of wisdom in order to foster a panorama of truth, objectivity and honest sensitivity to human needs and aspirations.

In this comprehensive book on homosexuality, Father Gerald D. Coleman, S.S. tackles an enormously difficult terrain, a journey with many possible pitfalls and dangerous twists in the road.

He pursues this journey with incomparable balance and good judgment, a "Pastoral Journey Toward the Truth," as the Introduction indicates, that is clearly rooted in the church's teachings and authentic pastoral ministry, while making this excursion lucid, candid, truthful and always hopeful.

Father Coleman places his discussion of homosexuality within the context of Pope John Paul II's *Veritatis Splendor*. This 1993 encyclical letter demonstrates that God is the fixed and basic point of reference for all morality. We are moral because of the deep conviction that God is good, and we who are created in God's likeness bear an exigency toward this good, this truth. Consequently, morality is not authorized by social convention, self-interest, or self-fulfillment. The moral life is always a response to God. We are moral to the extent that we mirror forth in our lives the person of Jesus, the One who perfectly interiorizes the presence of God.

Homosexuality: Catholic Teaching and Pastoral Practice consistently displays a reverence for the complexity of this issue, but a respect that is "wise," grounded in the church's authentic wisdom about the meaning of morality, and here specifically about the meaning of sexual morality. On a subject as difficult and at times as controverted as homosexuality, one does not always find the calm and the balance seen in this book.

In a 1993 interview with *America* executive editor Thomas H.

Stahel, *New Republic* editor Andrew Sullivan, who is a gay man and Catholic, made this point: "Undoubtedly the very fact of my existence at some level, in the public area, has provoked and prompted an enormous number of letters and an enormous amount of interest from people in exactly the same position...who want desperately to have a life that can be spiritually and morally whole. The church as presently constituted refuses to grapple with this desire...."

This book on homosexuality stands as a clear and sharp statement that Sullivan's claim is untrue. The Catholic Church does struggle with the desire of homosexual persons to be both spiritual and morally whole and Father Coleman kaleidoscopes in varied ways the map of the church's authentic care for homosexual people that provides a solid and peaceful ground for spiritual and moral maturation.

This is not an easy book. Father Coleman treats clearly and unambiguously the magisterium's teachings on this subject—and these principles cause some to turn away with anger and disappointment. The Church's pastoral ministry cannot be isolated or separated from her authentic teachings rooted in the life and teachings of Jesus. At the same time, the church's teachings need not be burdensome but can be a true challenge toward further growth and integrity for a Christian sexual person, one who struggles to better mirror forth the face of Jesus, to be good as God is good.

When readers complete this book, they will find an attitude toward homosexual women and men that is true, honest, deeply respectful and grounded in fine scholarship and research. Fr. Coleman convincingly underscores the church's helpful teaching in the 1986 *Letter to the Bishops of the Catholic Church on the Pastoral Care of Homosexual Persons* from the Congregation for the Doctrine of the Faith:

> The human person, made in the image and likeness of God, can hardly be adequately described by a reductionist reference to his or her sexual orientation. Everyone living on the face of the earth has personal problems and difficulties, but challenges to growth, strength, talents and gifts as well. Today, the Church provides a badly needed context for the care of the human person when she refuses to consider the person as a "heterosexual" or a "homosexual" and insists that every person has a fundamental identity: a creature of God, and by grace, His child and heir to eternal life (n 16).

Introduction

A PASTORAL JOURNEY TOWARD THE TRUTH

This book addresses a complex, sensitive and at times volatile question. Homosexuality is often one of those "test cases"[1] which raises multiple responses and an array of reactions. One writer has commented that, "In the 1990s homosexuality will be what the abortion issue has been in the 1980s." This book thus sets out on a perilous journey—mainly due to the fervent beliefs of numerous people on this subject.

A book about homosexuality is also and inevitably a volume about homosexual people who represent, in a phrase used by James and Evelyn Whitehead, a "vulnerable part of the body Christian."[2] Because so many homosexual people are indeed vulnerable, lonely, ostracized and angry, I do not approach this task lightly and certainly not without trepidation.

We all come to this subject not only with opinions or convictions but with deep levels of emotional response—far beyond the rational. My primary method will be to present information as clearly as possible on each of the subjects addressed; to raise important questions; and to do all of this within the context of the church's teachings, presuppositions and viewpoints regarding love and the question of human sexuality. I am profoundly aware that not all of the questions about homosexuality have clear and immediate responses. At the same time, I am conscious of the fact that over the centuries the church has taught and still teaches important parameters that color the landscape of human sexuality. Lisa Sowle Cahill has rightly remarked, "The horizon against which all moral activity is to be evaluated is the communal life as body of Christ in the world."[3]

In the encyclical letter of Pope John Paul II, *Veritatis Splendor,*[4] certain parameters are set out for properly interpreting church teaching on moral matters. As I commence this book on concerns about homosexuality and homosexual people, it is helpful to me and for the reader to outline some critical areas of importance in the encyclical:

1

1. This book embarks on a pastoral journey toward the truth. *Veritatis Splendor* speaks of such a journey (n 31) but emphasizes that the "respect due to the journey of conscience" of every person should not be such that personal freedom becomes an absolute and thus the sole criterion for values. As the encyclical teaches, personal sincerity, authenticity and "being at peace with oneself" can never substitute for truth (n 32). As we strive to help ourselves and others to form right judgments, then, we can never blur or compromise the church's authentic teachings on homosexuality and homosexuality activity. *Veritatis Splendor* explains:

> This is so not only because freedom of conscience is never freedom "from" the truth but always and only freedom "in" the truth, but also because the Magisterium does not bring to the Christian conscience truths which are extraneous to it....The Church puts herself always and only at the *service of conscience*...helping it not to swerve from the truth about the good of men, but rather, especially in more difficult questions, to attain the truth with certainty and to abide in it (n 64).

A fundamental task of this book, then, is to present the church's teachings clearly in order to endorse rather than hinder true personal freedom.

2. The human person cannot be reduced to a freedom which is self-designing (n 18). Respecting persons can never imply using them as means, but rather respecting certain fundamental goods—one of which is the unity and inseparability of body and soul (nn 49–50). Consequently, homosexual genital activity—no matter how sincerely intended or contextualized—can never be evaluated as distinct from its effect on one's whole person, one's soul. All human acts bear anthropological and ontological consequences.

3. A "pastoral journey" through the difficult questions surrounding homosexuality cannot endorse or advocate pastoral solutions which contradict or conflict with the church's moral norms, as such solutions are *de facto* destructive of authentic human freedom and dignity. It is pastorally wrong and inappropriate to suggest, then, a type of double standard or "double status" (n 56) which sets forth the church's moral teaching on one level, but because of circumstances

and situations, permits immoral acts on the existential level, allowing one to do in practice and in good conscience what is an intrinsically evil act. The encyclical specifically warns against this type of split pedagogy:

> A separation, or even an opposition, is thus established in some cases between the teaching of the precept, which is valid in general, and the norm of the individual conscience, which would in fact make the final decision about what is good and what is evil. On this basis, an attempt is made to legitimize so-called "pastoral" solutions contrary to the teaching of the Magisterium, and to justify a "creative" hermeneutic according to which the moral conscience is in no way obliged, in every case, by a particular negative precept (n 56).

This point does not contradict the church's traditional teaching about the relationship between objective wrong and subjective culpability, but it does raise up the importance of avoiding pastoral solutions that are in direct contradiction to the church's authentic teaching.

Having now outlined the parameters that will guide this book, an important question needs to be addressed: If this subject is so volatile, why tackle such a work?

In February, 1993, I gave a presentation at the Los Angeles Religious Education Congress on pastoral questions relating to homosexuality. I was overwhelmed by the fact that two thousand people registered for this workshop. The presence of so many people, along with their obvious attentiveness and subsequent seriousness of comments and questions, indicated to me that the question of homosexuality is an important moral and pastoral one in today's church. In addition, I have had pastoral relationships with Christians of homosexual orientation. I have prayed, thought and read a great deal on the issue; but my learning began as I listened to and observed and loved particular people for whom this is not just an issue but a personal reality.

Let me begin, then, with this question: What is your mental image of homosexual people?[5] When I say *homosexual person*, what kind of individual comes to mind? The militant activist, wearing leather, screaming obscenities? Someone looking for partners in a park or public restroom? A child molester? Flamboyantly effeminate men? Mean-looking women? If so, your image needs revising. These types are out there—and we have seen them at protests and in parades. But these people I do not know personally. The people I have met of homosexual orientation look just like heterosexual people. They lead ordinary lives, have the same concerns that everyone else has, and are not out to molest or seduce anyone. They work, they go to church, they pray, they love their families. If you do not know this, you need to: most homosexual people are what you would call ordinary people. There is a sexual aspect to their lives, but as with most of us, it is not the main part of who they/we are. It is thus not insignificant that the *Letter to the Bishops of the Catholic Church on the Pastoral Care of Homosexual Persons* of the Congregation for the Doctrine of the Faith teaches that "The human person, made in the image and likeness of God, can hardly be adequately described by a reductionist reference to his or her sexual orientation."[6]

The word *homosexual* is "fundamentally" an adjective which defines only one aspect of a person. No matter what value judgments are to be placed on homosexual orientation or behavior, we start here: we are speaking of authentic human beings who are like all other human beings.

As I will point out, statistics regarding homosexual persons are quite contradictory. The Kinsey Report indicated that about ten percent of the population is homosexual. A recent study[7] claims that it is closer to one percent. In all likelihood, both studies are flawed. The numbers are somewhere in between. Part of the difficulty is that a great many people in varying degrees have had inclinations and/or behaviors that are both heterosexual and homosexual: i.e., there is a broad continuum of heterosexual and homosexual inclinations. There are people who have never had a sexual *thought* in their lives that involved their own gender. There are other people who have never had a sexual thought in their lives that involved the opposite gender. In the middle there are a great many people who have had on some occasion a sexual fantasy about someone of their own sex.

What about the issue of choice? Do people take up homosexual ways by choice? Some do. Some are experimenters, sexual adventurers, who turn to homosexuality as a type of recreation. Others are profoundly lonely people, longing for someone to love them; and unable to find anyone of the opposite sex who will, they turn for comfort to someone of their own sex.

There are other people, for physiological reasons we are only beginning to understand, who are from their earliest recollections drawn exclusively toward love of their own sex (homophilia). I have known such people, and it is wrong to apply to them the phrase: "sexual preference." For them, it is not a preference. With them we speak of "definitive homosexuality" or "homosexual orientation."

Clearly there are a number of misconceptions about homosexuality that must be clarified:

1. It is false to assert that all people who experience attraction to someone of their own sex are definitive homosexual persons. As already pointed out, there is a broad continuum of heterosexual and/or homosexual predispositions, feelings and behaviors. We live in a culture which is overwhelmingly obsessed with sex and also has an oversimplified view of heterosexuality/homosexuality. For example, a young woman has a sexual fantasy about another woman and leaps to the conclusion: "I must be a lesbian woman." A young man forms a deep, emotional bond with another man and finds himself with certain sexual feelings and thinks, "I'm a gay man." This can be a false presumption and it can become a source of terrible confusion and anxiety especially in many who are young and sometimes leads them to tragic choices.

I offer this pastoral word especially to the young: If you experience a sexual attraction to someone of your own sex, do not leap to the conclusion that you are now defined as a homosexual person. Do not allow anyone to "force you out of the closet." Do not act on your sexual feelings. Do not panic over them. Talk to some adult you can trust in order to sort out and understand these feelings. Discerning one's basic sexual orientation is a longer, more complex process.

2. It is false to conclude that all homosexual persons choose their orientation or could choose to change their orientation. There is a growing body of evidence that definitive homosexuality is biologically determined: i.e., there are some people who may well be born with a fixed orientation toward homosexuality. They do not choose their desire any more than heterosexual people choose theirs.

3. It is false to claim that parents are somehow to blame for the homosexuality of their children. Some followers of Sigmund Freud

observed that many homosexual men have domineering mothers and passive, weak, emotionally absent fathers. There may well be family factors in the complexity of homosexuality. There are certainly cases where sexual abuse in the home has led to what is called situational homosexuality. However, if definitive homosexuality is biologically determined, it is no one's "fault." We now realize, for example, that the frequent instance of emotional distance in a father of a homosexual young man might well be the result of perceived homosexuality. The boy is different and the father does not know how to relate, so he withdraws, and perhaps the mother steps in to compensate. If you have a son or daughter who sustains a homosexual orientation, I have this pastoral word for you: It is not your fault. It is not your son or daughter's fault. It is a mystery. For the most part, homosexuality simply happens.

4. It is false to claim that all homosexual persons are promiscuous. This simply is not true. It is true that in the United States and elsewhere there is a rather promiscuous gay and lesbian subculture. Multiple partners and one-night stands are, for some, the rule. Many in this group have sex with hundreds of people, perhaps a thousand in a life-time. This subculture is disturbing, exploitive, and lewd, and its representatives are the ones who are too often highlighted by the media in Gay Pride Parades.

My point: Many people have singled out the more extreme members of a subculture and conclude that these represent all or even most homosexual persons. And all of this gets labeled "The Gay Life-style." There are many homosexual men and women who have nothing to do with this "life-style," and are as appalled by it as anyone else. To take the crowd who have sunk to the lowest level and lump all homosexual people into that picture is simply wrong. It is something on the order of saying: "Let me show you what heterosexuals are like," and point to the raunchiest of swinging singles bars. In his book *Is It A Choice?*[8] Eric Marcus writes about this so-called "gay life style":

> Not long ago, just after moving back to New York, a woman friend of mine told me that she was worried I'd go out and lead a wild "gay life style." I don't know how many times I've said there is no such thing as a "gay life

style," wild or otherwise, but I knew exactly what my friend was talking about....

As hard as it might be to believe, there is no such thing as a "gay life style," just as there is no such thing as a heterosexual life style. Gay and lesbian people, like heterosexual people, live in a variety of ways, from poor to middle-class to nouveau riche, from urban to rural.[9]

James B. Nelson[10] has outlined four classical ways that heterosexual people respond to homosexual people:

1. The first level of response is: Rejecting-Punitive. The person who holds this stance unconditionally rejects homosexuality as in any way legitimate and, at the same time, bears a punitive attitude toward gay and lesbian persons. For many centuries stoning, burning, sexual mutilation, and the death penalty were fairly common treatments for discovered homosexual people—an example of the rejecting-punitive motif. This attitude is rooted in familiar stereotypes: all lesbian women are tough and all gay men effeminate; homosexual persons are compulsive and sex-hungry; they are by nature promiscuous; gay men have an inherent tendency toward child molestation.

2. The second level is: Rejecting-Nonpunitive. Homosexuality is viewed as being always wrong, but homosexual persons can be treated with forgiving grace. In *Church Dogmatics*, Karl Barth represents this motif well: Homosexual activity is unnatural and violates the command of the creator. However, the central theme of the gospel is God's overwhelming grace in Jesus Christ. *Homosexual acts* must be condemned, but in light of grace the homosexual person must not.[11] Others argue in this motif that human dignity is threatened by gay/lesbian relationships. Homosexuality is an illness comparable to alcoholism, and sheer acceptance of it would have "implications for our view of marriage, the limitations appropriate to sexual activity, the raising of children, and the structure of the family."[12] This view equates, according to Nelson, an aversion to homosexual activity with an aversion to persons and thus maintains that homosexuality is idolatrous because it is basically self-worship and narcissistic: the gay person is simply loving in the other the reflection of the self.

Nelson seems to be using this "level of response" as characteristic of the position of the Catholic Church. I think this is a false assumption which tends to misrepresent the nuanced complexity of Catholic teaching. As we will see, the church does not condemn the homosexual orientation, but does still hold that our attitudes and assumptions about homosexuality must be such that we do not equate homosexuality with heterosexuality. In the church's teaching, hetero-sexuality is normative and genital activity is legitimate only in the context of heterosexual marriage.

3. The third position is: Qualified Acceptance. Here one takes the view that homosexuality is tolerable *if* it is irreversible and if a relationship is monogamous. Here one is troubled by homosexual behavior but views the stable, faithful homosexual relationship as a lesser evil than a homosexuality that is promiscuous. Helmut Thielicke argues, for example, that some homosexual persons "because of their vitality" are not able to practice abstinence. If this is the case, they should structure their sexual relationships "in an ethi-cally responsible way" (adult, fully-committed relationships). They should make the best of their painful situations without idealizing them or pretending that they are normal.[13]

4. The fourth level of response is: Full Acceptance. This view places homosexuality on a par with heterosexuality. The sins of exploitive, hurtful or promiscuous sex are equally condemned in homosexuality and heterosexuality. But where the love is faithful and caring, both forms are equally accepted and blessed. This position rests on the conviction that same-sex relationships can richly express and be the vehicle of God's humanizing intentions. In 1963, the English Friends stated in *Towards A Quaker View of Sex*, "One should no more deplore 'homosexuality' than left-handedness....Homosexual affection can be as selfless as heterosexual affection, and therefore we cannot see that it is in some way morally worse."[14]

In chapter 4 I will deal specifically with the Catholic teaching on homosexuality and homosexual activity; and chapters 5 and 6 will deal with certain pastoral conclusions which flow from this teaching. As we will see, I believe that none of Nelson's four levels of response capture the church's teachings on this question.

Whereas Nelson has outlined four possible ways heterosexual persons view homosexual persons, there are three general approaches one can locate in morally evaluating homosexual *activity*:

1. Homosexual Acts Are Wrong: The homosexual person may

not be responsible for his or her condition and compulsion may diminish subjective responsibility. The homosexual person is bound to develop self-control. It is critical to remember that homosexual activity is never procreative and is thus a serious transgression of the divine will. The homosexual act is a deviation of the normal attraction of man for woman.[15]

2. Homosexual Acts Are Neutral: This view holds that homosexual acts *for the homosexual* are moral for these reasons: (a) homosexuality is a God-created way of protecting the human race on this planet from over–population; (b) homosexuality makes available opportunities for love for someone who is unable to find love in heterosexual relations; and (c) homosexuality provides an outlet for the expression of the human personality for those who cannot express themselves fully within heterosexuality. In this view, human sexuality in itself is neutral and moral judgement about it cannot be based on objective sexual behavior. In *A Place at the Table*, Bruce Bawer makes this point, "In and of itself, homosexuality is morally neutral and without interest."[16]

3. Homosexual Acts Are Wrong–But Homosexual Behavior *for some people* Does Not Fall under the Total Condemnation of the First Approach: Some hold that in certain circumstances homosexual behavior can be morally acceptable since there is nothing else that the person can do. The main ethical argument here is that if the homosexual relationship contributes to the humanization of the person(s), even though it is not the ideal, it should be accepted by the church, even though the church must encourage fidelity to one partner. This approach does not endorse homosexuality but concludes that for some persons a homosexual relationship might truly be the "lesser of the two evils"—i.e., lesser than promiscuity.[17]

What do we say to homosexual Christians about moral limits? What does the church say about how life is to be lived? We hold up the standard of chastity—the virtue by which one integrates one's sexuality according to the moral demands of one's state in life. For the homosexual person, chastity demands abstinence from genital sexual activity, as chastity necessitates abstinence for all unmarried individuals. Chastity presupposes both self-control and openness to life and interpersonal love which goes beyond the mere desire for physical pleasure. In particular, desire for union with another must not degenerate into a craving to possess and dominate. Chastity calls us to affirm and respect the value of the person in every situation.

Chastity is an expression of moral goodness in the sexual sphere. It is a source of spiritual energy by which, overcoming selfishness and aggressiveness, we are able to act lovingly under the pressure of sexual emotion. Chastity makes a basic contribution to an authentic appreciation of human dignity.

Citing the Congregation for Catholic Education's document *Educational Guidance in Human Love*, the U.S. bishops' document *Human Sexuality* teaches:

> Chastity "consists in self-control, in the capacity of guiding the sexual instinct to the service of love and of integrating it in the development of the person." Chastity is often misunderstood as simply a suppression or deliberate inhibition of sexual thoughts, feelings, and actions. However, chastity truly consists in the long-term integration of one's thoughts, feelings and actions in a way that values, esteems, and respects the dignity of oneself and others. Chastity frees us from the tendency to act in a manipulative or exploitative manner in our relationships and enables us to show true love and kindness always.[18]

Chastity requires us to authentically learn self-control, a characteristic which presupposes such virtues as modesty, temperance, and respect for one's life and the life of others. It is not prudish but sensible to maintain that modesty and temperance both involve a sense of balance, an ability to dress and act appropriately in given situations. For Christians, the context for sexual intercourse is the committed, monogamous marriage of husband and wife. This is the biblical norm. In the church, those who are married are called to express their sexual faithfulness in the discipline of monogamy. In the church, those who are not married are called to express their sexual faithfulness through the discipline of chastity (the virtue of chastity is not synonymous with an interior calling to celibacy). Chastity is certainly misunderstood and maligned in our sex-obsessed culture. However, chastity is possible. It is a worthy way of being faithful. It is a witness.

There are those who do their very best to live chastely, and fail. What are we to do? We meet them with forgiveness, as we have been forgiven. We give them our patient support and our empathetic encouragement. We recall the *Principles to Guide Confessors in Questions of Homosexuality* of the National Conference of Catholic Bishops: "The confessor should encourage the person to form stable relationships with persons of both sexes."[19] These *Principles* go on to say that "If a homosexual [person] has progressed under the direction of a confessor, but in the effort to develop a stable relationship with a given person has *occasionally* fallen into a sin of impurity, he should be absolved and instructed to take measures to avoid the elements which lead to sin without breaking off a friendship which has helped him grow as a person."[20] It is clearly far better for homosexual persons to live a stable and chaste life than to engage in multiple, secretive and promiscuous affairs. It is difficult to be faithful without a faithful community of support. We cannot abandon our homosexual brothers and sisters to unbearable loneliness or to the one community that will accept them—the community in which anything goes.

It is pastorally imperative, then, that the church minister to homosexual persons in a way which always upholds the virtue of chastity and challenges all sexually active homosexual relationships, even if these relationships are monogamous. I will return to this point in chapter 5.

One way that the church becomes an instrument of the Spirit's transformation of human lives toward freedom and holiness is by embracing all who enter. We must dream of a church where no one must struggle alone with who they are; where those who find them-selves with a homosexual orientation can be accepted with empathetic love, prayers and support; where parents of homosexual children can tell of their pain and of their love; where no one has to hide and slow-ly die of loneliness in the house of God. The church must have wel-coming and strengthening arms—like the arms of Christ. Can we do that? Can we not do this and be the church of the living Christ? Lawler, Boyle and May have written in *Catholic Sexual Ethics*:

> There are many things homosexual lovers may share and which may form a basis for their life together....Persons of a homosexual orientation deserve the love and support of the Christian community. They are called to friendship with God and to holiness of life, as are all human persons; and they have distinctive heavy burdens to bear. If, as

many homosexual [persons] do, they carry their burdens
with generous and chaste fidelity, they support and
strengthen all Christians. They become witnesses to the
nobility of making great personal sacrifices to guard the
great human goods sexuality is ordered to. Should they fall
in their human weakness, they should still receive the compassionate concern that all persons long for.[21]

The church has a great many things to offer to homosexual people. We have stories to tell; we have news to share, we have faith,
hope, love, and all the gifts of the Christian community, including
words about discipline and discipleship and holiness of living. We
have much to say to homosexual people—and much to learn from
homosexual people. But none of it can be heard, none of it learned,
none of the words of Christ can get through, none of the freeing and
transforming gift can be given, as long as our posture toward homosexual people is defensive or recoiling in repugnance or fear.

Thomas Merton points to an experience one day in 1958 when
he had gone into town on an errand:

In Louisville, at the corner of Fourth and Walnut, in the
center of the shopping district, I was suddenly overwhelmed with the realization that I loved all those people,
that they were mine and I theirs, that we could not be alone
to one another even though we were total strangers....The
whole illusion of a separate holy existence is a dream.[22]

As church, we need to capture this experience as our own in order
to sense that homosexual people are truly our brothers and sisters.

Chapter 1

WHAT DOES IT MEAN TO BE HOMOSEXUAL?

In 1981 the Archdiocese of Baltimore established one of the first official diocesan ministries for lesbian and gay Catholics after issuing a theological rationale for such a ministry. The statement said that the homosexual orientation is "in no way held to be a sinful condition" and that like heterosexuality it represents the starting point for one's response to Christ.[1] This assertion is clearly in conformity with various magisterial teachings. For example, *Persona humana* affirms that "...[T]he human person is so profoundly affected by sexuality that it must be considered one of the factors which give to each individual's life the principal traits that distinguish it" (n 1). This *Declaration* specifically asserts:

> ...[I]t is from sexuality that the human person receives the characteristics which, on the biological, psychological and spiritual levels make the person a man or woman, and thereby largely condition his or her progress towards maturity and insertion into society.[2]

In 1978 Karol Wojtyla (now Pope John Paul II) wrote that sexual ethics possess "such powerful anthropological implications" that it has become the battlefield for a "struggle concerning the dignity and meaning of humanity itself."[3] It is indeed necessary, then, to approach the question of homosexuality with the needed respect and reverence due to all questions regarding human sexuality. This "battlefield" can be viewed in these few examples:

At his trial Oscar Wilde defined homosexuality as "the love that dares not speak its name."[4] The *Letter to the Bishops of the Catholic Church on the Pastoral Care of Homosexual Persons* of the Congregation for the Doctrine of the Faith[5] begins by stating, "The issue of homosexuality and the moral evaluation of homosexual acts have increasingly become a matter of public debate, even in Catholic circles."[6] James P. Hanigan specifically subtitles his work on

13

Homosexuality as *"The Test Case for Christian Sexual Ethics."*[7] In *Embracing the Exile*, John E. Fortunato writes:

> For some gay Christians the pain of their journeys may have been greater; for some it is much less. Their story lines probably go very differently. But my guess is that the major components are common to us all....The denial of our gayness for some period. The questioning of our faith. The seeming irreconcilability of our sexual and spiritual lives. The schizophrenia. The feelings of unworthiness. The guilt. The loneliness. The hiding. The closets. And a sense of being on the fringes, cut off, banished. The story within the story belongs to all of us who are gay.[8]

In 1935, in his compassionate "Letter to an American Mother" whose son was homosexual, Sigmund Freud wrote:

> Homosexuality is assuredly no advantage, but it is nothing to be ashamed of, no vice, no degradation, it cannot be classified as an illness....Many highly respected individuals of ancient and modern times have been homosexuals, several of the greatest men among them (Plato, Michelangelo, Leonardo de Vinci, etc.). It is a great injustice to persecute homosexuality as a crime, and cruelty too.[9]

From this brief overview, it is clear that homosexuality is an extremely sensitive, delicate and complicated question. To treat homosexuality otherwise is to deal with this question with less than an attitude of respect, humility, nuance and analysis that is truly called for.

Although Freud equivocated about whether or not homosexuality was in itself pathological, he did not consider homosexual persons as "sick." In a 1903 interview published in the newspaper *Die Zeit* he stated:

> I am...of the firm conviction that homosexuals must not be treated as sick people....Wouldn't that oblige us to characterize as sick many great thinkers and scholars...whom we admire precisely because of their mental health? Homosexual persons are not sick.[10]

Toward a Definition

What is a homosexual orientation? Definitions vary widely and thus it is helpful to view *examples* of the types of "definitions" one finds:

1. Homosexual persons are "those individuals who more or less chronically feel an urgent sexual desire towards, and a sexual responsiveness to, members of their own sex, and who seek gratification of this desire predominantly with members of their own sex...."[11]
2. A homosexual person is "one who is motivated, in adult life, by a definite preferential erotic attraction to members of the same sex and who usually (but not necessarily) engages in overt sexual relations with them...."[12]
3. Homosexuality is "a *preference* on the part of *adults*, for *sexual* behavior with members of their own sex."[13]
4. Homosexual persons are those "who feel comfortable and affirmed when intimate with other members of the same sex, while with the other sex, they feel weak, resentful, scared, or simply indifferent, or less comfortable when genital intimacy is possible or occurs...."[14]

Each of these four "definitions" carries a certain bias. For example, the first definition presumes that homosexuality is a *chronic* condition and thus necessarily denotes a compulsivity. The second and third definitions use the word *preferential*, thus giving the impression that the homosexual person has made a *choice* regarding his or her sexual orientation. The fourth definition represents a homosexual person as being distant from and resentful toward members of the opposite sex. These so-called definitions all misrepresent the homosexual orientation by including these types of biases.

Although no one "definition" completely captures all that needs to be said about the homosexual orientation, the definition given in the *Encyclopedia of Bioethics* seems to represent this orientation most accurately and unbiasedly:

A homosexual person sustains "a predominant, persistent and exclusive psychosexual attraction toward members of the same sex. A homosexual person is one who feels sexual

desire for and a sexual responsiveness to persons of the
same sex and who seeks or would like to seek actual sexual
fulfillment of this desire by sexual acts with a person of the
same sex.[15]

This definition of homosexuality is a useful one because it contains
certain commonly employed understandings: that homosexuality is an
integral part of one's psychosexual makeup; this psychosexual orientation indicates a fundamental attraction toward persons of the same
sex, but does not preclude an interest in, care for and attraction toward
members of the opposite sex; respects the important distinction that
the homosexual person has a desire for and a psychosexual responsiveness to persons of the same sex and would like to act upon this
sexual fulfillment, but perhaps might not do so, for any number of
complicated reasons. Consequently, a person can be homosexual in
orientation without having acted upon this psychosexual attraction.[16,]
Eric Marcus confirms this point:

Sexual orientation…has everything to do with feelings of
attraction and nothing to do with actual sexual experience.
As you grow through childhood, you become aware of
your sexual feelings. That awareness, whether it's attraction to the same sex, the opposite sex, or both sexes, does
not require actual sexual experience. If you think back to
your own early awareness of sexual feelings, more likely
than not, you knew whether you were attracted to members
of the same sex, the opposite sex, or both long before
becoming sexually active.[17]

Two further nuances are important: Common usage denotes the
homosexual person as one who sustains all the components mentioned
in the definition from the *Encyclopedia of Bioethics*. On the other
hand, a *gay person* is one who has "publicly" identified himself or herself as a homosexual person and has made this fact known to at least
one other individual. More specifically, *gay* designates a man who is to
a greater or lesser extent publicly comfortable being known as a homosexual person.[18] The *lesbian* person is the female homosexual who is,
like the gay man, known to some extent as being a homosexual person.
Secondly, there is unfortunately a certain "gay subculture"

which takes a narrowly deterministic view of homosexuality and believes that there are correct and incorrect ways of being a homosexual person.[19] In this view, homosexuality is an act of emancipation, political rebellion, social experimentation, and cultural self-assertion. This view understands homosexuality as something which makes a person essentially different. Bruce Bawer puts it this way:

> As gay visibility has grown steadily over the past couple of decades, the subculture, with its narrow sense of what it means to be gay, has played a key role in defining homosexuality for the general public. Subculture-oriented gays visit schools to talk to young people about "gay life," by which they mean gay life as it is understood by the subculture. They develop university-level Gay Studies programs in which the subculture's view of homosexuality is presented to students, gay and straight, as the definitive truth about the subject. Subculture-oriented gays form political action groups that tell politicians what gay voters want.[20]

This type of view is harmful to a more holistic attitude which understands homosexuality as described in the *Encyclopedia of Bioethics*. In addition, this attitude inevitably condones homosexual activity, a viewpoint which the church does not sanction.

Sexual Identity

Each person experiences his or her sexual life within certain limitations, mainly rooted in gender self-assessment. This gender self-assessment moves along three separate dimensions: gender identity, sexual orientation, and sexual intention.[21]

These three dimensions, separately or together, are basically parts of a subjective, psychological, intrapsychic phenomenon. As one facet of a many-faceted sense of self, sexual identity exists with other identities, such as political, ethnic, religious, generational, vocational. Although there are important objective, behavioral aspects of sexual identity, its uniqueness can be more clearly perceived from its subjective aspects.

A. Gender Identity

Gender identity is the first aspect of sexual identity to form. The child develops a sense of being a *boy* or *girl* early in the second year of life, probably based upon an inconspicuous, repetitive, labelling process under way since birth. In other words, while a person is born with a given *sex* (male or female), an individual *learns* his or her *gender*. A child is taught its gender and subtly steered into various directions by the family. Simone de Beauvoir remarked, for example, "No one is born a woman."[22] In other words, one is born female, but in order to become fully a woman, she has the task of learning and living her femininity. She does this by taking into account, often unconsciously, the models and images provided by one's family and cultural settings.

Families and cultural groups have many conventional, and some very unique, attitudes about appropriate behaviors for boys and girls. By accepting their labels and the early steering, most children "choose" to be further influenced in a masculine or feminine direction. Perhaps as many as 90% of children develop what is known as a core gender identity, consonant with their biologic sex, by the middle or end of the third year of life. As a consequence of establishing core gender identity, boys and girls will maintain a relatively consistent sense of themselves as boys or girls, and become preoccupied with behaving in an acceptable masculine or feminine fashion. Because of this vital consequence, core gender identity can be considered the psychological foundation of sexuality.

Cultural forces—e.g., television, playmates, educational systems, adolescent subcultures, specific cultural experiences—impact on the child to shape the evolution of gender self-images. Beyond adolescence, "normal" generally refers to the absence of concern about masculinity or femininity. Clearly, then, an individual is normally born with a given sex (male or female) but one's gender (masculine or feminine) is a learned phenomenon. Adult gender identity disorders represent the failures to comfortably resolve the problem every toddler faces: "Am I a boy or a girl? Is that all right with me?"

B. Sexual Orientation

The second dimension of sexual identity is sexual orientation, which also has subjective and objective aspects. Adult subjective orientation refers to the sex of people or mental images of people that attract and provoke sexual arousal. Adults can be considered heteroerotic if the great majority of images, fantasies, and attractions associated with sexual arousal concern members of the opposite sex. Homoerotic adults think about, are attracted to, or aroused by images of persons of the same sex. Bioerotic individuals have the ability to become sexually aroused by images of both sexes. Sexual orientation is also reflected in adult behavior. Adults are generally classified as heterosexual, homosexual, or bisexual individuals, depending on the biologic sex of their partners and their own set of images and attractions.

The two aspects of sexual orientation are not always consistent: a homoerotic woman may behave heterosexually; a man who behaves bisexually may be entirely homoerotic; a heteroerotic man may engage in homosexual behavior. The homoerotic nature of male orientation is usually consciously manifested several years before heteroerotic orientation. Onset of partner sexual behavior and masturbation also tends to be earlier in homoerotic grade school and junior high students. The opposite patterns tend to be true for homoerotic and heteroerotic girls—i.e., female homoerotic orientation tends to manifest itself later than female heteroeroticism.[23]

Despite many assumptions, homosexuality, heterosexuality, and bisexuality are not *preferences*. Each is a sexuoerotic orientation or status.[24] They are no more chosen than is a native language. The roots of sexuoerotic status are complex and reflect either the "nature" or "nurture" school of thought (which we will deal with later in this book).

C. Sexual Intention

Sexual intention is not sexual acting-out, but refers rather to what a person actually wants to do with his or her sexual partner. It constitutes the final dimension of sexual identity. Conventional sexual intentions include a wide variety of behaviors, such as kissing, caressing, genital union, which are mutually pleasurable to consenting persons. Conventional intentions involve giving and receiving pleasure. While the behavioral repertoire of conventional intention is usually wide, the fantasy repertoire may be much wider. Unconventional sexual intentions involve raw or disguised aggression toward a victim, rather than mutual pleasure. The victim may be the self or another person. In addition, they are often relatively limited to a few behaviors that provoke arousal. Sadism, masochistic degradation, exhibitionism, voyeurism, rape, and pedophilia/ephebophilia are examples of unconventional developmental outcomes of intention. Erotic intention refers to the intrapsychic fantasy aspects. Behavioral intention refers to what is actually acted out.

What might we conclude? Each of these three dimensions of sexual identity (gender, orientation, and intention) can be thought of as structures of the mind created through the process of development. These structures remain relatively fixed throughout adulthood. In general, gender identity is more fixed than sexual orientation, which, in turn, is more enduring than sexual intention. The constancy of the structures is not absolute, however. Dramatic shifts in each dimension of sexual identity have been reported, and many unreported shifts have been observed clinically. Nonetheless, the relative stability of these structures should be emphasized. It is not surprising, however, to realize that a "normal" feminine, heteroerotic, heterosexual woman with peaceable intentions may, e.g., occasionally experience homoerotic images. In other words, the subjective side of sexual identity is quite private and extremely complex. Vincent Genovesi's comment is helpful:

> The meaning of sexuality is not up for grabs; rather, the meaning of sexuality is something derived from the meaning of our lives as human beings. As a people of faith, moreover, we realize that we have been loved into being. We live because God loves us, and insofar as we live with his life we are enabled to love even as he has first loved us....Our sexuality plays a crucial role in our ability to answer this call to love. We say this because human sexuality is "both the physiological and psychological grounding of our capacity to love." It is "a basic way in which we profess both our incompleteness and our relatedness. It is God's ingenious way of calling us into communion with others through our need to reach out and touch and embrace—emotionally, intellectually and physically." Our sexuality is simply essential both to our becoming fully human and to our human becoming.[25]

In light of this distinction among gender, orientation and intention, it is important to explore what many authors call homophilia. Homophilia is defined as a fixed, unalterable orientation to same-sex love.[26] Homophilia is a term aimed at affirming the homosexual individual as a person and exploring the concept of sexual orientation especially as it relates to other areas of an individual's life. Human sexuality studies indicate that sexual orientation has several components including—but not limited to—genital behavior. Sexual orientation is also related to intimacy needs, interpersonal communication, and relationships involving companionship and mutual support. For those authors, it is important, then, to distinguish homophilia from the components of sexual orientation that are more directly related to genital pleasure. These authors would therefore assess homophilia itself not only not morally wrong, but "normal."

Is this distinction between the homophilia and homogenital aspects of homosexuality helpful?

The 1986 Vatican *Letter to the Bishops* teaches that "...the particular inclination of the homosexual person is not a sin" (n 3). But number 3 also states that this "particular inclination" is "ordered to an intrinsic moral evil" and "thus" is "an objective disorder." This teaching must be adequately situated, however, within the context of the teaching of the 1975 document *Persona humana*, which teaches that some persons are *definitively* homosexual because of an innate instinct or a constitution which is incurable (n 3). Therefore, homosexuality (or homophilia) for some persons constitutes an innate constitutional fact. Consequently, the *Letter* asserts that homosexual people are more than their sexual *expression* and affirms that "a homosexual person, as every human being, deeply needs to be nourished at many different levels simultaneously" (n 16).

What conclusions can be reached? Sexual orientation is not fundamentally or even primarily a tendency toward *acts*, but rather a psychosexual, intrapsychic attraction toward particular individual *persons*. This is not to give an "overly benign" interpretation to the homosexual orientation but to realize that one's sexual orientation is not fundamentally a tendency toward sexual activity but rather an intrapsychic dimension of one's personality. This fact was recognized in *Principles to Guide Confessors in Questions of Homosexuality* (1973) when it recognized that the "deeper need of any human being is for friendship rather than genital expression...."[27]

In light of this conclusion, Marcus' definition of a homosexual person is accurate: "A homosexual person is a man or woman whose feelings of sexual attraction are for someone of the same sex....In contrast, a heterosexual [person] is a man or woman whose feelings of sexual attraction are for the opposite sex."[28]

Self-Awareness

The assessment of one's gender identity is no easy matter and an individual comes to an authentic sense of his or her own sexual orientation only slowly. In assessing one's sexual orientation, in this case one's homosexuality, three levels of evaluation/assessment are important:

1. *The Level of Attraction:* Here a person assesses with honesty and integrity both one's dreams and fantasies, as well as one's conscious attractions: e.g., When I walk down a street, when I walk along a beach, who is the first sort of person I tend to notice—a man or a woman? Or when I enter a room, do I tend as a general rule to notice the men or the women? Hanigan puts it this way:

> I find, for one instance, that in classes or lectures before a sexually diverse audience, I usually become aware that there are physically attractive women in the audience, and some not so attractive. But I do not have a clue as to whether there are physically attractive men present. From the depths of preconscious awareness springs the unreflexive knowledge of and consequent relatedness to members of the opposite sex as potentially desirable or undesirable sexual partners or sexual aggressors which generates a range of feeling and emotional tone toward them which is simply different than what is felt toward members of the same sex.[29]

2. *The Level of Arousal:* Here one faces an important question: What type of persons do I find sexually erotic and arousing?

3. *The Level of Experience:* Here one evaluates actual sexual experiences (e.g., kissing; holding hands) and, if present, genital experiences. For example, it is possible that an individual is a pseudo-homosexual[30] and experiencing an experimental stage in one's sexual life-experience; or one may find that a homosexual genital experience was not satisfying, comforting, or erotically stimulating. Such experiences must be carefully assessed and weighed in order to evaluate precisely one's level of experience.[31]

Sexuality is not an "all or nothing" behavior, any more than intelligence or athletic ability.[32] Sexuality forms a continuum, with homosexuality on one end and heterosexuality on the other. Thus, men who define themselves as heterosexual may well have males in their lives whom they deeply love; and women who define themselves as homosexual persons may have men in their lives whom they deeply love. Consequently, it is more realistic to think in terms of being "more" (predominantly) heterosexual than homosexual or "more" (predominantly) homosexual than heterosexual.[33]

The scale developed by Alfred Kinsey and his associates for their reports on male and female sexual behavior reflects the actual experience of human sexual attraction and desire more accurately than does a radical opposition between homosexual and heterosexual experience.[34]

On a scale of zero through six, with exclusive homosexual (6) and heterosexual orientations (0) at either extreme, most human beings fall somewhere between the two extremes. In terms of their fantasies, dreams, feelings, curiosity, experiences of sexual attraction and interest, as well as their overt behavior, some degree of homosexual and heterosexual attraction and desire is known to most people. One does not have to understand or accept the Freudian theory that everyone at birth is polymorphously perverse[35] to recognize the truth manifested in Kinsey's scale. The evidence, e.g., of fairly widespread, but wholly transitory, homosexual behavior in places where there are no members of the opposite sex (e.g. prisons and single sex boarding schools) is a confirmation of some degree of homosexual inclination and desire in many people whose sexual orientation is fundamentally heterosexual. Conversely, the desire and ability of many homosexually inclined people to enter into and sustain for a period of time a heterosexual relationship confirms Kinsey's findings as well. In addition, there are a number of social and demographic variables which may be of equal or greater importance in the analysis of one's sexual orientation: e.g., class, race, culture, income and religion. Bell and Weinberg conclude:

> Before one can say very much about a person on the basis of his or her sexual orientation, one must make a comprehensive appraisal of the relationship among a host of features pertaining to the person's life and decide very little about him or her until a more complete and highly developed picture appears.[36]

A word should be added here regarding the 1973 decision of the American Psychiatric Association (APA). In the *Diagnostic and*

Statistical Manual of Mental Disorders, 3rd edition, the category of
Homosexuality is replaced by Ego-dystonic Homosexuality, described
in this fashion: "The essential features are a desire to acquire or
increase heterosexual arousal, so that heterosexual relationships can
be initiated or maintained, and a sustained pattern of overt homosexual arousal that the individual explicitly states has been unwanted and a
persistent source of distress."[37] The *Manual* goes on to describe Ego-
syntonic Homosexuality as no longer "classified as a mental disorder."[38] In this form (Ego-syntonic) an individual is not upset by his or
her orientation.

In 1974, a significant minority of the members of the APA did
not accept the *Manual's* revision of the category of homosexuality.
Representative of the minority, Dr. Irving Bieber objected to the
revised classification on the score that it is a developmental abnormality, although not a disease or mental illness. It might be called heterosexual dysfunction or inadequacy.[39]

James D. Whitehead and Evelyn Eaton Whitehead have developed a pastorally helpful guide to assist persons in self-acceptance of
their homosexuality.[40] They employ the metaphor of a *journey* or *passage*, an image well known within biblical stories: e.g., Abraham
leaving home; the Exodus event; the Exile; the Diaspora; the itinerant
movements of Jesus (Matthew 11:11). While we all tend to desire per-
manence ("Let us build three tents here," Luke 9:33), as Christians
our fidelity is pledged, since Abraham and Moses, to a God whose
revelations require uprooting and repeated departures. Christians thus
recognize their lives as *journeys* with a direction and a purpose.

A journey normally involves the important paradox of *passage*,
a movement which always involves loss and gain: it is a time of peril
and possibility. During a passage we become vulnerable to both loss
and unexpected grace. The Whiteheads give two examples:

> In the death of a parent we lose our beginning and our
> security. That buffer between us and the world, that guar-
> antor of meaning and security, which we may have experi-
> enced as often in conflict as in affection, is taken from us.
> We are, at last, orphaned. Stripped gradually or suddenly of
> this important person—this part of myself—I may well
> become disoriented, alone on my life journey in a new and
> frightening way.

In a very different experience of a beginning friendship, a similar dynamic is at play: amid the excitement and enthusiasm of a deepening relationship we may feel a growing threat. If I admit this person into my heart, I will have to change. This is not because I am selfish or shallow, but simply because my heart will have a new occupant. Most threatened, perhaps, is my sense of independence: to allow you into my life I will have to let go of some of how I have been until now.[41]

A passage begins, then, in disorientation and with the threat of loss. It matures into a second stage as we allow ourselves to fully experience and to name this loss. The terror of a passage appears in this "in-between time." How do I know I can survive without the security and dependability of my parent? How can I be sure that this growing friendship will be better than my well-defended independence? A passage is a narrow, dark subterranean journey; it is something that we "under go." At the same time, however, this time of vulnerability and loss is also a time of grace. We find unexpected strengths; we are startled by our ability to risk and to trust; we emerge not just different, but stronger.

Using this metaphor of journey/passage, the Whiteheads suggest that there are three passages for an individual who is coming to grips with his or her own homosexual orientation.

1. *The Interior Passage:* This first passage is more like a revolution and conversion. This is a passage from the closet of ignorance or denial to the light of self-acceptance. This is the passage when one accepts and defends one's own sexual identity. This passage is interior in two senses: it takes place *within* the individual; and it takes place apart from questions of interpersonal expressions of affection and commitment. Douglas C. Kimmel suggests that self-identification as homosexual occurs only in one's early twenties.[42] Daniel Levinson's research also endorses the point that many people today require most of the decade of their twenties to come to a sense of their sexual identity.[43]

2. *The Passage of Intimacy:* A second passage appears in the life journey of homosexual people when they experience an invitation or challenge to share themselves with *others*. In the second passage one is being led to a mode of presence with others where one is known for who one is. In this passage there is both a need and a desire to be

known and to be loved for who one is. The Whiteheads point out that this second passage merits "special scrutiny":

> A common place in both gay and straight experience is a plunge into a second passage of interpersonal intimacy without first traversing the interior passage of self-acceptance.[44]

In this passage a person announces him or herself to others in the hope that if he or she is loved, this love will bring about a greater sense of self-acceptance. In light of the distinctions already made, the journey from passage one to passage two is the movement from being homosexual to being a gay man/lesbian woman.

3. *The Public Passage:* For some gay and lesbian Christians a third passage appears in their life journey. This is the transition into being recognized as homosexual and Christian in the public world. This public passage may not be taken by all gay or lesbian persons. The Whiteheads raise questions here about the possible motives which would incline a person to make this third passage. An obvious motive is an exhibitionist one: a compulsive desire to be seen and recognized. However, at the other end of the motivational continuum is the motive for generativity: i.e., an impulse to care for and contribute to the next generation. In other words, a person's homosexual life becomes a public witness to being both homosexual and Christian. In this way, one's generativity provides a public observable model of homosexual Christian life. The Whiteheads wisely counsel, "One cannot enter this passage simply because it is 'the thing to do' or because others have made it. A Christian enters it because he is invited to do so, because he senses himself so called."[45]

While I find this threefold progression quite helpful, I do have these cautions: first, progression from one stage to another is not simply a natural progression, but a careful process of integration and self-assessment; second, the process of movement from stage one to stages two and three should not be interpreted as endorsing homosexual activity; and third, only the most weighty reason(s) justifies the movement into the third stage because too often in the public mind this third stage is automatically equated with homosexual activity.

What conclusions are important here? Many people are not able to conceive of homosexuality as a possibility for authentic love: i.e., homosexuality is kept on the level of a physical, sexual urge or drive. It is very important to keep in mind that one's sexual orientation is integral to one's very self. In other words, one's homosexual orientation does not simply encompass sexual desires, but influences (though it does not determine) the ways one thinks, the ways one decides, the ways one responds, the ways one relates, the ways one creates and structures his or her whole world. All these actions are influenced by one's orientation. While it is possible to make a distinction between an individual's orientation and activity, it is also important to understand that it is impossible to quarantine orientation from the rest of one's life.[46] This point is articulated well in *Human Sexuality: A Catholic Perspective for Education and Lifelong Learning*:

> Sexuality…is a fundamental dimension of every human being. It is reflected physiologically, psychologically, and relationally in a person's gender identity as well as in one's primary sexual orientation and behavior.[47]

It is important to state here that a person who is homosexual and has not made this self-awareness known to others (has not "come out") can surely be as honest, integral and self-possessed (ego-syntonic [see note 18]) as a gay or lesbian person. In other words, the impression should never be given that honesty and integrity are qualities possessed only by those who have made the public step in homosexual "levels of awareness."

In addition, "coming out" is not something one does once and then forgets about it. For gay and lesbian people who choose to live "out of the closet," coming out is something they may do almost every day. Marcus gives this example:

> I sat down next to a woman on a train from New York to Washington the other day, and within minutes she asked me if I was married. I said that I wasn't. She then asked if I had a girlfriend. I said that I didn't, and she asked if I would be interested in meeting her sister. I could have just said no, and left it at that, but if I were straight, I might have been interested in meeting her sister. The truth was, because I'm gay, it would have been an inappropriate

match, so I told her that I was flattered, but that I was gay and her sister probably wouldn't be interested in me.[48]

Paradoxically, although a gay son or lesbian daughter who comes out of the closet is now free of the burden of hiding the truth, parents most often find themselves in a closet of their own, hiding the truth about their gay or lesbian child. Every time a parent is faced with a question like, "Is your son married?" or "Is your daughter dating anyone?" parents have to decide what to say.

Another agonizing difficulty in this coming out process is captured by Amity Pierce Buxton in *The Other Side of the Closet*, a book about the coming-out crisis for heterosexual spouses of gay and lesbian people. Heterosexual spouses greet the disclosure as a denial of the relationship. She writes that "Shocked spouses typically feel rejected sexually and bereft of the mates that they thought they had....Although relieved to know the reason behind changes in their partner's behavior or problems in marital sex, most feel hurt, angry and helpless."[49] Although their homosexual spouses most often feel relief stepping out of the closet, and are likely to receive support from other gay and lesbian people, the heterosexual spouses suddenly find themselves in a closet of their own, fearful of telling anyone the truth about their gay or lesbian spouse. This difficulty necessitates a great deal of pastoral concern on the part of the Church's ministers.

Statistics

Estimates of the number of people in the population whose sexual orientation is exclusively or predominantly toward members of the same sex vary rather widely, often in accord with the sexual orientation of those making the estimates. Complicating the question of numbers still more is the problem of what one means by homosexual orientation. The term itself—orientation—in its remote origins stems from architecture, where it signifies the alignment of temples and churches on an east-west axis (from *origins*, "east"). In psychology it has come to mean awareness of one's position or direction with reference to time, place or identity of persons; also it denotes a tendency to move toward a source of stimulation or a particular direction, as in tropisms. From this nexus it is but a short step to the concept of sexual orientation. The widespread adoption of the expression is related to the 1970s popularity of such compounds as action-oriented, identity-oriented, and success-oriented. It is possible that the semantic modulation into the erotic sphere was anticipated by the late nineteenth-century German use, with respect to sex of the term *Richtung*, "direction."

Using the most restricted definition and taking the most conservative statistics, about 4 to 5% of the population should be counted as predominantly homosexual in orientation.[50] The 1990 edition of the *Encyclopedia Americana* states that "In Western Cultures, 4 to 8% of males and 2 to 4% of females are predominantly or exclusively homosexual in behavior."[51] In the *Official Statements from Religious Bodies and Ecumenical Organizations* of 1991, the point is made that "It is difficult if not impossible to determine the number of homosexuals in the general community. Reasonable estimates suggest that between 4 and 10% of the total population are exclusively homosexual. In terms of absolute numbers this cannot be dismissed as trivial. Many more pass through a homosexual phase in their lives and while such statistics are to be treated with reserve, they do indicate a sizable proportion of the population."[52]

The San Francisco-based magazine *Ten Percent*, a national quarterly devoted to gay culture, has consistently maintained the 10% number for gay men in the United States. However, in April of 1993 a survey was published by the Battelle Human Affairs Research Center in Seattle, published by the Alan Guttmacher Institute and financed by the National Institute of Child Health and Human Development, a Federal agency. In this survey of American males, only 2% reported a homosexual experience over the past decade and only 1% describe themselves as exclusively homosexual. These new findings are in line with a series of surveys of sexual practices done in each of the last four years by researchers at the University of Chicago, and with recently published reports from Britain, France and Denmark.[53]

The Guttmacher study, one of the most thorough reports on male sexual behavior ever done, found that only 1% of the 3,321 men surveyed said they consider themselves exclusively homosexual. Many gay leaders have attempted to discredit this 1% figure, pointing out that people are reluctant to discuss their most intimate sexual nature with a clipboard-bearing stranger, even in surveys like this one where the interviews were conducted face-to-face in a subject's home (in Seattle, Washington) and with a guarantee of confidentiality.[54]

Frances Kunreuther, the Executive Director of the Hetrick-Martin Institute, the nation's largest social service agency for gay youth, has critiqued this recent survey by indicating that "Sexual orientation is a lot more than sexual behavior. It is about how we fall in love." In addition, several critics have pointed out that the survey was limited to men between 20 and 39, a period in which many adults have still not come to terms with their sexual orientation. What does it matter? In the political realm, power depends partly on numbers, so the new data may weaken the gay rights movement in its attempt to ward off laws in several states that would allow discrimination against homosexuals. On this point, however, the *New York Times* has remarked, "But in terms of civil rights, the size of the homosexual population should not be permitted to matter at all. Fair, nondiscriminatory treatment ought to be the right of all Americans, whether they are a tiny group or a multitude."

Language

A final word needs to be added regarding language use and homosexuality. From earliest recorded history we have evidence that certain names were not to be uttered because of the dangers that surrounded them. With regard to homosexuality this factor has entered in through the Judeo-Christian proscription of sodomy.[55] Thus we encounter such expressions as "the nameless sin," "the crime against nature," and so on. There is also a common type of "deletion," as when an individual will ask another, "Is he *that way?*" or "Is she one of *them?*"[56]

Against this background of euphemistic language, the open use of hostile language gains a particularly aggressive edge. One person calling another "queer" or "faggot" may be extremely damaging to the self-image of the one so named. Dating mostly from the 19th and 20th centuries, there are in English numerous slang terms for homosexual people, mostly devised by heterosexuals, thus tending to express in their meaning or derivation the hostility, the contempt, the hatred, and the fear that heterosexual people have felt toward homosexual people.[57] Gay and lesbian people have themselves adopted many of these terms, because until recently their understanding of themselves and their sexuality differed little from the views of the society in which they lived. By far the largest number of male slang terms fall into the categories of male passivity and effeminacy, which imply the renunciation of one's maleness. Another common practice is to apply a word that has female reference. The most direct method is to use a female name for a male. The oldest known slang term "Molly" is an example.

Terms for lesbian women are far less common than those for homosexual men, a fact that is consonant with the greater invisibility of lesbian women in the past. The oldest term seems to be "dyke," a term which derives from the late 19th century slang "dike," meaning "to dress up formally or elegantly."

That the understanding and perceptions involved are so frequently wrong makes the task of overcoming prejudice and ill-will so much harder. It is thus no accident that English has so few slang terms that mean "homosexual," pure and simple, without reference to sexual roles and acts.

One of the most contemptuous slang terms for homosexual men is "faggot" which carries overtones of effeminacy and cowardice. Inasmuch as its use is widespread and its origins usually misunderstood, it deserves some consideration here. One of the most persistent myths that has gained a foothold in the gay movement is the belief that "faggot" derives from the basic meaning of "bundle of sticks used to light a fire," with the historical commentary that when witches were burned at the stake, "only presumed male homosexuals were considered low enough to help kindle the fires."

The ultimate origin of the word is a Germanic term represented by the Norwegian dialect words *fagg* (bundle/heap) and *bagge* (obese/clumsy creature). From the latter are derived such Romance words as *bagasse* (French) and *bagascia* (Italian), this latter term meaning "prostitute," whose meaning matches that of the American English *faggot/fag*. It should be evident that this word and the ideas that have been mistakenly associated with it serve no useful function whatsoever, except to demean homosexual persons. The sooner such words are abandoned, the better.

The word "fairy" derived from the French *feerie*, the name of the mythical realm of the supernatural beings, was one of the commonest terms for the homosexual male in America in the 1925–1960 period. The word designated the more stereotypical or "obvious" sort of homosexual person, with the semantic link supplied by the notion of the delicate and fastidious that had attached itself to the expression, so that it was transferred effortlessly to a dainty and effeminate type of male.

In 20th century America the epithet "queer" has probably been the most popular vernacular term of abuse for homosexual people. The meaning is probably rooted in the use of "queer" for counterfeit (coin or bank note) in the mid-18th century, with the antonym "straight"; hence an expression popular in the recent past, "Queer as a three-dollar bill." As used for homosexual people, the term has connoted strangeness and "otherness," rooted in the sense that gay people were marginal to society's mainstream.

In the late medieval period, the concept developed of a "vicious homosexual inclination," so vicious, in fact, that the vice became "unmentionable," as though it did not exist.[58] Slang terminology for homosexual persons continues this viciousness and has nothing to do with the "homosexual orientation" as properly understood. Consequently, when teachers and ministers within the church hear such terms being used, it is important to remind the user of every person's human dignity.[59]

The strong assertion made in the 1986 *Letter to the Bishops* is most pertinent here:

> It is deplorable that homosexual persons have been and are the object of violent malice in speech or in action. Such treatment deserves condemnation from the Church's pastors wherever it occurs. It reveals a kind of disregard for others which endangers the most fundamental principles of a healthy society. The intrinsic dignity of each person must always be respected in word, in action and in law.[60]

Chapter 2

ORIGINS OF HOMOSEXUALITY

In his book *Is It A Choice?* Eric Marcus writes:

No one becomes a homosexual anymore than a man or woman becomes a heterosexual. Feelings of attraction for one sex or the other are something we become aware of as we grow up. Where exactly these feelings come from and why some of us have strong heterosexual feelings while others have strong homosexual feelings remains a mystery.

Just as heterosexual people don't choose their feelings of sexual attraction, gay and lesbian people don't choose theirs. All of us become aware of our feelings of sexual attraction as we grow, whether those feelings are for someone of the same sex, the opposite sex or both sexes.[1]

Despite such assertions and despite all the research into sexual orientation, we *de facto* know very little about the development of heterosexuality, bisexuality, and homosexuality. Social scientists have proposed many theories to explain sexual orientation, but none have been conclusively proven true.[2] One author puts it this way:

The biggest problem most people have in understanding homosexuality is that they think of it as a single way of feeling and acting, and therefore look for a single way of explaining it. But...there are a number of very different kinds of homosexuality. It doesn't make sense to think that they all have the same cause, that there is a single explanation for all of them. It makes much better sense to look for different explanations for the different kinds of homosexuality. The question to ask is: "Which of these explanations account for some kinds of homosexuality...?" And the answer is that nearly all of them explain some kinds of homosexuality but not others—and that most homosexuali-

33

ty involves several of these explanations at once, several causes working together.[3]

The 1990 *Kinsey Institute Report on Sex* asserts that no one knows what "causes" homosexuality, as no one knows what "causes" heterosexuality. The Report states:

> Many theories have been proposed, but so far most have not held up under careful scrutiny and none have been proven. In fact, scientists probably have a clearer idea of what does "not" cause a homosexual orientation. Children raised by gay or lesbian parents or couples, for instance, are *no* more likely to grow up to be homosexual than are children raised by heterosexual parents....
>
> It also is not true that people become homosexuals because they were seduced by an older person of the same sex in their youth. The childhood and adolescent sexual experiences of both homosexuals and heterosexuals are fairly similar, except that homosexuals recall later that they found opposite-sex encounters less satisfying than did heterosexuals.
>
> Current theory is that there probably are many different developmental paths by which a person can come to be homosexual, bisexual or heterosexual.[4]

In 1948, the Kinsey Institute published a homosexual-heterosexual rating scale, ranging from zero (0) for exclusively heterosexual behavior to six (6) for exclusively homosexual behavior. Drawing on an admittedly limited population of white, middle-class males between 16 and 55 during a three-year period, Kinsey determined that there were a few men falling at either end, but that most fell somewhere along the continuum: i.e., they had engaged, to varying degrees, in both heterosexual and homosexual activities.

In 1986, the Kinsey Institute held a symposium for 50 eminent researchers from various fields, including anthropology, psychology, biology, history, medicine, psychiatry, and sociology, to reexamine the issue of sexual orientation and assess the usefulness of the scale. The symposium, published as the book *Homosexuality/Heterosexuality:*

Concepts of Sexual Orientation, was notable for the conclusions that were not drawn. The researchers unanimously challenged the idea, upon which the original Kinsey scale had been based, that sex acts *per se* measured sexual orientation. Instead, they agreed that the behavioral scale—measuring the sexual acts a person engages in— had to be balanced with other scales measuring love, sexual attraction, fantasy, and self-identification—all of which could change over time. According to the Kinsey Institute, then, there is probably no essential heterosexual or homosexual nature but many "homosexualities" and "heterosexualities" that characterize people. In other words, according to their report, sexual orientation is multidimensional, situational, and contextual.

Australian clinical psychologist Vivienne C. Cass of Murdoch University has identified a six-stage process of homosexual identity formation for gay men and lesbian women of all ages that sidesteps the social rigidities of sexual categorization. According to Cass, the process begins when a person recognizes that there is "something" about his or her behavior (including actions, feelings, thoughts) that could be called homosexual. After going through various stages of denial, confusion, self-realization, disclosure, and quest for approval, such individuals finally acquire a degree of mature self-acceptance in which sexual orientation is conceived as only part of a complex self— not the total identity. There is nothing inherent or inevitable within a person controlling the process, which grows out of a complex interaction between the individual and the environment. It can be set into motion at any time during the life cycle, and may be terminated at any stage along the way.[5]

As we shall see, most scientific theories on the causes of homosexuality reflect the classic debate on whether a person's makeup is the product of biology or environment. Many researchers speculate that homosexuality is a by-product of upbringing, especially a child's relationship with his or her parents. Other researchers have focused instead on physical causes, such as brain structure or hormone exposure while in the womb. Recent research locating differences within the brains of heterosexual and homosexual men has added new data to the biological side of the nature versus nurture controversy.[6]

In the 1880s, homosexuality was largely viewed as a sickness, which has had a lingering effect on general perceptions of homosexual men and women. When homosexuality was/is considered a sickness, a perverse condition, it demanded a cure and many physicians began an all-out campaign to find such a cure. Trying to locate same-sex desire in the body, physicians pointed to the structure of the pelvis, the size of the penis, to body hair. They warned of the deep-voiced female or the contralto male. They associated homosexuality with degeneracy, then genius and then misguided parenting. And with speculations about cause came attempts at treatment: castration, hypnosis, electric shock, hysterectomies, and later, in a slightly less brutal era, psychoanalysis.[7]

As we now begin our study of various points of view regarding causes for homosexuality, we must keep in mind some critical issues-of-interpretation:

1. Vatican II's *Pastoral Constitution on the Church in the Modern World (Gaudium et Spes)* affirms that "in pastoral care, appropriate use must be made not only of theological principles, but also the findings of the secular sciences, especially psychology and sociology" in order to blend modern science and its theories and understanding of the most recent discoveries with Christian morality and doctrine."(n 62) In other words, Christian and Catholic morality on the question of homosexuality must be consistently attuned to the insights and discoveries of secular sciences on this subject.

2. Many persons have strong objections to this search for a cause or causes of homosexuality as such an attitude inevitably leads to the impression that there is something "wrong" with being a homosexual person and thus there is a need to find out *why* a person has a homosexual orientation. We do not expend this type of effort, for instance, in seeking the cause or causes of heterosexuality. We must be pastorally attentive to this concern.

3. Eric Marcus has written that in any study of the cause/causes of homosexuality, it is always critical to "tell the truth" about who the homosexual person truly is. Marcus has written:

When I heard Dan Quayle say on "Good Morning America" and "Prime Time Live" that I had made the "wrong choice," I wanted to ask him what choice he was referring to. When I realized I was gay I also realized I *did* have a choice, but not between homosexuality and heterosexuality. I could choose to live in the closet, maybe even marry a woman and pretend to be who I'm not, or I could be honest about who I am and live my life openly—no easy thing to do. I didn't choose to be gay, but I did choose to tell the truth.

In a television interview...President Bush said that he would still love his grandchild if he found out he was gay, but he wouldn't want him to promote his gay lifestyle. Would somebody please tell me what a gay lifestyle is? One may choose a country-club lifestyle, a Western lifestyle, a city lifestyle, but there is no such thing as a gay lifestyle—just as there is no such thing as a heterosexual lifestyle. Homosexual lifestyles, like heterosexual lifestyles, run the gamut. They defy classification. It is pastorally critical, therefore, to "tell the truth" about homosexual persons in this search for a cause/causes.[8]

In discussing sexual orientation, adult subjective orientation refers to the intrapsychic images of people that attract and provoke sexual arousal. Adults can be considered homoerotic who think about, are attracted to, or aroused by images of persons of the same sex. Consequently, any attempt to search out the causes of one's homosexuality is by necessity going to be as complex and as limited as would be the search for the origins and roots of one's heterosexuality or bisexuality. As noted above, there are a number of writers who argue that all research into the "causes" of homosexuality is intrinsically hostile to homosexual persons.[9] These writers suggest that such research is motivated by the premise that homosexuality is pathological and is most often grounded in rigid assumptions about what constitutes true "maleness and femaleness." In addition, the debate about the major causes for a homosexual orientation very much depend on one's "definition" of homosexuality. So-called *essentialists* consider homosexuality as referring to an individual's inner, authentic self: that one's sexual orientation is intimately intertwined with one's identity as a human being. Most defenders of homosexual rights then argue that expression of this identity is essential to human wholeness.

On the other hand, the so-called *constructivists* argue that homosexuality is a behavior and perhaps a preference for certain behaviors, the meaning of which is ambiguous for the understanding or labeling of a person. In this view, homosexuality should not be considered an identity as such, especially because homosexual behavior takes varied forms from culture to culture.[10] The landmark work in this constructivist approach is Greenberg's *The Construction of Homosexuality*.[11]

Recognizing the necessary care that must be had in approaching this subject, we can indicate that the major causes for a homosexual orientation that have been proposed include genetic, prenatal/hormonal, adult (postnatal)/hormonal, and psychological factors.[12]

A. Genetic Factors

Early research[13] into the causes of homosexuality suggested a strong genetic component, but these results did not withstand further tests. It is generally concluded today that studies of frequency of homosexuality in identical and fraternal twins, and in near-relatives of homosexuals, suggest that there is some degree of genetic influence in the development of the homosexual orientation operative in some persons.[14]

In 1991 Simon LeVay, a biologist at the Salk Institute for Biological Studies in San Diego, California, published research indicating that variations in sexual orientation may be the result of differences in brain structure.[15] LeVay has found that in homosexual men part of the anterior hypothalamus—a brain region that governs sexual behavior—has the anatomical form usually found in women rather than the form typical of heterosexual men. LeVay's is the second report of a difference between the brains of homosexual and heterosexual men, though it is the first to find such a difference in the hypothalamus, which is known to be a source of sexual urges.[16] That connection raises the possibility that this difference may not only correlate with homosexuality but also play a role in causing it.

Either interpretation—correlation or cause—suggests that some biological difference is at the root of homosexuality. This "difference" is potentially explosive:

> Homophobes could exploit the result by pointing to the brain "defect" in homosexuals; they might even envision screening for homosexuality *in utero*. Others may interpret the data as evidence that homosexuality is as natural a variation from the average as left-handedness. And many gays will see LeVay's finding as welcome confirmation of what

they have always believed. "If it's true, the implications are amazing," says Dennis Landis, a neurologist who studies brain structure at Case Western Reserve University. "It would begin to suggest why male homosexuality is present in most human populations, despite cultural constraints. It suggests it's a biological phenomenon."[17]

This finding has important implications for science as well as society. Not only does it link sexual orientation to a structure within the brain, it also adds to a small but growing body of observations suggesting that many structural differences in the brain—including those that distinguish typical male and female brains—may be determined by prenatal hormone levels. Some of those differences may play a role in sexual behavior as well as in cognitive differences between men and women.

Scientists at McMaster University in Ontario report that on measures of visual-spacial ability where consistent differences have been observed between males and females, male homosexuals fall between the two sexes. Neuroscientist Sandra Witelson and psychologist Cheryl M. McCormick reported, "It is as if, in some cognitive respects, they are neurologically a third sex."[18]

These researchers administered three tests of spacial ability (where males excel) and two measuring verbal fluency (where females show a small advantage) to three groups of 38 subjects each: homosexual men, heterosexual men, and heterosexual women. Witelson reports that: "The cognitive pattern of homosexual men was significantly different from heterosexual men but not significantly different from that of heterosexual women." These results—like those from other studies on homosexuality—are consistent with the hypothesis that homosexuals are exposed to atypical levels of prenatal sex hormones.

In the spacial tests, heterosexual males had the highest scores, followed by homosexual males, and then females. This pattern was particularly pronounced among right-handers in a test where subjects had to visualize the water level in a tilted glass. In a measure of verbal fluency, the order was reversed: Women scored highest, followed by the homosexual men, and then the heterosexual men.

Witelson believes that evidence from anatomical, genetic, hormonal, and neuropsychological research is converging to suggest that "sexual orientation...is part of a larger constellation of cognitive attributes." She adds that all this may lead to an explanation for "the apparently greater prevalence and ability of homosexual men compared to heterosexual men in some professions." However, the bewilderingly complex relationships between brain anatomy, prenatal sex hormones, handedness, and homosexuality still need a great deal of study.[19]

LeVay points out that his finding contains no direct evidence that the difference he has observed actually causes homosexuality. LeVay knew that the research team of Roger Gorski at the University of California, Los Angeles, had examined postmortem human brains and found two regions, or nuclei, in the anterior hypothalamus that are more than twice as large in men as they are in women. LeVay extended the study to homosexual men, using brains of men who had died of AIDS. In most of the 19 homosexuals he looked at, he found that one of these nuclei, called INAH-3, was smaller than it is in heterosexual men—in fact it was the same size as it is in women.

AIDS provides the first chance to study the brains of homosexual men, according to LeVay, since male homosexuality is a risk factor for the disease, and AIDS patients are often categorized by risk group. The brains of lesbian women are more difficult to obtain for research, since lesbian women are not generally at risk for AIDS, and sexual orientation is rarely recorded in deaths from other causes.

Could the differences LeVay saw be due to AIDS rather than to homosexuality? "AIDS pathologies...could influence the size of the nuclei," maintains one scientist with Gorski at U.C.L.A. who studies the INAH nuclei. She notes, however, that LeVay found that heterosexual men had large INAH-3 nuclei, whether they had died from AIDS or from other causes. This has led some scientists to conclude that "LeVay is probably correct."

Dr. Richard Swaab, a neuroscientist at the Netherlands Institute for Brain Research in Amsterdam, applauds LeVay's finding, because it builds on his own group's discovery, reported in 1990 in *Brain Research* of the first known structural difference between the brains of homosexual and heterosexual men. Swaab's team found that the suprachiasmatic nucleus (SEN), a part of the brain that governs daily rhythms, is twice as large in homosexual men as it is in the typical heterosexual brain.

Sandra J. Witelson and her colleagues at McMaster University have proposed that the brain is a mosaic of areas that may respond to sex hormones at various times during early development. Typical female or male hormone levels would produce a typical female or male brain, Dr. Witelson maintains. But unusual levels of sex hormones at any given time may switch the development at susceptible brain areas. She writes that "This could cause different areas in the same brain to undergo different sexual differentiation."[20] Depending on levels and timing, sex hormones could influence handedness, sexual orientation, or other characteristics.

Witelson emphasizes that her model is speculative, based on a rather eclectic assortment of data. But that model—and LeVay's finding—raise questions that offer a program for future research. Does INAH-3 have sex-hormone receptors, for instance, indicating that it could be influenced by those hormones? And when during brain development does the difference between the sexes emerge?

No matter how such questions are answered, it may be difficult ever to establish that INAH-3 or any other brain structure actually causes homosexuality, or to rule out the possibility that childhood or adolescent experience may have altered the size of INAH-3 in homosexual people. But Witelson, for one, is not discouraged: "The important [point] is that several independent studies have shown that various brain structures are different between people of different sexual orientation."

These findings of LeVay have important moral and scientific implications:

1. These studies not only link sexual orientation to a structure within the brain, but they add to a small but growing body of observations suggesting that many structural differences in the brain—including those that distinguish typical male and female brains—may be determined by prenatal hormone levels. Some of those differences may play a role in sexual behavior as well as in cognitive differences between men and women.

2. If it is clearly demonstrated that homosexual behavior is the product of genetics and biochemistry rather than culture, a broad reappraisal of homosexuality will undoubtedly ensue. LeVay and others feel on this point that this research will eventually help remove the stigma of being a homosexual person.

3. Some have criticized LeVay's research from the point of view that he is a biased observer: i.e., he is a gay man himself, and this fact predates his research and somehow affects the results. This is a fair question for any researcher and doubly so in this case, since the analytical method required by the kind of work LeVay does is unavoidably subjective. At the same time, however, it is impossible for any researcher to divorce him or herself from personal history. If one studies Alzheimer's disease because one's husband has Alzheimer's, one also has a personal interest—but not necessarily a negatively prejudicial interest. As one writer remarks, "If you're doing an important study, hopefully you'll have some passion for it." [21]

The scientific research of Michael Bailey (Northwestern University) and Richard Pillard (Boston University School of Medicine) likewise demonstrates that male sexual orientation is substantially genetic. Pillard and his colleagues recruited several hundred women and men, about half of them lesbian or gay and half of them heterosexual. They attempted to find out what they could about the sexuality of their 500 brothers and sisters. The pattern was striking. As compared with heterosexuals, gay men and lesbian women had four to five times as many homosexual siblings (brothers more often than sisters). Pillard comments:

> Our studies also confirm the observation, first made a hundred years ago, that in childhood gay men and (less often) lesbian women tend to display gender nonconformity; i.e., they behave in ways typical of the other sex. Nonconforming boys "dress up," play with dolls, and choose girls as playmates. Nonconforming girls are "tomboys" who like rough sports and boys' clothing and are often leaders in their play groups. This behavior often begins as soon as they are old enough to show typical gender differences in their style of play. Although not proof that sexual orientation has a hereditary basis, the evidence of homosexuality's roots in early gender nonconformity does refute the popular theory that it results from seduction or developmental conflicts of adolescence.[22]

Pillard and Bailey also compared monozygotic (genetically

identical) twins with dizygotic (fraternal) twins and adopted brothers with biological brothers. Data from 150 gay and 11 bisexual men and their 121 twin and adopted brothers showed that identical twins had the highest concordance rate for homosexuality. That rate was 50%, which suggests that both genes and environment play a role in determining sexual orientation. Fraternal twins had the same concordance rate as biological brothers who were not twins. Adopted brothers, even though most of them joined the family in infancy, had the lowest concordance rate. This result suggests that even a shared family environment does not necessarily influence sexual orientation.[23]

In July of 1993 a team of National Institutes of Health scientists published a landmark study in *Science* maintaining that they have identified a small stretch of genetic material that is linked to male homosexuality. By analyzing the pattern of inherited genetic markers in homosexual brothers, these scientists determined that a sequence of DNA related to homosexuality is localized on the tip of the X chromosome, which is passed from mother to child. This research is the first detection of a distinct region of the chromosome that could explain sexual orientation in men.

The research found that 33 of 40 pairs of gay brothers (83%) inherited identical sequences of DNA in this one region of the X chromosome, called "Xq28." (The "q" refers to the location on the longer of the two arms of the chromosome; the "28" refers to its placement on the arm.) It is unclear how the genetic mechanism works. It might act directly on the brain, by controlling exposure of the fetal brain to sexual hormones. Or it may act indirectly by influencing temperament or personality traits.

The INAH scientists do not know why 7 of the 40 pairs of gay brothers did not inherit the genetic marker. One scientist speculates that these gay men may have inherited other genes associated with homosexuality or may have been influenced by environmental factors or life experiences. Other nongenetic factors also may play a contributing role. The trait for sexual orientation differs from that of, e.g., eye color, which is 100% dependent on genetics. It may be more a characteristic like height, which is about 90% genetic, but also affected by nutrition.[24]

How might we conclude this section? According to Chandler

Burr, a journalist who is writing a book on the subject of biology and homosexuality:

> The evidence, although preliminary, strongly indicates a genetic and biological basis for all sexual orientation. We see this in the work of scientists Michael Bailey and Richard Pillard, who have done studies on twins and gay and lesbian siblings. For example, they found that with identical twins, where one twin is gay, the other twin has an approximately 50% chance of being gay. In fraternal twins [separate eggs], if one sibling is gay, there is a 16% chance the other sibling will be gay. And in non-genetically related adopted brothers and sisters, where one sibling is gay or lesbian, there is a 9% chance that the other sibling will be homosexual, which is approximately the normal statistical incidence in the general population. These results, which indicate that sexual orientation is governed primarily by genetics, have been confirmed dramatically in other laboratories in the United States.[25]

In his study, Hamer and his colleagues recruited 76 homosexual men and traced out pedigrees for each, determining which other members of each family were themselves homosexual. They found 13.5% of the gay men's brothers to be homosexual—much higher than the rate of 2% or so that the Hamer group measured in the general population. Earlier studies had also found that brothers of homosexual men are more likely to be homosexual than are men in the general population.

But once Hamer and his colleagues ventured outside the immediate family, they found something new. Hamer states, "When we collected the family histories, we saw more gay relatives on the maternal side than on the paternal side. In particular, they found homosexuality to be significantly more common among maternal uncles of gay men and among cousins who were sons of maternal aunts than it is among males in the general population.

This implied that, for some male homosexuals at least, the trait is passed through female members of the family. And this in turn gave the researchers an obvious place to start looking for a homosexuality gene: the X chromosome, the only chromosome inherited exclusively from the mother.

Hamer warns, however, that this one site cannot explain all male homosexuality. Although his pedigree analysis showed that the homosexuality trait is usually maternally inherited, he did see some families where the traits seemed to be passed paternally. And even among his 40 sets of brothers, chosen so that there was no evidence of trait passing through male family members, seven sets of brothers did not share the stretch of Xq28 where the gene appears to lie. Hamer concludes, then, that it seems likely that homosexuality arises from a variety of causes, genetic and perhaps environmental as well.[26]

Chandler Burr ends his superb study on "Homosexuality and Biology" by stating: "Five decades of psychiatric evidence demonstrates that homosexuality is immutable, and nonpathological, and a growing body of more recent evidence implicates biology in the development of sexual orientation."[27] It is important, therefore, that we continue to stay atuned to the biological implications in the study of sexual orientation.

B. Prenatal/Hormonal Factors

Several studies have administered abnormal sex hormone levels to animal fetuses in their mothers' wombs to study the effects this has on sexual differentiation and development of sexual behavior patterns in adult animals. It has been shown that the right dose of sex hormones given to an animal fetus at a critical time can result in that animal showing sexually "inverted behavior" when mature, including homosexual behaviors exhibited in conjunction with mating. These effects are complex and multifaceted, and have been taken by some as evidence suggesting that similar hormone variations must be causal factors in human homosexuality.[28]

While experiments directly manipulating hormones in the womb cannot be performed with human fetuses, a number of naturally and accidentally occurring medical conditions have served almost as "quasi-experiments." These studies have shown that some human fetuses exposed to abnormal hormonal levels during development can show radically altered physical development, brain functioning, gender orientation, and sexual behavior of the person.

Does this research suggest that prenatal hormonal factors cause homosexuality? There are theorists who propose that the animal experiments and their human "quasi-experimental" parallels strongly suggest that homosexuality is biologically determined.[29] These theorists specifically propose that human sexual orientation is largely determined between the second and fifth month of pregnancy by fetal exposure to the principal sex hormones. Because of the problems regarding the applicability of the animal research to humans and the fact that few of the human "quasi-experiments" deal with homosexuality in isolation, it is critical to examine the three major types of direct evidence of this hypothesis.

The first group of evidences are the reports suggesting that the brains and/or entire neurohormonal systems of male homosexuals (no significant research in this area has been conducted with lesbian women) are different from their heterosexual peers, being significantly "feminized." For instance, some research suggests that homosexual men are less right-handed than heterosexual men,[30] that they have different mental abilities than heterosexual men based on different brain structures,[31] and that their hormonal response to an injection of estrogen is more like a woman's than a heterosexual man's (or at least is intermediate between those extremes). At the present time, there is significant reason to doubt the persuasiveness of the evidence on each of these points.

The second type of evidence for prenatal causation suggests that the most powerful predictor of adult male homosexuality is striking gender non-conformity or inappropriateness early in childhood. In other words, boys who are strikingly effeminate as young children appear to be much more likely to become homosexual men than their more typically masculine peers.[32] Some effeminate children do not grow up homosexual, however, and many homosexual people do not report gender-inappropriate behavior as children. There is no conclusive evidence for why early gender behavior distortion occurs. While some regard it as evidence for the prenatal hormone hypothesis, there is some evidence that the causes could be psychological.[33]

Finally, research has been cited which lends indirect support to the prenatal cause hypothesis. The most frequently cited are those showing that an unusual number of homosexual people were born to German women who were pregnant during World War II.[34] These researchers argue that the stress of war produced hormone disturbances which produced homosexuality in the children.

What conclusions can be reached? While there is an impressive amount of research cited in favor of the prenatal causation hypothesis, the direct research in support of this hypothesis is far from conclusive. It seems most reasonable to conclude that prenatal/hormonal influences may be a facilitating contributing cause of homosexual orientation in some individuals. These influences cannot be considered operative in all homosexual persons, and there is no evidence that such factors can by themselves "cause" homosexuality.[35]

C. Adult Postnatal/Hormonal Factors

There are still anecdotes reported suggesting that male and female homosexuals have too much or too little of certain sex hormones compared to others, or that they have too much of the hormones of persons of the other gender. The research in this area is quite clear, however, that there is no substantial hormonal difference between homosexual people and their comparable heterosexual peers. Research which was once thought to show such differences has been shown to be plagued by inaccurate methods of measuring hormones and inaccurate ways of categorizing the sexual preferences of subjects in the studies.[36]

D. Psychological Factors

Psychoanalytic theory is the "standard" psychological theory of causation and almost all of the psychoanalytic research has been directed at male homosexuality. In this view, homosexuality is due primarily to a profound disturbance in parent-child relationships.[37] If a boy has a father who is distant, unavailable, or rejecting; and a mother who is overly warm, smothering, and controlling, the boy's desire to identify with the father may be frustrated. An ambivalent feeling of fear of and yet longing for closeness with another male may result. A smothering relationship with the mother can make sexual relationships with women threatening. This in turn can lead to avoidance of normal heterosexual activities both because of fear of the aggressiveness of other males with whom the boy is competing and fear of the sexuality of women. At the same time, the boy is attracted to other men because of his longing for closeness to a male. There is some evidence that similar dynamics are present for lesbian women as well, where the major disturbance seems to be in the relationship with the mother. Lesbian women report greater than expected frequencies of rejecting and negative relationships with their mothers.[38]

The evidence of this basic theory is substantial, yet inconclusive. Much of the research is based upon the clinical impressions of practicing psychoanalysts, and some see the evidence as contaminated by the biases of the therapists. The bulk of empirical research[39] on the families of homosexual people documents patterns that would be predicted by the psychoanalytic theory, even though it cannot be argued that those results support only that theory.[40]

Several studies have produced evidence that would seem to contradict the psychoanalytic hypothesis.[41] It seems that there is not enough evidence to prove the psychoanalytic hypothesis, but there is too much evidence to dismiss it at this time.

The other major type of psychological theory is learning theory. These hypotheses suggest that early sexual and other learning experiences shape sexual orientation. For instance, the first sexual experiences of a boy shape the sexual orientation: e.g., the first sexual experiences of a boy with troubled family relationships and a preexisting tendency toward effeminate behavior may be more likely to cause homosexuality. Such early experiences could shape the child's perception of himself, his sexual fantasies, and his choices of subsequent sexual experiences, with the eventual result of adult homosexual orientation. The evidence in support of the learning approach is much less substantial and more indirect than that of the psychoanalytic hypotheses.[42]

Interest has been demonstrated recently in the psychological theory of causation to Joseph Nicolosi's reparative therapy for male homosexuality.[43] While I do not entirely agree with Nicolosi's argument, I think that it is important to include his work here since it receives so much attention. One of the main difficulties I have with Nicolosi's reparative therapy is that it assumes that there is no such reality as definitive homosexuality. In addition, Nicolosi's assumption might lead to the unrealistic expectation that definitive homosexuals can change their orientation. The "non-gay homosexual"[44] is a man who experiences a split between his value system and his sexual orientation. He is fundamentally identified with the heterosexual pattern of life. The non-gay homosexual feels his personal progress to be deeply encumbered by his same-sex attractions. Although Nicolosi does not use the term, the non-gay homosexual is the one who is dystonic about his sexuality: i.e., he is uncomfortable and non-accepting of his homosexuality.

Nicolosi maintains that homosexuality is a developmental problem that is almost always the result of difficulties in family relations, particularly between father and son. As a result of failure with father, a boy does not fully internalize male gender-identity, and develops homosexually.

As very young infants, both boys and girls are first identified with the mother, who is the first and primary source of nurturance and care. However, whereas the girl *maintains* primary identification with the mother, the boy later has the additional developmental task of shifting identification from the mother to the "second other." It is through his relationship with the father that the boy will change to a masculine identification, which is necessary if he is to develop a normal masculine personality. This additional developmental task for boys explains why they have more difficulty than girls in developing gender identity and may also explain the higher ratio of male to female homosexuality.

Nicolosi maintains that before a boy's third year, the father's most significant task is to protect his son against mother's impulses to prolong the mother-infant symbiosis. Through his example, the father demonstrates to the boy that it is possible to maintain an intimate but autonomous relationship with the mother. It is in this triangular relationship that the homosexual man's family background is commonly faulty. Typically, there is an overly close relationship between mother and son, with the father distant from both of them.

Nicolosi indicates that failure to gender-identify through relationship with the father may be due to many influences, including the following:

A. More Rewarding Relationship with Mother.

B. Lack of a Salient Father: i.e., a father's inability to elicit masculine identification in the son.

C. Failure to Encourage Autonomy: i.e., nurturance is not sufficient if the father fails to encourage the boy's own masculine autonomy—the father must upset the comfortable, nurturing, symbiotic relationship the boy has with the mother.

D. Father Absence: father-absence results in dependency, lack of
assertion and/or weak masculine identity.

Nicolosi then maintains that a poor relationship with the father mani-
fests itself later in a male homosexual's seeking of male attention and
companionship. He approvingly quotes Bieber: "We have come to the
conclusion that a constructive, supportive, warmly related father pre-
cludes the possibility of a homosexual son." Nicolosi nuances this
point by emphasizing that although heterosexual men may describe
their fathers unfavorably, homosexual men are stronger in their rejection of their father as a model. This appears to be a particularly differ-
entiating trait. When heterosexual men express disappointment with
their fathers, there is usually less frustration, bitterness, and a smol-
dering sense of victimization.

For the rest of his life, then, according to Nicolosi, the homosexual man tries to figure out his father, who always remains for him a
mystery. For him, both father and masculinity remain elusive and
mysterious. If the father was hostile and antagonistic, then he
becomes a "confounding mystery." If father was emotionally distant
and inadequate, then he becomes a "longing mystery."

This deficiency in father-son relationship accounts in Nicolosi's
framework as a major "predicator" of homosexuality. Nicolosi writes
that boys who have this type of inadequate relationship with their
fathers tend to be fearful of injury, avoiding physical fights, play more
with girls, and describe themselves as loners. He favorably cites
Aardweg who also maintains that poor peer relations can be identified
more often in the background of homosexual men.

In addition, Nicolosi indicates that many studies show the preho-
mosexual boy to be alienated from his body. He writes that clients
often describe an excessive modesty regarding early childhood; and
while this is a quality also seen in heterosexually developing boys, the
condition frequently continues into adulthood. This shyness may then
alternate with exhibitionism, which is an attempt to compensate for
the shyness. Because his maleness was overlooked, he later will have
a deficit—a need to be looked at and admired. Gay bars are thus often
places to receive male attention.

Clearly, in this model, genetics has no significant influence on
homosexuality. While there remains the possibility of some genetic
contribution to gender identity and thus sexual orientation, Nicolosi's

emphasis consistently returns to psychological and environmental causes. Believing homosexuality to be biologically determined discourages, he maintains, any attempts at growth beyond it. The so-called "homosexual gene" is mythical.

For most homosexual men, core gender-identity is intact, but there remains a private and subjective sense of simply not feeling fully male-identified. Nicolosi thus favorably quotes Bieber, "Every homosexual is a latent heterosexual." Gender-identity deficit is the internal, private sense of incompleteness or inadequacy about one's maleness, and this is not always evident in explicit effeminate traits. Homosexual conduct is used as an erotic bridge to gain entry into the special male world. It is a way of finding masculine acceptance—not through personal strength, but vicariously through erotic power. Since the homosexual male is particularly inclined to see relationships with men in terms of power, there is sometimes an overcompensation in power drive. There may also be a masochistic satisfaction in submission, which gives rise to same-sex clinging behavior. In almost every case, homosexual men report, according to Nicolosi, dependency problems, and their relationships often take on an addictive character.

Nicolosi concludes that two men can never "take in each other," in a full and open way. Not only is there a natural anatomical unsuitability, but an inherent psychological insufficiency as well. Both partners are coming together with some deficit. Each is symbolically and sexually attempting to find fulfillment of gender in the other person. But the other person is not whole, and so the relationship ends in disillusionment. Consequently, Nicolosi teaches that no man "can ever be truly at peace in living out a homosexual orientation." Consequently, motivation-to-change means that a "client" is ambivalent in rejecting a homosexual identity and is striving toward heterosexuality. Nicolosi summarizes his reparative therapy by indicating that there are four categories of male friendships for the homosexual man in an increasing order of reparative value:

A. Gay Friendships: Create the possibility of erotic attraction and a mutually exploitive sexual agenda. Honest friendship is contaminated by flirtation and vague innuendos, with each looking for clues of sexual receptivity from the other. Mutual game-playing and manipulation undermine efforts at establishing equality and mutuality, and diminish the value of this type of relationship.

B. Celibate Homosexual Friendships: With other dystonic homosexual men who offer an empathy and special understanding. However, they are limited to their potential to break down the male mystique, which is usually reserved for the straight man.

C. Heterosexual, Nonsexual Friendships: Of particular therapeutic value is the client's disclosure of his homosexual struggle to the straight friend.

D. Heterosexual Sexually Attractive Male Friendships: With men for whom the client feels an erotic attraction offer the greatest opportunity for healing. This transformational shift from sexual to fraternal is the essential healing of male homosexuality.

In light of all of these theories, what conclusions can be reached?

1. Researchers Bell, Weinberg, and Hammersmith questioned 979 homosexual people and 477 heterosexual people who made up a representative and matched sample of the total population. Their meticulous study took ten years to complete—three years in which to collect the data, five years to analyze it, and another two years to check it. They found that family backgrounds had little or no effect on a person's eventual sexual orientation. In critiquing psychological theories, then, and particularly that of Nicolosi, one of the central passages in this research study summarizes a critical point:

> For the benefit of readers who are concerned about what parents may do to influence their children's sexual preference, we would restate our findings another way. No particular phenomenon of family life can be singled out, on the basis of our findings, as especially consequential for either homosexual or heterosexual development. You may supply your sons with footballs and your daughters with dolls, but no one can guarantee that they will enjoy them. *What we seem to have identified...is a pattern of feelings and reactions within the child that cannot be traced back to a single social or sociological root*; indeed, homosexuality may arise from a biological precursor (as do left-handedness and allergies, e.g.) that parents cannot control.

In short, to concerned parents, we cannot recommend anything beyond the care, sympathy, and devotion that good
parents presumably lavish on all their children anyway.[45]

Accurate studies tell us there are neurotic family patterns and there
are loving family patterns. Both types of families produce heterosexual and homosexual children.

2. Current studies by Bailey, Pillard, LeVay, and the National
Institutes of Health indicate that sexual orientation is "substantially
genetic." Despite many attempts, there has been no clear demonstra-
tion that parental behavior, even a parent's homosexuality, affects
children's sexual orientation.

3. As of this writing, the cause/causes of homosexuality is/are
unknown; and the scientific study of sexuality is truly in its infancy.
Despite all the research into sexual orientation, we know very little
about the development of heterosexuality, bisexuality, and homosexuality. Social scientists have proposed many theories to explain sexual
orientation, but none have been conclusively proven true.

Perhaps this letter is a viable commentary:

Mother, I am gay. It took me a long time to admit that to
myself, and a long time to get up enough courage to tell
you. It is the way I am, and is something I realized way
back in Jr. High School. It is not something I chose to be—
anyone who would have you believe such a thing has not
gone through the pain that such a realization can bring, or
the bigotry and prejudice that exists for gay people in our
society. If being gay were a matter of choice, there would
be no gay people, as no one would choose it.

You also must not blame yourself. You no more caused my
sexuality than you caused me to be five foot eight. I would
never blame you, and you must not either. I can't stress this
enough. No one really knows what causes someone to be
homosexual, but it is known that an over-abundance or a
lack of mothering does not cause homosexuality. You cannot blame yourself—even if this is your first instinct. There
is nothing you could have done or did not do that would
change my sexuality.[46]

Conclusion

There is a general consensus today that no one theory of homosexuality can explain such a diverse phenomenon, as no one theory of heterosexuality can explain that diverse phenomenon. There is certainly no single genetic, hormonal or psychological cause of homosexual orientation. There appears to be a variety of factors which can provide a "push" in the direction of homosexuality for some persons. The complex of factors which result in the orientation toward homosexuality probably differs from person to person. While we do not know what causes the orientation, we undoubtedly know that the forces that go into the creation of a homosexual person are more complex and mysterious than most had earlier appreciated. There is, then, substantial reason to approach the scientific topic of homosexuality with caution, respect and humility, as the overwhelming complexity of the issue merits.[47]

A final word should be added about the possibility of changing one's homosexuality to heterosexuality. A number of studies have been conducted on this conversion and these studies claim a certain success rate. The psychological methods used have ranged from psychoanalysis[48] to directive behavioral sex therapy.[49] There has been at least one empirical research report of change via religious means for church lay counseling and healing ministry.[50] Reported success rates have never been outstanding or suggestive of an easy path to change for the homosexual person. These "success" rates have ranged from 33% to 50–60%. In *Homosexuality in Perspective* (1979), e.g., Masters and Johnson reported a 50–60% cure or improvement rate for highly motivated clients using sex therapy methods and behavior therapy methods. This report was later questioned, however, on the grounds of whether or not those studied were *de facto* truly homosexual or heterosexual people.

One author has said, pointing to the somewhat common and continued experience of homosexual feelings even when the "conversion" person is functioning heterosexually, "...the finding that one can with great effort graft apparently heterosexual behavior over an earlier homosexual orientation" is hardly a ringing endorsement of the change process.[51] Even the most optimistic advocates for change by psychological means conclude that change is most likely when motivation is strong, when there is a history of successful heterosexual functioning, when gender identity issues are not present, and when involvement in actual homosexual practice has been minimal.

Today there are many Christian ministries which attempt to provide opportunities for growth and healing for the homosexual.[52] Many of these groups are represented by the umbrella *Exodus International* organization. These groups offer a variety of approaches, but generally agree that change from homosexuality is a difficult and painful process of renouncing "sinful practices and attitudes" and reaching out to grasp the promise of God's help. These groups suggest that struggling with homosexual attraction is a lifelong task, but that the person who takes on that struggle can expect gradual change, especially with God's grace. Some aim for conversion to heterosexuality, others aim at freedom from overpowering homosexual impulses and an increasing capacity to experience one's sexuality as fully as would be desired for any Christian single person.

In an astonishing book entitled *Healing Your Family Tree*, Fr. John H. Hampsch maintains the questionable position that homosexuals "*can* (his emphasis) be cured of this ego-dystonic personality disorder, even if it is proven to be genetic in origin." Hampsch supports this "orientation reversal" by citing the work of organizations such as *Exodus International*. He claims that in order to be "cured" it is necessary to "submit with great humility to a deliverance prayer...," in order to be delivered from a spirit of homosexuality." Hampsch maintains that homosexuality is an "inherited bondage derived from ancestral sin that *sometimes* leaves one open to demonic intervention...," which is often at the root of this disorder."[53] Such harmful and misguided counsel is certainly different from the sound advice of Fr. John F. Harvey:

> ...(T)he moral law does not posit any obligation to take steps to change orientation. However desirable this change is, in our present state of knowledge we can give no guarantee that if one were to follow a certain program and plan of life to change orientation, this will always happen. Since, therefore, we cannot prove that such change will inevitably follow if we do certain things, we cannot impose an obligation to follow a certain psychological and spiritual program to change sexual orientation. This is based upon the ethical principle that one may not impose an obligation unless it is certain that it exists.[54]

Chapter 3

BIBLICAL DOCUMENTATION

The *Letter to the Bishops of the Catholic Church on the Pastoral Care of Homosexual Persons* situates its scriptural discussion of homosexuality within the theology of creation found in Genesis:

> Human beings...are nothing less than the work of God himself; and in the complementarity of the sexes, they are called to reflect the inner unity of the Creator. They do this in a striking way in their cooperation with him in the transmission of life by a mutual donation of the self to the other....To choose someone of the same sex for one's sexual activity is to annul the rich symbolism and meaning, not to mention the goals, of the Creator's sexual design. Homosexual activity is not a complementary union, able to transmit life; and so it thwarts the call to a life of that form of self-giving which the Gospel says is the essence of Christian living.[1]

Because of the critical nature of the scriptural documentation on this subject, it is important to outline carefully various points made in the *Letter* about the biblical data:

1. It is erroneous to claim that "Scripture has nothing to say on the subject of homosexuality."[2]
2. It is erroneous to claim that scripture "somehow tacitly approves" of homosexuality.[3]
3. It is erroneous to state that all biblical injunctions against homosexual activity are so culture-bound that "they are no longer applicable to contemporary life."[4]
4. There is a clear consistency in the Bible on the moral issue of homosexual behavior.[5]
5. The church's teaching on homosexual behavior is based upon the "constant biblical testimony."[6]

56

6. Scripture must be interpreted and properly understood only within the "Church's living Tradition."[7]
7. In the complementarity of the sexes, human beings reflect the inner unity of God, especially in their cooperation with God in the transmission of life and by a mutual donation of one to the other.[8]
8. This truth-of-complementarity has been obscured by sin, exampled in the story of Sodom in Genesis 19 where the moral judgment is made against homosexual relations.[9] In the New Testament, Paul uses homosexual behavior as an example of the human body clouded by sin: it is a form of idolatry and moral excess.[10]
9. It is only in the marital relationship that the use of the sexual faculty can be morally good. Consequently, a person who engages in homosexual activity acts immorally.[11]
10. Homosexual persons are often generous and giving of themselves but when they engage in homosexual genital activity, they are engaging in a non-complementary union, unable to transmit life.[12]

We need to carefully exegete the scriptural data *in light of* the church's tradition regarding homosexuality. Keeping *this* perspective in mind, we need to also recall that the concepts "homosexual" and "homosexuality" were unknown during the time of the Bible's composition. While scripture does speak about homosexuality, it does not recognize homosexuality as a sexual orientation as such, since the biblical writers took it for granted that all people were created with a natural attraction to members of the opposite sex and their genital activity would and should reflect this fact. Consequently, any homosexual behavior was likely to be judged from this perspective. In other words, the biblical writers were non-cognizant of the concept of a sexual orientation as such. It is helpful to look at the basic texts in the Bible which speak to this question:

Genesis 19:1–11

Genesis 18:20–21 reads,

Then the Lord said, "Because the outcry against Sodom and Gomorrah is great and their sin is very grave, I will go

down to see whether they have done altogether according
to the outcry which has come to me; and if not, I will
know."[13]

After Abraham converses with God about God's possible destruction
of the wicked people of Sodom, chapter 19 begins:

> The two angels came to Sodom in the evening; and Lot was
> sitting in the gate of Sodom. When Lot saw them, he rose to
> meet them, and bowed himself with his face to the earth,
> and said, "My lords, turn aside, I pray you, to your servant's
> house and spend the night, and wash your feet; then you
> may rise up early and go on your way." They said, "No; we
> will spend the night in the street." But he urged them strong-
> ly; so they turned aside to him and entered his house; and he
> made them a feast, and baked unleavened bread, and they
> ate. But before they lay down, the men of the city, the men
> of Sodom, both young and old, all the people to the last
> man, surrounded the house; and they called to Lot, "Where
> are the men who came to you tonight? Bring them out to us,
> that we may know them." Lot went out of the door to the
> men, shut the door after him, and said, "I beg you, my
> brothers, do not act so wickedly. Behold, I have two daugh-
> ters who have not known man; let me bring them out to you,
> and do to them as you please; only do nothing to these men,
> for they have come under the shelter of my roof." But they
> said, "Stand back!" And they said, "This fellow came to
> sojourn, and he would play the judge! Now we will deal
> worse with you than with them." Then they pressed hard
> against the man Lot, and drew near to break the door. But
> the men put forth their hands and brought Lot into the house
> to them, and shut the door. And they struck with blindness
> the men who were at the door of the house, both small and
> great, so that they wearied themselves groping for the door.

After further discussion between the angels and Lot, verses 24-29
conclude:

> Then the Lord rained on Sodom and Gomorrah brimstone
> and fire from the Lord out of heaven; and he overthrew

those cities, and all the valley, and all the inhabitants of the cities, and what grew on the ground....So it was that, when God destroyed the cities of the valley, God remembered Abraham, and sent Lot out of the midst of the overthrow, when he overthrew the cities in which Lot dwelt.

Victor Paul Furnish in *The Moral Teaching of Paul*[14] writes that "later biblical writers were not themselves preoccupied with [the] homosexual dimension" of this story.[15] For example, Jeremiah writes that Sodom's sins were adultery, persistent lying and an unwillingness to repent (23:14). Ezekiel claims that the crimes of Sodom's people were "pride, gluttony, arrogance [and] complacency"; moreover, the inhabitants of Sodom "never helped the poor and needy; they were proud and engaged in filthy practices..." (16:49–50). The Wisdom of Solomon identifies the evils of Sodom as folly, insolence and inhospitality (19:13–14). Sirach indicates simply that God "did not spare the people with whom Lot lived, whom he abhorred for their pride" (16:8).

Jesus makes reference to Sodom in Luke 10:10–12 and Matthew 10:14–15. Jesus seems to associate Sodom with the evil of inhospitality. However, there are two late New Testament texts (2 Peter 2:4–10 and Jude 6–7) which do give a predominantly sexual interpretation to the Sodom story.

It seems clear, then, that the citizens of Sodom were involved in numerous offenses. In this regard, it must be remembered that God's decision to destroy Sodom and the surrounding cities was made *prior* to the angelic visit. That is what Abraham's great debate with God was all about (Genesis 18:22–33). The messengers were sent from God to warn Lot and his family to flee, regardless of the reception the messengers themselves received.

Homosexual activity, therefore, was one among many sins for which scripture condemns Sodom. The word "know" in the story is paralleled in Judges 19:22–30 where the word is quite literally translated as "to have intercourse with," which was also the way this word was used in Genesis 4, and commonly in the Old Testament. The point is inescapable: whereas sexual intercourse was legitimate in Genesis 4, because Adam and Eve had been given to each other in marriage, it was an abomination and an act of wickedness in Genesis 19 and in Judges 19, because the relationship is not marital but is one of contemplated homosexual rape. As the *Letter to the Bishops* points out, "...in Genesis 19:1–11...the deterioration due to sin continues in the story of Sodom. There can be no doubt of the moral judgment made there against homosexual relations."[16]

In *Women and Sexuality*, Lisa Sowle Cahill adds yet another dimension-of-interpretation to this story:

> The historical setting renders the act an outrage not only as an instance of sexual violence, but also because it would have amounted to a vile betrayal of the duty of hospitality, without which travelers could not even have survived in the deserts of the ancient Near East. Lot's proposed resolution of the affront is a frightening revelation of the dark side of a male piety only too ready to identify women's social and religious status in terms of the worth of their sexuality to fathers and husbands....Lot was willing to sacrifice his two daughters as an offering to the assailants, and proferred them with the encouragement that they were virgins. To have raped them would apparently have fallen significantly short of the "wickedness" about to be perpetrated on the pair of male visitors.[17]

2 Peter 2:7 interprets one of the sins of Sodom and Gomorrah as "licentiousness" and Jude 7 identifies one of the sins of these cities as "unnatural lust." It is important to conclude, then, that Sodom and Gomorrah were condemned by God for many crimes including homosexual activity. One author writes, "The biblical authors held strong and varying opinions on the sin of Sodom, but none of them equated that sin with homosexual practices."[18] Such an assertion is simply untrue.

John Boswell's *Christianity, Social Tolerance, and Homosexuality*[19] is often cited as a fundamental text for properly interpreting the biblical materials. However, from my research it seems that Boswell tends to misrepresent the authentic meaning of the scriptural texts in many instances. Whether his is a natural error in research or a conscious advocacy stance, it tends to explain away what biblical scholars see as more complex, often negative texts about homosexuality.

He suggests, for example, that Sodom was destroyed *merely* because of "inhospitable treatment of visitors sent from the Lord."[20] Boswell states that the men of Sodom *simply* desired to "know" (get acquainted with) the strangers.[21] Boswell concludes, "There is no sexual interest of any sort in the incident."[22] Such an interpretation is erroneous and should sustain no credibility.

Leviticus 18:21b–23 and 20:13

I am the Lord. You shall not lie with a male as with a woman; it is an abomination. And you shall not lie with any beast and defile yourself with it, neither shall any woman give herself to a beast to lie with it; it is perversion....

If a man lies with a male as with a woman, both of them have committed an abomination; they shall be put to death, their blood is upon them.

The earliest specific law against homosexual activity in Israel occurs in Leviticus 20:13. The same law is present in Leviticus 18, but without reference to the death penalty. The Holiness Code in which the law stands (Leviticus 17–26) had its origin in the 6th century B.C. The purpose of this legislation, made plain early on in the code, was to establish the "holiness" of the Israelites over against their neighbors:

You shall not do as they do in the land of Egypt, where you dwelt, and you shall not do as they do in the land of Canaan, to which I am bringing you. You shall not walk in their statutes. You shall do my ordinances and keep my statutes and walk in them. I am the Lord your God (18:3–4).

In this Holiness Code the people of Israel were required to maintain their identity and integrity as the people of the one true God. The prohibition of males lying with males, like many of the other laws in this code, sought to identify and condemn practices that had been, and ought always to remain, essentially foreign to Israel's life.[23]

Some have argued that what is really being proscribed here is either a kind of homosexual temple prostitution or the imposition of sex by one man on another, by one woman on another or by a human being on an animal.[24] In other words, homosexual rape is forbidden, as is bestiality.

On the contrary, the words "as with a woman" suggest that what is permissible for a man to do with a woman is not permissible for him to do with another man. Consequently, these passages seem to indicate that what is permitted between the sexes in marriage is not permitted between members of the same sex. Some authors tend to so overly-contextualize the Leviticus texts as to make the homosexual content of the condemnation unimportant: i.e., in the code homosexual activity is condemned because of its perceived association with peoples and practices the Israelites found reprehensible and threatening and most particularly because such practices were associated with idolatry and cultic impurity; and homosexual behavior would make no sense to an underpopulated people that depended on fertility for their very survival.[25] While such interpretations can be helpful in understanding the general context of the time, it is wrong to conclude that *at the same time* the texts do not condemn homosexual activity.

Boswell simply exegetes the Levitical texts against homosexual behavior as "ceremonially unclean" behavior[26] and not as "inherently evil" behavior. He concludes, "...the Levitical regulations...are manifestly irrelevant in explaining Christian hostility to gay sexuality."[27] Such an assertion is false and contradicts a number of the points of exegesis raised already in the C.D.F. *Letter.*

1 Corinthians 6:9–11 and 1 Timothy 1:8–11

Do you not know that the unrighteous will not inherit the kingdom of God? Do not be deceived; neither the immoral, nor idolaters, nor adulterers, nor homosexuals [sodomites], nor thieves, nor the greedy, nor drunkards, nor revilers, nor robbers will inherit the kingdom of God. And such were some of you. But you were washed, you were sanctified, you were justified in the name of the Lord Jesus Christ and in the spirit of our God (1 Cor. 6).

Now we know that the law is good, if anyone uses it lawfully, understanding this, that the law is not laid down for the just but for the lawless and disobedient, for the ungodly and sinners, for the unholy and profane, for murderers of fathers and murderers of mothers, for man slayers, immoral persons, sodomites, kidnappers, liars, perjurers, and whatever else is contrary to sound doctrine, in accordance with the glorious gospel of the blessed God with which I have been entrusted (1 Timothy 1).

Furnish suggests three important points that should be kept in mind when studying the Pauline/deutro-Pauline texts:

1. The concepts "homosexual" and "homosexuality" as a sexual orientation were unknown in Paul's day. These terms presume an understanding of human sexuality that was possible only with the advent of modern psychological and sociological analysis.[28] Ancient writers did not know, for example, of our concept of "sexual orientation." Dio Chrysostom, for instance, presumed that the same lusts that drove men to engage female prostitutes could drive them eventually to seduce other men.[29] Similarly, Philo wrote of the sodomites' sexual intercourse with men as if it were one form of their "mad lust for women." Moreover, these writers and their contemporaries presumed that one could by force of will control these appetites and conform oneself to the sexual behavior dictated by reason or by "the law of nature."[30]

2. Homosexual behavior was invariably associated with insatiable lust and avarice. Seneca, for instance, portrayed it as a rich man's sport.[31]

3. Writers of this period were convinced that homosexual behavior necessarily involved one person's exploitation of another. For example, the influence of Stoicism was widespread, and is detectable not only in several of the writers of the period but also in the teaching of St. Paul.

In the 1 Timothy 1 text, "sodomites" is used for the original Greek term *arsenokoitai*, which literally means "[men] who have intercourse with [other] males." In *The New Testament and Homosexuality*,[32] Robin Scroggs argues for this translation of 1 Timothy 1:

(U)nderstanding this, that the law is not laid down for the just but for the lawless, rebellious, impious, sinner, unholy, profane, patricide, matricide, murderer, *pornoi*, *arsenokoitai*, *andrapodistai*, liar, and perjurer and whatever else is contrary to sound doctrine....

Scroggs demonstrates that *pornos* means "male prostitute": the one who sells himself, or the slave in the brothel house (in normal Greek usage); in the New Testament usage, it normally means sexual crimes in general. Since *pornos* is here juxtaposed to *arsenokoites*, it may have the same meaning vis-à-vis *arsenokoites* as does *malakos* in 1 Corinthians 6, the first term denoting the passive homosexual role and the second term the active. Scroggs then concludes that the phrase could be translated, "Male prostitutes, males who lie [with them] and slave dealers [who procure them] (*andrapodistai*)."

Scroggs' point becomes more evident when analyzing the 1 Corinthians 6 text. The two Greek words in question here are *malakoi* and *arsenokoitai*. The root meaning of the first term is "soft" or "weak," and by extension, "effeminate" (as in fact some translations render this text). It is significant that this is the very term that a number of writers at the time used to describe "call-boys," those who offered their bodies for pay to older males. However, the term can denote men as well as boys. *A Greek-English Lexicon of the New Testament and Other Early Christian Literature* indicates that *malakoi* denotes "men and boys who allow themselves to be misused homosexually."[33] That Paul is using it in a sexual sense here seems likely, because it stands in a list where several other terms referring to sexual immorality also appear, including "fornicators" and "adulterers."

Although 1 Corinthians 6:9 is the first documented use of the word *arsenokoitai*, it is difficult to avoid the conclusion that it refers to males who engage in sexual activity with other males. The juxtaposed term *malakoi* supports this interpretation. Scroggs argues that the word is simply a literal rendering in Greek of the Hebrew phrase *mishkav zakur*, "lying with a male," the usual way of referring to male homosexual intercourse in early rabbinic literature. Both arsenokoites and *mishkav zakur* appear to be terms coined from the prohibition of homosexual acts in Leviticus 18:22–23 and 20:13.

Since *malakoi* would refer to the "effeminate" or passive partner in such a relationship, *arsenokoitai* doubtlessly refers to the male who assumes the more active role. Furnish thus translates the phrase in 1 Corinthians 6:9–11 as, "Don't deceive yourselves: Neither the sexually immoral, nor idolaters, nor adulterers, nor effeminate males, nor men who have sex with them, nor thieves, nor money-grabbers, nor drunkards, nor slanderers, nor swindlers will get into God's kingdom."[34]

What, then, did Paul have in mind as he recites a list of vices which includes reference to "effeminate males" and "men who have sex with them"? Given what we have learned from the forms of homosexual activity with which Paul's world was most familiar, it would appear that these references are respectively to youthful call-boys and their customers. According to various ancient writers who condemn this practice, the one partner has violated the male role that by nature is his; and, by taking advantage of this, the other partner has also violated his proper role. Such conduct Paul regards as one of the forms of unrighteousness by which "unbelievers" are distinguished from "saints." It is untrue to conclude, then, as Boswell does, that "There is no clear condemnation of homosexual acts in the verses in question."[35]

Romans 1:22–27

Claiming to be wise, they became fools, and exchanged the glory of the immortal God for images resembling mortal man or birds or animals or reptiles. Therefore, God gave them up in the lusts of their hearts to impurity, to the dishonoring of their bodies among themselves, because they exchanged the truth about God for a lie and worshiped and served the creature rather than the Creator, who is blessed forever! Amen. For this reason God gave them up to dishonorable passions. Their women exchanged natural relations for unnatural, and the men likewise gave up natural relationships with women and were consumed with passion for one another, men committing shameless acts with men and receiving in their own persons the due penalty for their error.

Richard B. Hayes has given us an important context with which to interpret this text.[36] Hayes indicates that a *keynote* for understanding this text is to appreciate Paul's basic theological view that the believer was to proclaim God's righteousness (God's faithfulness and justice). God's wrath is thus displayed against those who do not acknowledge and honor him. In Paul's theology, all depravities *follow from* the human person's *unrighteousness*; and this is the meaning of the "exchange" rhetoric: because some persons fell into idolatry and "exchanged" worship of the true God for false gods, God "exchanged" in them the natural for the unnatural. In this light, it is important to note that this is the first and only time in the whole Bible that one encounters the condemnation of female homosexual activity.

In this text, Paul, like his non-Christian contemporaries, supposes that homosexual behavior is something *freely chosen* by an individual; in Greek and in English the verbs "exchanged" and "gave up" imply a conscious decision to act in one way rather than another. Paul associates this choice with *insatiable lust*; the men, he writes, were "consumed with passion for one another." Paul regards such activity as *a violation of the created order*: "natural" heterosexual relations were abandoned in favor of those which were "against nature." It is not surprising, then, to find Paul including sexual immoralities among those vices to which the pagans had been led by their own idolatry: lustful impurity and the degradation of their bodies (1:24), and "dishonorable passions" as evidenced by homosexual intercourse (1:26–27). In this connection he too can speak of the Gentiles having received "the due penalty for their error" (1:27). The "due penalty" indicates the very "exchange" itself, rather than some form of venereal disease or even (incredibly) AIDS, as some have recently suggested.

Scroggs and many contemporary writers seek to answer the question, "What specifically was it that the New Testament was reacting to when it speaks of what we might term 'homosexuality'?" As we have seen, Scroggs makes a good case for the position that the New Testament (especially Paul) was reacting against pederasty. Scroggs and others then imply that since this is the case, it is not correct to further draw conclusions about the New Testament position on other forms of homosexual activity. In other words, one can say nothing based on the New Testament about whether it condemns any other form of homosexual behavior. This argument is flawed.

To discern what particular form/manifestation of a phenomenon an author is reacting to is not the same thing as to say why he is reacting against it. In other words, the specific manifestation is not the cause. Scroggs and others have to a certain extent confused these two things. For example, let us say that a series of particularly heinous murders have taken place over recent months, murders of a ritual nature which in some way mock the church. Under such circumstances, if church spokesmen were interviewed by the news media they might well express their indignation and utter disapproval of this particular form of murder. They might even dwell on the fact that the form in question is especially despicable. But would it be correct to conclude that they are not really opposed to murder as such but only to *this particular form of murder*? Of course not. The same thing is true of the New Testament's view of homosexual activity. In other words, Scroggs and others have made a very good and convincing case for the position that pederasty was most probably the particular form of homosexuality to which the New Testament is by-and-large reacting. But this does not mean that the New Testament opposes only pederasty, but would find other types of homosexual behavior permissible. Consequently, the question comes down to this: Did/would Paul see a homosexual relationship by mutual consent as against God's will or not?

In Romans 1:26–27 when Paul speaks of "natural" sexual relations versus "unnatural," Scroggs and others deny that this has anything to do with "any theories of natural law."[37] Even though pederasty may be the example of such behavior Paul had in mind, it seems a strain on credibility to think that he does not mean "unnatural" in somewhat the same sense we would now use the term in reference to deviant sexual activity. What Paul writes in these verses seems to bear this out. Note also that he uses the language of "males with males" (rather than men with men), and not "men with boys," as one might expect if the reference were only to pederasty. Given the reference to the "unnatural" quality of this behavior, and the generic terms "male(s)" and "female(s)" and the unique reference to female homosexual activity, it is difficult not to conclude that Paul is referring to something more than pederasty.

While it may be possible to demonstrate certain specific manifestations of homosexual behavior that New Testament authors probably had in mind in their anti-homosexual statements (e.g., pederasty), this does not prove that these remarks were limited to this one manifestation of such behavior. However widespread pederasty may have been in the Mediterranean world of the first century, surely no one could claim that sexual activity between adult males was unknown then, even though it may be less well documented. Pauline and deutero-Pauline texts provide some evidence to support the contention that the condemnation was in fact broader. First, evidence comes from what New Testament authors *do not say*. Nowhere *in the New Testament* can one find reference to any sexual vice specifically referring to "boys." The extra-biblical *Didache*, on the other hand, contains a list of moral prohibitions based upon the decalogue in which *ou paidophthoreseis* ("thou shalt not corrupt boys") occurs between "thou shalt not commit adultery" and "thou shalt not commit fornication" (*Didache* 2:2)—thus it is connected to the 6th commandment. Furthermore, *arsenokoitai* cannot be restricted to minors nor, as mentioned earlier, can *malakoi*.

Second, we should look again at what the New Testament authors *do say*. The term they use in contexts condemning homosexual behavior is *arsenokoitai* (1 Corinthians 6:9; 1 Timothy 1:10). Like rabbinic *mishkav zakur*, this is undoubtedly a coinage based on Leviticus 18:22 and 20:13, the Old Testament passages that provide the clearest and strongest condemnation of homosexual activity. There is no evidence to suggest that the Leviticus texts refer to acts committed with boys rather than men, and this holds true for the rabbinic expression as well. Because of the widespread phenomenon of pederasty in New Testament times, it is quite possible that pederasty was the *specific form* of homosexual behavior that New Testament writers would have come into contact with most often. But this does not mean it was the only form they had in mind. The fact that Paul and the author of 1 Timothy made use of a term based on the legal texts in Leviticus, passages rejecting homosexual acts *in general*, supports the view that what they were condemning was broader than pederasty. These facts make it impossible to endorse Scroggs' conclusion: "Biblical judgments about homosexuality are not relevant to today's debate."[38]

In addition, the New Testament's clear pro-marriage statements are of vital importance in expressing its view about homosexuality. This is a point of major significance and should not be overlooked.

Although it cannot be proven absolutely from scriptural evidence alone, there appears to be sufficient basis from which to assert that both the Old and New Testament writers express disapproval of homosexual behavior *per se*. The reasons are not always clearly stated, which certainly makes the biblical, moral and pastoral task more difficult.[39]

Some authors have also argued that there are biblical passages that portray same-sex relationships in highly positive terms.[40] The example most often cited is the relationship between Jonathan and David (1 Samuel 18:1–4; 20:30; 20:40–41; 2 Samuel 1:26). These authors usually suggest that Jonathan and David enjoyed a "physical relationship," witnessed to by the bonding and depth that existed between them. In *Jonathan Loved David: Homosexuality in Biblical Times*,[41] Horner reviews the Middle Eastern background in which the Bible was written (largely the Gilgamesh Epic and certain Hittite laws) and concludes that homosexuality was widely tolerated in this area. He maintains that this provides the viewpoint against which the Old Testament texts should be interpreted. He argues that David and Jonathan loved each other "physically," and that the "possibility" exists of understanding Naomi and Ruth's relationship in the same way (Ruth 1:16–17). The Leviticus texts proscribing homosexual acts (18:22; 20:13) do not seem to disturb Horner, since the Holiness Code is exilic and thus in his view reflects a later attitude toward homosexuality.

He maintains that "abomination" in these passages refers to "idolatry"; hence the proscribed actions are not condemned on ethical grounds. As for Paul,[42] Horner maintains that his statements against homosexuality come out of a mind-set that views the flesh as evil. Finally, Horner states, since Jesus' most intimate associates were men, "at least he was not the type of person who would have displayed any hostility toward those who might have had homosexual relationships."

In light of this type of "interpretation," it is critical to note that the language describing the type of relationship between David and Jonathan is largely drawn from treaty terminology (e.g., 1 Samuel 18:1). The laws in Leviticus 18:6–23 represent a stratum of older legal material which has been inserted into a later parenetic context condemning pagan cultic practices. Therefore, one may not use this later context as a basis for interpreting terms integral to the earlier stratum. There is no doubt that in various parts of Samuel 1 and 2, a description is given of a warm and affectionate friendship between Jonathan and David.[43] While their relationship can properly be interpreted as a "good friendship," nothing is said explicitly at all about a homosexual dimension to this relationship. Horner conjectures that Saul discovered the nature of the relationship between his son and David and plotted to kill David. Fortunately, Jonathan was able to warn him and Jonathan remained with his wife and father after David fled. Eventually Saul and Jonathan were killed together in battle. On

hearing of this tragic event, David composed a moving elegy in testimony to his love for the two men (2 Samuel 1:19–27). The key verse
is 1:26 where David writes:

> I am distressed for you, my brother Jonathan; very pleasant
> have you been to me; your love to me was wonderful,
> passing the love of women.

Taken out of context such a declaration seems to offer some credibility for Horner's interpretation. However, since there is no explicit
treatment of the matter of homosexuality and since both Jonathan and
David were married (David eight times with many children), and
since the language describing their relationship is mainly drawn from
treaty terminology, it seems inaccurate and biblically unwarranted to
conclude that the relationship between David and Jonathan was
homosexual in nature.[44]

Pastoral Conclusions

1. While individual biblical texts must be interpreted carefully
and contextually, there is no doubt that both the Old Testament and
the New Testament prohibit homosexual conduct. Even the absence of
any explicit teaching from Jesus does not counteract this point.

2. In his classic work on homosexuality, Bailey states that
"...We have decisive Biblical authority for censoring the conduct of
those whom we may describe as male perverts...."[45] Bailey and others
conclude that: "To such situations it can hardly be said that the New
Testament speaks, since the condition of inversion with all its special
problems, was quite unknown at that time."

John McNeill has argued in a similar fashion:

> (B)oth in the Old and the New Testaments, wherever the
> Bible clearly seems to refer to homosexual activity, we
> must recognize a judgment of condemnation. However,
> every text dealing with homosexual activity also refers to
> aggravating circumstances such as idolatry, sacred prostitu-
> tion, promiscuity, violent rape, seduction of children, and
> violation of guests' rights. As a result one can never be sure
> to what extent the condemnation is of homosexual activi-

ties as such or only of homosexual activities under these circumstances.[46]

This same interpretation is given by Scanzoni and Mollenkott:

A careful examination of what the Bible says about issues relating to homosexuality still leaves us with many unanswered questions. For one thing, the idea of a life-long homosexual orientation or "condition" is never mentioned in the Bible....(F)urthermore, [it] does not mention the possibility of a permanent, committed relationship of love between homosexuals analogous to heterosexual marriage.[47]

In light of these types of inadequate interpretations, it is critical to recall the point made in the *Letter to the Bishops*:

It is likewise essential to recognize that the Scriptures are not properly understood when they are interpreted in a way which contradicts the Church's living Tradition. To be correct, the interpretation of Scripture must be in substantial accord with that Tradition (n 5).

It is important to affirm, then, the historical and human character of the Bible. At the same time, however, neither attribute describes the Bible's final reality. It is only when we recognize the Bible as the word of God and the book of the church that we name its full and intended reality.[48]

It is critical to note as well that along with the Catholic tradition on this subject, a number of Protestant exegetes trace the condemnation of homosexual behavior to the doctrine of creation in Genesis 1–3. Williams is representative when, following Eichrodt and Von Rad, he writes that: "The primal form of humanity is the fellowship of man and woman....The old myths of the androgynous (bisexual and unisexual) Man are rejected and all ambiguity in the relationship between the sexes is removed."[49] For many Protestant writers there is something so basic about the potential for male-female covenanting that no other sexual structuring can hope to achieve the same kind of appropriate fellowship.

3. R.A.F. MacKenzie has written that "The Scripture contains revelations...but not all Scripture is revelation. All Scripture is

inspired, but not all is revealed. Similarly, tradition comes to include much that is only of human origin, however venerable and valuable…(needing constant interpretation and commentary in succeeding ages)."[50] This means that the scriptures, as critical as they are, are not totally sufficient in isolation. The tradition of Christian wisdom, the knowledge available in the natural and social sciences, the contemporary experience of the faithful, and the insight that comes only through prayer and the anguished searching of a restless heart, are all components of a fuller process of ethical discernment. Therefore, in facing the question about the morality of homosexual activity, we cannot be content solely with exploring the Biblical material, but also must search the tradition of the church on this subject. The teaching church continues to interpret the scriptures as opposed to all homosexual conduct.

4. While the Bible is clear about homosexual activity, it is also clear about hate. Hate is wrong. It is wrong to draw a circle around a group of people and hate them because of who they are, whether the excuse is race, sexual orientation, ethnic origin, or sex. This hate is wrong whether it is expressed in physical attacks, murder, a snicker, or silence. There is nothing in the Bible that gives us permission to hate people because of who they are. *Veritatis Splendor* warns that: "Such understanding never means compromising and falsifying the standard of good and evil in order to adapt it to particular circumstances" (n 104). This is sound advice that should be followed, but advice that can be heeded without rancor and hatred of persons.

5. In 1 Corinthians 6:9–11 Paul condemns all sorts of unrighteous people [e.g., idolaters; adulterers; thieves; the greedy; drunkards; revilers; robbers]: he does not *single out* homosexual persons. Paul is making the point by this list of immoral practices that we are all in need of grace. If there is any portion of these texts that we should especially underline, it is Romans 2:1:

> Therefore, you have no excuse…whoever you are, when you judge another; for in passing judgment upon him you condemn yourself, because you, the judge, are doing the very same things.

Chapter 4

HOMOSEXUALITY IN CHURCH TEACHING

Situating the church's teachings on homosexuality in a proper context is vitally important. In a provocative article entitled "Preaching and Teaching Sexuality: The Dilemmas and Possibilities" in the April 1993 edition of *Chicago Studies*,[1] Louis J. Cameli asks the question: "Do we know what we are doing when we preach on sexuality?" This is a pivotal question in assessing church teaching on the question of homosexuality as well: i.e., Do we know what we are doing when we teach about homosexuality? "Teaching" includes a range of activities such as preaching, instructing, and counselling. Cameli maintains that people respond to this question dependent on whether or not they are self-confident about the questions of sexuality.[2]

While the "confident" do not form a uniform cohort, some of the confident belong to the so-called "right wing," those who carry the banners of conservative Christianity or traditional Catholicism. They know exactly what they are doing in teaching on matters of sexuality. Cameli comments, "They repeat sometimes angrily and sometimes menacingly but always forcefully and, usually, abstractly the principles contained in official Church teaching."[3]

Another group shares the confident attitude of the "traditionalists." This group includes members of the so-called "left wing," who represent a more progressive Catholicism. They apologize for the past and regret that church teaching has confused and disturbed people, robbing them of the joys of sex. Their message means to liberate people: "Sex is good. Enjoy yourselves. We're sorry about things you've heard from the church."

Quite different from these two, we find numerous groups of teachers who lack the confidence which seems so abundant among the "traditionalists" and "progressives." Their lack of confidence is born of a confusing web of questions: e.g., Is church teaching in the areas of sexuality out of step?

When one looks at our social situation, there is considerable misery. A permissive and runaway sexuality seems to breed violence,

73

exploitation, sickness and death. Cameli remarks, "People are certainly no happier for all the social permissions they have to act on their sexual instincts....Could official Church teaching be the answer after all?"[4]

None of these approaches are pedagogically helpful when dealing with church teaching. The mere repetition of the teaching encapsulated in abstract principles does a disservice to the power of the teaching for inviting persons into a deeper and more abundant life in God.

It is important, then, to always teach about sexuality with humility. This does not mean assuming a waffling stance or being apologetic about what one has to say. Cameli writes:

> Humility in the realm of sexuality means that the *ecclesia docens*, the teaching Church, is also the *ecclesia discens*, the learning Church, and candidly admit that Church teaching is open to further development. Again, this does not mean that the teaching is reversible or subject to a radical revision. Rather, development in sexual moral teaching...means that deeper insights are to be had, that the Spirit continues to guide the Church in paths of fuller understanding, and that more appropriate communication can be devised.[5]

Humility in teaching sexual morality means that the church finds no embarrassment in sharing the dilemmas and questions which do not have easy answers or solutions. Sharing the questions and sharing honestly and openly the "loose ends" would go far to make the presentation of Catholic teaching on sexual morality appear to be more adequate. The Vatican's 1986 *Letter to the Bishops* on homosexuality, for example, names homosexuality a "complex issue" and encourages the need for more "study" and "well-balanced counsel" on this difficult subject (n 2).

The church should not retreat from its sense of the truth about human sexuality. At the same time, however, the church must humbly admit that questions and dilemmas remain. The church must continue to dialogue with the human sciences in order to humbly interface about questions of human sexuality. Religious faith does not replace research. Faith which takes into account human sciences in the area of sexual morality moves a great deal in the direction of helping the church authentically express its sexual teachings.

Humility presupposes, then, a respect for the particular problems and unanswered questions which plague the complex area of human sexuality. At the same time, however, humility cannot assume that there is no truth in these matters or that all teaching on these concerns can change. As this chapter unfolds, we will see that the church has a clear landscape for understanding human sexuality and thus humility can never be equated with a lack of direction or a belief that certain teachings have not reached a level of moral maturity.

Veritatis Splendor acknowledges the importance of interdisciplinary studies (n 30), but does rightly warn against the use of behavioral sciences which deny "the very reality of human freedom." (n 33) As we continue this study of homosexuality, then, we do so mindful of the encyclical's concern not to take as our standard "the results of a statistical study of concrete human behavior patterns and the opinions about morality encountered in the majority of people" (n 46).

In her book *Between the Sexes*, Lisa Sowle Cahill raises this question:

> Sexual morality is a difficult subject, one that impinges in a most intimate and often painful way on the consciences, identities, anxieties and hopes of those who address it. In the churches, as in the wider culture, sexuality has been a source of division, exclusion, suffering, and even hatred....Various theological and moral perceptions of sexuality still need to be formulated with an appropriate degree of humility as well as honesty....How shall the homosexual's situation be understood after empirical studies have indicated the relative uncontrollability of sexual orientation, along with the fundamental relation of sexuality to identity and personality?[6]

We thus approach the question of homosexuality in church teachings with needed humility, but also with a clear awareness that there are parameters-of-truth which help guide us through these difficult questions.

A. The Thomistic Tradition

In his teaching on sexuality, St. Thomas Aquinas made a distinction between sexual sins "against nature" (*contra naturam*) and "according to nature" (*secundum naturam*).[7]

Thomas explains this distinction:

(a) In sins according to nature (*peccata secundum naturam*), the sin is determined as being "contrary to right reason": e.g., fornication, rape, incest, adultery, sacrilege.
The lack of conformity to right reason is common to all sexual sins.

(b) In sins against nature (*peccata contra naturam*), the sin contains an *additional* aspect: it is not only against reason but it is also inconsistent with the end of the venereal act, i.e., the begetting of children: e.g., masturbation, bestiality, homosexual activity, contraception.

Thomas did not determine the objective gravity of sin simply according to its external consequences, but by the inner disharmony which sin brings to a person: i.e., the ontological disharmony, rather than the psychological effects it may produce. *Veritatis Splendor* makes this same point:

If the object of the concrete action is not in harmony with the true good of the person, the choice of that action makes our will and ourselves morally evil, thus putting us in conflict with our ultimate end, the supreme good, God himself (n 72).

For Thomas, unnatural sexual sins are unreasonable because they attack a fundamental ontological order. These acts always violate an intelligible good: e.g., homosexual activity is a generic act which is always forbidden, and needs no further specification.[8] For Thomas, therefore, certain acts are always forbidden, no matter what the circumstances.[9]

It has become part of Catholic tradition, following upon this Thomistic background, that there are certain acts that are intrinsically evil (*intrinsece malum*), and therefore can never be done. As one example, the manuals of moral theology listed "Sex outside the marriage contract" (i.e., the free exercise of the sexual faculty, apart from normal sexual intercourse within a marriage relationship) was prohibited, no matter what the intention or the situation.

An act is intrinsically evil when its essential core is so gravely evil that no actual or possible set of circumstances, whatever goodness they may contain, could render an instance of that act good in the concrete; i.e., it is impossible for any individual act's particular features to possess sufficient goodness to outweigh or even equal the evil of its common features. Therefore, the act *as a concrete whole* always possesses more evil than good. In other words, the essential core is so evil that its evilness diffuses and corrodes the act as a whole, and overrides whatever goodness the particular features may have, notwithstanding that a particular feature considered in isolation from the whole act may have more good than evil. One author offers this example:

> In my judgment, "slavery"—either on an individual or institutional level—is intrinsically evil. Slavery here is defined as an established or settled type of interpersonal relatedness—a *modus vivendi*, if you will—in which the self treats the other solely as a means and not as an end, or treats him merely as an object, thing or function and not as a person. As so defined, slavery so gravely violates the constituent values of community—equality, freedom and justice—that I cannot conceive of a situation in which it would be morally justifiable.[10]

In 1975, the Congregation for the Doctrine of the Faith published *Persona Humana, (The Declaration on Certain Questions Concerning Sexual Ethics)*. It specifically states that, according to the Christian tradition, right reason and the church's teaching, every direct violation of the moral order of sexuality is objectively serious because in the moral order of sexuality such high values of human life are involved.[11]

Veritatis Splendor recalls and reemphasizes this teaching about intrinsically evil acts. In chapter two, number 4, "acting morally good" is a matter of human freedom choosing to act "in conformity with man's true good" (n 72). The *Catechism of the Catholic Church* likewise teaches that "There are concrete acts that it is always wrong to choose, because their choice entails a disorder of the will, i.e., a moral evil" (n 1761).

The 1995 encyclical of Pope John Paul II *Evangelium Vitae* also restates this tradition:

The negative moral precepts, which declare that the choice
of certain actions is morally unacceptable, have an absolute
value for human freedom: they are valid always and everywhere, without exception. They make it clear that the
choice of certain ways of acting is radically incompatible
with the love of God and with the dignity of the person
created in his image. Such choices cannot be redeemed by
the goodness of any intention or of any consequences; they
are irrevocably opposed to the bond between persons; they
contradict the fundamental decision to direct one's life to
God....The "no" which they unconditionally require makes
clear the absolute limit beneath which free individuals cannot lower themselves (n 75).[11a]

The *Catechism of the Catholic Church, Veritatis Splendor* and
Evangelium Vitae all clearly affirm the Church's teaching that there
are certain acts that by their very nature are incapable of being
ordered to God because they radically contradict the good of the
human person. Homogenital activity is such an act since it violates
human integrity and is offensive to human dignity (see n 80 of
Veritatis Splendor).

Patrick J. Boyle gives us this historical view:

Throughout the many centuries of its existence, the magisterium of the Church has not hesitated to call certain moral
acts evil in themselves. In recent times Vatican II has reiterated many of these morally evil acts. Such acts as infanti-
cide, euthanasia, genocide, suicide, and devastation of
entire cities with their inhabitants were considered by the
council fathers as intrinsically evil acts. Pope Pius XII,
John XXIII, Paul VI taught that abortion was intrinsically
evil. Paul VI stated that all means of artificial birth control
were objectively evil. Fornication, adultery and sodomy
were condemned by the Sacred Congregation for the
Doctrine of the Faith. Thus, the magisterium has consistently asserted its competency in designating certain acts
intrinsically evil....[12]

How might we pastorally understand this question of intrinsic evil?

(1) These "negative precepts" may never serve as intentions for human action.
(2) These norms are universal and admit of no exception.
(3) These norms present a point of reference: i.e., every action that is objectively and intrinsically evil (*intrinsece malum*) must be absolutely avoided.
(4) The functions of these norms serve as guides to right actualization and are thus indispensably important.

Veritatis Splendor concludes its treatment of intrinsically evil acts by affirming:

> As is evident, in the question of the morality of human acts, and in particular the question of whether there exists intrinsically evil acts, we find ourselves faced with the question of man himself, of his truth and of the moral consequences flowing from that truth. By acknowledging and teaching the existence of intrinsic evil in given human acts, the Church remains faithful to the integral truth about man; she thus respects and promotes man in his dignity and vocation (n 83).

Regarding human sexuality, Boyle raises certain positive benefits of this teaching for the pastoral life of the church:

> If understood correctly, it could generate a respect for the importance of sex. It could show that sex should not be used at one's whim. Another advantage in the traditional teaching is the security of knowing which acts are bad and to be avoided by the faithful. A third advantage consists in the uniformity in counselling which the traditional teaching provided. In other words, such acts as masturbation and fornication are evil for all irrespective of circumstances or proportionate reason....It is evident that the traditional teaching on the gravity of matter in sexual sins separated sins against chastity from most of the other sins. This separation had the positive effect of engendering a certain fear

of unchastity. It marked the virtue out as something special. This positive attitude is created in much the same way
that the prohibitions against the taking of one's own life
and against abortion implicitly create the positive attitude
in an individual of a great respect for life. Even in war
time, soldiers who have witnessed death or who have been
forced to take a life often grow in this respect for life
because they see the finality of death.[13]

In concluding this treatment of St. Thomas and the tradition that
followed him, we need to turn here to a critical text in St. Thomas'
Summa Theologiae.[14] In his treatment of "Pleasure," St. Thomas concludes article 7:

Now with regard to pleasures of either of these two kinds,
there are some which are unnatural, absolutely speaking,
but may be called natural from a particular point of view.
For it sometimes happens that one of the principles which
is natural to the species as a whole has broken down in one
of its individual members; the result can be that something
which runs counter to the nature of the species as a rule,
happens to be in harmony with nature for a particular individual: as it becomes natural for a vessel of water which
has been heated to give out heat. Thus something which is
"against human nature," either as regards reason or as
regards physical preservation, may happen to be in harmony with the natural needs of *this* man because in him nature
is ailing. He may be ailing physically: either from some
particular complaint, as fever-patients find sweet things
bitter and vice versa; or from some dispositional disorder,
as some find pleasure in eating earth or coals. He may be
ailing psychologically, as some men by habituation come
to take pleasure in cannibalism, or in copulation with
beasts or with their own sex, or in other things not in
accord with human nature.[15]

Thomas understood homosexual activity (*in coitu masculorum*)
unnatural for the human species, absolutely speaking. In his teaching,
however, it was possible for some "breakdown" to occur in an individ-

ual member, thus making "copulation with one's own sex" connatural for an individual (*huic homini connaturale*) in whom "nature is ailing." Thomas would certainly not condone such activity or understand it as "natural," as he referred to such activity as an "unnatural crime."[16]

B. Principles To Guide Confessors in Questions of Homosexuality

In 1973 the National Conference of Catholic Bishops published a paper whose Foreword reads:

> This paper has been approved by the Bishops' Committee on Pastoral Research and Practices for distribution to priest-confessors who deal with the moral and pastoral problems of homosexuals.

> In the Committee's judgment, the paper contains a valuable digest of traditional and contemporary theological thought on this complex question. It is made available in the hope that homosexuals who seek the Church's aid may find in the priests they consult an ever more effective channel of Christ's grace and mercy.

What are the main features of these *Principles*?

These *Principles* understand the homosexual person to be "an adult" whose sexual orientation is "predominantly toward persons of the same sex."[17] This opening "definition" is quite important for it recognizes that an individual must reach some stage of maturity ("an adult person") to sustain the capacity to identify his or her sexual orientation. In addition, this understanding recognizes that one's sexual orientation is not an "all or nothing" reality.[18] As we have seen, sexuality forms a continuum with homosexuality on one end and heterosexuality on the other. Thus, men who define themselves as heterosexual may well have males in their lives whom they deeply love; and women who define themselves as homosexual may have men in their lives whom they deeply love. Consequently, it is more realistic to think in terms of being "more" (predominantly) heterosexual than homosexual or "more" (predominantly) homosexual than heterosexual. In addition, at different points in one's life, a person may gravitate more toward one end of the scale then the other (e.g., through experimental or variational homosexual experiences).

In this regard, it is important to realize that sexuality can be either psychological or physical or both: e.g., a person could be both psychologically and physically homosexual; a person could be both psychologically and physically heterosexual; a person could be psychologically homosexual but not physically, i.e., have a homosexual orientation but not actualize it physically; a person could be psychologically heterosexual but not physically, i.e., have a heterosexual orientation but not actualize it physically; a person could have a homosexual psychological orientation but engage in heterosexual physical behavior; a person could have a heterosexual psychological orientation and engage in homosexual behavior.

When the *Principles* assert therefore that a homosexual person is "oriented predominantly toward persons of the same sex," it is supporting the view that sexual orientation is not dichotomous, i.e., heterosexual or homosexual. Over 40 years ago, Kinsey, Pomeroy and Martin asserted:

> The world is not divided into sheep and goats. Not all are black nor all things white. It is a fundamental of taxonomy that nature rarely deals with discreet categories and tries to force facts into separate pigeonholes. The living world is a continuum in each and every one of its aspects. The sooner we learn this concerning human sexual behavior the sooner we shall reach a sounder understanding of the realities of sex.[19]

It is doubtlessly for this reason that the *Principles* recognize homosexuality as a "complex question" and encourage confessors to "avoid both harshness and permissiveness."

The *Principles* stress the moral questions of homosexual acts and the importance of the complementarity of the marital union of husband and wife. The *Principles* teach that: "Two homosexuals cannot complement one another in the same way as male and female."[20]

Marc Oraison emphasizes this same point in *The Homosexual Question*:

In speaking of a homosexual relationship the term *couple* is thus not suitable; *pair* fits better. We should say, "A pair of friends." The current meaning of *couple* is based on sexual difference and the possibility of fertility. On the other hand, the homosexual relationship is based on the impossibility of dealing with the other. So I hope my readers will go along with the word *pair*. I will use it as a step toward a more accurate vocabulary....[21]

The *Principles* thus affirm that authentic sexual complementarity can only take place within the heterosexual, marital context.

Most significantly, the *Principles* assert that a person "discovers" that he or she is homosexual: "In every case he *discovers* an already existent condition."[22] This same point is made in *Human Sexuality: A Catholic Perspective for Education and Lifelong Learning* (1990) from the United States Catholic Conference:

Sexuality...is a fundamental dimension of every human being. It is reflected physiologically, psychologically, and relationaly in a person's gender identity as well as in one's primary sexual orientation and behavior. For some young men and women, this means a discovery that one is homosexual, i.e., that one's "sexual inclinations are oriented predominantly toward persons of the same sex."[23]

When an individual *discovers* himself or herself to be homosexual, what does this imply? The 1977 document of the National Conference of Catholic Bishops, *Sharing the Light of Faith: National Catechetical Directory for Catholics in the United States*, teaches:

Sexuality is an important element of human personality, an integral part of one's overall consciousness. It is both a central aspect of one's self-understanding (i.e., as male or female) and a crucial factor in one's relationship with others.[24]

The 1983 document of the Congregation for Catholic Education's *Educational Guidance in Human Love*, also affirms:

Sexuality is a fundamental component of personality, one of its modes of being, of manifestation, of communicating with others, of feeling, of expressing and of living human love. Therefore, it is an integral part of the development of the personality and of its educative process.[25]

In this document's 4th section, "Some particular problems," the Congregation wrote:

Homosexuality, which impedes the person's acquisition of sexual maturity, whether from the individual point of view or the interpersonal, is a problem which must be faced in all objectivity by the pupil and the educator when the case presents itself.

Pastorally, these homosexuals must be received with understanding and supported in the hope of overcoming their personal difficulties and their social mal-adaptation. Their culpability will be judged with prudence; but no pastoral method can be used which, holding these acts conform to the condition of these persons, accord them a moral justification....

It will be the duty of the family and the teacher to seek first of all to identify the factors which drive towards homosexuality....More particularly, in seeking the causes of this disorder, the family and the teacher will have to take account of the elements of judgment proposed by the ecclesiastical Magisterium, and be served by the contribution which various disciplines can offer. The causes having been sought and understood, the family and the teacher will have an efficacious help in the process of integral growth: welcoming with understanding, creating a climate of hope, encouraging the emancipation of the individual and his or her growth in self-control, promoting an authentic moral force towards conversion to the love of God and neighbor, suggesting—if necessary—medical- psychological assistance from persons attentive to and respectful of the teaching of the Church.[26]

The *Principles* are in conformity with other church teachings about human sexuality: Human sexuality must be considered one of our principle traits, an integral part of our personality, and a fundamental dimension of every human being. One's sexual orientation is not chosen, but is discovered. The *Principles* thus state: "...One cannot pinpoint precisely the *decisive* factors in the history of any homosexual person."[27]

The *Principles* respect to a great extent the sense-of-responsibility present in an adult homosexual person, while recognizing that this "degree of freedom" varies from one homosexual individual to another. In this light, the *Principles* conclude that "Each homosexual [person] has the obligation to control his tendency by every means within his power, particularly by psychological and spiritual counsel."[28] The document particularly affirms:

> It is difficult for the homosexual [person] to remain chaste in his environment, and he may slip into sin for a variety of reasons, including loneliness and compulsive tendencies and the pull of homosexual companions. But, generally, he is responsible for his actions, and the worst thing that a confessor can say is that the homosexual [person] is not responsible for his actions.[29]

The *Principles* hold homosexual people in high regard for their capacity for authentic freedom. As the document strongly counsels modesty, chastity and care about environment and friendships, it asserts:

> The priest...should show the person that he can live chastely in the world by means of a plan of life, which will include personal meditative prayer, spiritual reading, reception of the sacraments, and some specific work of charity in the world. Two other elements which should be stressed are regular access to spiritual direction and the formation of a stable friendship with at least one person. One of the greatest difficulties for the homosexual [person] is the formation of such a friendship.[30]

The document is realistic about a type of homosexual environment which can be a threat and "occasion of sin"[31] to a homosexual individual who is authentically striving to live a chaste and holy life. The *Principles* affirm the possibility that a person with a homosexual orientation "can have an abiding relationship with another homosexual person without genital sexual expression."[32]

The *Principles* urge the confessor to encourage the "permanent"[33] homosexual person to form a stable relationship "with another homosexual individual"[34] and counsels:

> If a homosexual [person] has progressed under the direction of a confessor, but in the effort to develop a stable relationship with a given person has *occasionally* fallen into a sin of impurity, he should be absolved and instructed to take measures to avoid the elements which lead to sin without breaking off a friendship which has helped him grow as a person. If the relationship, however, has reached a stage where the homosexual [person] is not able to avoid overt actions, he should be admonished to break off the relationship.[35]

To properly appreciate this point, it is important to revisit the church's traditional moral and pastoral teaching regarding the principle of gradualism. To live an authentic life of holiness and prayer calls for a deep personal conversion, a conversion that oftentimes necessitates gradual change and development.[36] This principle of gradualism is consistent with the church's moral tradition[37] and finds a clear articulation in Pope John Paul II's *Apostolic Exhortation on the Family*:

> What is needed is a continuous, permanent conversion which, while requiring an interior detachment from every evil and an adherence to good in its fullness, is brought about concretely in steps which lead us ever forward. Thus, a dynamic process develops, one which advances gradually with the progressive integration of the gifts of God and the demands of His definitive and absolute love in the entire personal and social life of man.[38]

The pope affirmed this same principle in his Address to the College of Cardinals on 5 November 1979:

> Solidarity means above all a proper understanding and then proper action, not on the basis of what corresponds to the concept of the person offering help, but on the basis of what corresponds to the real needs of the person being helped, and what corresponds to his or her dignity.

The principle of gradualism thus recognizes that personal movement toward greater good and deeper personal integrity is gradual and progressive and is brought about only "in steps." Every minister in the church must carefully discern this "dynamic process" within the "person being helped." Authentic ministry cannot ignore the church's authentic teachings on human sexuality and the objective immorality of homosexual activity. At the same time, this ministry must be rooted in an authentic interpretation of the principle of gradualism.

Veritatis Splendor reminds us that conscience formation must be a "continuous conversion to what is true and to what is good" (n 64). The authentic application of the principle of gradualism builds on the point raised in the encyclical:

> ...(T)emptations can be overcome, sins can be avoided, because together with the commandments the Lord gives us the possibility of keeping them....Keeping God's law in particular situations can be difficult, but it is never impossible. This is the constant teaching of the Church's tradition....Man always has before him the spiritual horizon of hope....Christ has redeemed us! This means that he has given us the possibility of realizing the entire truth of our being; he has set our freedom free from the domination of concupiscence....(W)hat is unacceptable is the atttitude of one who makes his own weakness the criterion of the truth about the good, so that he can feel self-justified, without even the need to have recourse to God and his mercy (nn 102–103).

Many homosexual people find their lives to be lonely and their sexuality to be a burden. While this is not so in all cases, it is a fact with some persons. It is the need for closeness and intimacy that leads a homosexual person to seek a stable relationship with another individual. The church teaches that homosexual activity in such unions, or in any situation, is morally unacceptable. The principle of gradualism recognizes this fact but assists the person toward a progressive assimilation of the church's moral values. Authentic ministry demands an awareness that purification and growth in holiness come about gradually. Instant serenity is almost never the human reality. Every person of faith must cope with his or her personal sinfulness and human limitations. These vary from person to person and are frequently complex and discouraging. But all persons, even in spite of limitations and failure, must continue to grow in holiness of life.

This principle of gradualism has roots within the scriptural ethical tradition[39] where there is, on the one hand, an awareness of human sinfulness and, on the other hand, a recognition of the inexhaustible vastness of God's love and grace. Any failure, then, to realize totally at this moment everything that one is called to be and to do does not negate the possibility of future success. We are all sinners; but we can be healed and forgiven.

C. Declaration on Certain Questions Concerning Sexual Ethics
(*Persona Humana*)

In 1975 the Congregation for the Doctrine of the Faith promulgated *Persona humana*. This *Declaration* deals with the natural law as understood in the church's tradition and comments on three specific sexual examples, in light of natural law theory: conjugal acts, homosexual acts, and masturbation. Concerning homosexual activity, the *Declaration* asserts that there are those who claim that homosexual activity "between certain people" is permissible and this "indulgent" interpretation warrants the magisterium's comment:

> A distinction is drawn…between homosexuals whose tendency comes from a false education, from a lack of normal sexual development, from habit, from bad example, or from other similar causes, and is transitory or at least not incurable; and homosexuals who are definitively such because of some kind of innate instinct or a pathological constitution judged to be incurable.

> In regard to this second category of subjects, some people conclude that their tendency is so natural that it justifies in

their case homosexual relations within a sincere communion of life and love analogous to marriage, insofar as such homosexuals feel incapable of enduring a solitary life.[40]

The *Declaration* affirms that homosexual people are to be treated with "understanding and sustained in the hope of overcoming their personal difficulties and their inability to fit into society." The *Declaration* counsels that their "culpability will be judged with prudence." At the same time, however, *Persona humana* teaches:

> For according to the objective moral order, homosexual relations are acts which lack an essential and indispensable finality....(H)omosexual acts are intrinsically disordered and can in no case be approved.[41]

We find here the traditional teaching of the church that condemns all homosexual activity—even when these homosexual relations are taking place within a "sincere communion of life and love analogous to marriage." In other words, no "right intention" or set of circumstances justifies homosexual activity.

This same point is made in *Veritatis Splendor*:

> If acts are intrinsically evil, a good intention or particular circumstances can diminish their evil, but they cannot remove it. They remain "irremediably" evil acts; *per se* and in themselves they are not capable of being ordered to God and to the good of the person....Consequently, circumstances or intentions can never transform an act intrinsically evil by virtue of its object into an act "subjectively" good or defensible as a choice (n 81).

In addition (and this becomes an important point when this same Congregation issues in 1986 its *Letter to the Bishops of the Catholic Church on the Pastoral Care of Homosexual Persons*), *Persona humana* speaks *mainly* about homosexual activity, and not *per se* about homosexuality. This fact led some to conclude that the magisterium was indicating that while homosexual acts are intrinsically disordered, homosexuality itself is not, and perhaps is a good or at least a neutral fact in a person's life. We will return to this point in analyzing the 1986 *Letter*.

D. To Live in Christ Jesus

In 1976 the National Conference of Catholic Bishops issued a pastoral letter entitled *To Live in Christ Jesus: A Pastoral Reflection On the Moral Life*. In this letter the bishops of the United States wished to discuss certain moral questions concerning the dignity of human persons in light of Christian faith and the power of the Spirit within us. The bishops wrote:

> His [Christ's] life challenges the lives we lead. He began His ministry by calling us to change our lives completely. His very first word summons us to turn away from sin, turn toward God, and receive the gift of the Spirit.[42]

To Live in Christ Jesus teaches that morality is not something imposed on us from without, but is ingrained in our being: it is the way we accept our humanity as restored to us in Christ. In this light, the bishops teach:

> Some persons find themselves through no fault of their own to have a homosexual orientation. Homosexuals, like everyone else, should not suffer from prejudice against their basic human rights. They have a right to respect, friendship, and justice. They should have an active role in the Christian community. Homosexual activity, however, as distinguished from homosexual orientation, is morally wrong. Like heterosexual persons, homosexuals are called to give witness to chastity, avoiding, with God's grace, behavior which is wrong for them, just as non-married sexual relations are wrong for heterosexuals. Nonetheless, because heterosexuals can usually look forward to marriage, and homosexuals, while their orientation continues, might not, the Christian community should provide them a special degree of pastoral understanding and care.[43]

There are certain critical points in this teaching:

1. Some individual's "find themselves" to be homosexual. It is not helpful to speak of a homosexual *preference*, as this word gives the impression that someone *chooses* his or her sexual orientation. It is better to speak of a heterosexual or homosexual *orientation*. I noted

in the Introduction that some people might well "take up homosexual ways by choice:" e.g., for purposes of experimentation; or reaction to earlier sexual abuse. This does not imply, however, that one fundamentally chooses his or her sexual orientation.

2. It is wrong to demonstrate or express prejudice against a person because of his or her sexual orientation: all persons have basic human rights which include the right to respect, friendship, and justice.

3. Homosexual persons have a right to an active role in the Christian community. This active role is to be measured over against a homosexual person's witness of a chaste life. What does this mean?

A person seeking maturity and balance, someone striving to live Christian love, "practices the virtue of chastity by cultivating modesty in behavior, dress and speech, resisting lustful desires and temptations, rejecting masturbation, avoiding pornography and indecent entertainment of every kind, and encouraging social and legal policies which accord respect for human sexuality."[44] Chastity requires us to authentically learn self-control, a characteristic which presupposes such virtues as modesty, temperance, and respect for one's life and the life of others (a point also made in *Principles to Guide Confessors in Questions of Homosexuality*).[45]

To Live in Christ Jesus calls all men and women to live chastely, while recognizing the particular difficulties incumbent on the homosexual person—thus indicating the need for "a special degree of pastoral understanding and care." It is important in this context to say something about the realities of loneliness and intimacy that every human being must strive to balance.[46] Oftentimes, despite a variety of relationships and commitments, there are lonely times that perhaps touch the life of single people more profoundly. Sometimes, these are moments of uncertainty, of pain, of a sense of isolation. No bromide immediately erases such feelings. But it is equally vital to recall that moments of loneliness can be potentially fruitful times, even if not particularly happy times. In these moments of loneliness one can encounter God, face-to-face as it were, if one learns to "let go," trusting that God is there. While God is tangibly present in life's moments of intimacy, God also can be experienced powerfully in life's moments of loneliness.[47]

E. Letter to the Bishops of the Catholic Church on the Pastoral Care of Homosexual Persons

On October 1, 1986, the Congregation for the Doctrine of the Faith issued the *Letter to the Bishops of the Catholic Church on the Pastoral Care of Homosexual Persons*. This *Letter* revisits the 1975 document *Declaration on Certain Questions Concerning Sexual Ethics* and points out that the Declaration "...took note of the distinction commonly drawn between the homosexual condition or tendency and individual homosexual actions. These were described as deprived of their essential and indispensable finality, as being 'intrinsically disordered', and able in no case to be approved of."[48] The *Letter* then comments:

> In the discussion which followed the publication of the Declaration, however, an overly benign interpretation was given to the homosexual condition itself, some going so far as to call it neutral, or even good.[49]

The *Letter* was concerned about interpretations which understood the homosexual orientation itself in a non-moral or amoral way: i.e., the homosexual condition *per se* as neutral. The *Letter* exegetes such interpretations as "benign" and generated the need for clarification.

In his article "Toward an Understanding of the Letter on the Pastoral Care of Homosexual Persons,"[50] Archbishop John R. Quinn of San Francisco summarized the various reasons why this *Letter* was written: the increasing public debate about homosexuality; the enunciation of positions incompatible with the teaching of the church; the increasing positive appraisal of the homosexual orientation itself; and a certain militant aspect within the homosexual communities which tend to trivialize sexuality and the central importance of marriage and family life.

A guiding statement for proper interpretation of this *Letter* is found in number 16:

> The human person, made in the image and likeness of God, can hardly be adequately described by a reductionist reference to his or her sexual orientation. Everyone living on the face of the earth has personal problems and difficulties,

but challenges to growth, strength, talents and gifts as well. Today, the Church provides a badly needed context for the care of the human person when she refuses to consider the person as a "heterosexual" or a "homosexual" and insists that every person has a fundamental identity: a creature of God, and by grace, His child and heir to eternal life.

The *Letter* does uphold, then, the human dignity of every homosexual person as a "creature of God." The *Letter* teaches: "…(T)he transcendent nature of the human person" must never be denied and the "supernatural vocation of every individual" must always be affirmed. It is out of *this* belief and counsel that the *Letter* must be properly read and interpreted.

The biblical data employed in the *Letter* (especially seen in number 6) relies heavily on the theology of creation found in the book of Genesis. The *Letter* affirms that God fashioned humankind, male and female, in his own image and likeness and thus all human beings are "nothing less than the work of God himself." Number 6 also insists that "the complementarity of the sexes" is a reflection of the inner unity of God himself.[51] Specifically, husband and wife accomplish this reflection "in their cooperation with Him in the transmission of life by a mutual donation of the self to the other."

The *Letter* makes reference to texts both in the Old and New Testaments and affirms that in various ways moral judgments are made "against homosexual relations." Numbers 6 and 7 of the *Letter* insist that the biblical testimony concludes that persons "engaging in homosexual behavior" act immorally. This conclusion rests on the Genesis vision of God's sexual design concerning complete complementarity of the male and female and the responsibility for the transmission of human life.

At the same time, it is of significance to note that number 7 affirms that "homosexual persons are…often generous and giving of themselves." The thrust of the biblical teaching, however, is that when such persons engage in homosexual activity, they do not give themselves to "a life of that form of self-giving which the Gospel says is the essence of Christian living."

The biblical data regarding homosexuality and homosexual activity is extremely complex and should never lead to a simple condemnation of all homosexual persons who engage in homosexual activity. As the 1975 *Declaration* of the C.D.F. pointed out, "...homosexuals must certainly be treated with understanding and sustained in the hope of overcoming their personal difficulties and their inability to fit into society. Their culpability will be judged with prudence."[52] The *Letter* thus indicates, "...the particular inclination of the homosexual person is not a sin."[53]

The most difficult section of this *Letter* is found in number 3:

> Although the particular inclination of the homosexual person is not a sin, it is a more or less strong tendency ordered toward an intrinsic moral evil; and thus the inclination itself must be seen as an objective disorder.

As we have already seen, the church teaches that homosexual acts cannot be fit objects for deliberate moral choice because they are always "disordered" in the scholastic or Thomistic sense. The *Letter* is emphasizing this point—especially in light of the phrase already referred to in this same paragraph, "The particular inclination of the homosexual person is not a sin..."

How are we to understand this notion of an "objective disorder"? Archbishop John R. Quinn explains it in this manner:

> This is philosophical language. The inclination is a disorder because it is directed to an object that is disordered. The inclination and the object are in the same order philosophically....In trying to understand this affirmation, we should avert to two things. First, every person has disordered inclinations. For instance, the inclination to rash judgment is disordered, the inclination to cowardice, the inclination to hypocrisy—these are all disordered inclinations. Consequently, homosexual persons are not the only ones who have disordered inclinations. Second, the letter does not say that the homosexual person is disordered. The inclination, not the person, is described as disordered. Speaking of the homosexual person, the letter states that the Church "refuses to consider the person as a 'heterosexual' or a 'homosexual' and insists that every person has a fundamental identity: a creature of God and, by grace, His child and heir to eternal life...." Consequently, the docu-

ment affirms the spiritual and human dignity of the homosexual *person* while placing a negative moral judgment on
homosexual *acts* and a negative philosophical judgment on
the homosexual *inclination* or orientation, which it clearly
states is not a sin or moral evil.[54]

Archbishop Quinn's interpretation of the "objective disorder" is certainly helpful in that it stresses the fact that the *Letter* is using "philosophical language."

P. A. van Gennip[55] helps to further clarify "objective disorder."
He maintains that human imperfection had previously been discussed
in the more specific expressions of either illness or sin: "Illness is a
catch-all for human imperfection in the *natural* order; sin is the same
thing in the *moral* order. It seems that the term, 'objective disorder' is
deliberately chosen to avoid both these terms."[56] Van Gennip asserts
that if "illness" were chosen, the possibility of affirming free will in
order to choose continence would have become very minimal. If "sin"
were chosen, the possibility of speaking of free will would not even
have been necessary. Thus the choice of "objective disorder"—a concept which expresses the evil of the inclination/orientation and at the
same time allowing for some sensible motivation for continence.

One final point. Ronald Modras argues in "Pope John Paul II's
Theology of the Body"[57] that the "objective disorder" must be understood within the pope's theology of the "nuptial meaning" of the
body.[58] In his theology of the body, the pope used words like "imbalance" and "distortion" to describe the concupiscence or "lust of the
flesh" that is now a permanent element or "disposition derived from
man's sinfulness." The human heart has become a "battlefield"
between the "sincere giving" that is love and the lust that seeks to
"appropriate" another as an object of enjoyment. Because of the first
sin, "'The desire of the body' is more powerful than 'the desire of the
mind.'" We can become gifts to and for one another only if we have
self-control. Concupiscence "limits" and "reduces" self-control and
makes us "ashamed" of our bodies. It is within this context of concupiscence that a proper context is set for an understanding of homosexuality as a "disorder." Modras explains,

> The word should not be taken to mean a psychological or
> even a moral disorder, since the letter makes clear that the

homosexual condition is not a sin. Within the framework of the pope's theology, however, homosexuality is the result of sin. God simply could not, would not, and did not create homosexuals as such. The homosexual condition is a result of the first sin, an aspect or form of the concupiscence that is the condition of us all. Unwilled, spontaneous sexual attraction or desire for someone of the same sex is a "disorder" in the same way that unwilled, spontaneous sexual attraction or desire for anyone is an "imbalance" and "distortion."[59]

The *Letter* also expresses concern that the church should not be manipulated to give her support to laws and statutes which would consider homosexuality as something other than what the biblical testimony affirms. The church's tradition consistently defends and promotes family life and this *Letter* takes pains to safeguard the centrality of the family. Number 9 of the *Letter* reiterates this point by stating that homosexual activity must never be considered as equivalent to "the sexual expression of conjugal love."

The *Letter* deplores all violent speech and action aimed at homosexual persons.[60] The *Letter* asserts that all such violence "deserves condemnation from the Church's pastors whenever it occurs." In harmony with the 1975 *Declaration*, the *Letter* affirms the church's moral and pastoral tradition that generalizations are never permissible when assessing "individual cases." We must avoid all forms of reductionism:

> ...(C)ircumstances may exist, or may have existed in the past, which would reduce or remove the culpability of the individual in a given instance; or other circumstances may increase it. What is at all costs to be avoided is the unfounded and demeaning assumption that the sexual behavior of homosexual persons is always and totally compulsive and therefore inculpable. What is essential is that the fundamental liberty which characterizes the human person and gives him his dignity may be recognized as belonging to the homosexual person as well. As in every conversion from evil, the abandonment of homosexual

activity will require a profound collaboration of the individual with God's liberating grace.[61]

The *Letter* reaffirms the church's teaching that homosexuality *per se* carries its own burdens and thus calls upon homosexual persons to unite their sufferings and difficulties to the sacrifice of the Lord's cross.[62] As with all Christian men and women, the homosexual person needs to place his or her life within the context of the paschal mystery and attempt to deeply appreciate "the sacrifice of the Lord" as "a source of self-giving" which will save the homosexual person from a way of life which constantly threatens to destroy this person.

What conclusions might we reach from this *Letter*?

1. Homosexuality is a variation in human sexual orientation that occurs consistently even though with less frequency than heterosexuality.[63] This fact sustains certain implications for moral judgment: If certain biological or psychological conditions constantly recur in human societies, then the members of those societies have the obligation to enhance human life as far as possible in the midst of those conditions, whether the conditions themselves are desirable or undesirable.

2. Procreation is understood in the Catholic tradition as integrally connected with the moral significance of sexuality itself: procreation is seen as a form of service to the species and to particular civil and religious communities. This social dimension of sexual ethics is clearly evident, e.g., in Augustine's articulation of marriage's "three goods." Biblical resources bear out this same perspective. Therefore, love, commitment and friendship between spouses are perceived by biblical and classical authors as ancillary goods.

In addition, in both Old and New Testaments, perspectives on sexuality favor the institutionalization of sexuality in heterosexual, monogamist, permanent and procreative marriage. Certain sexual acts are prohibited because they are incompatible with the life of faith in the covenant community: e.g., adultery, fornication, and homosexual activity.

3. Every member of the church must be especially attentive to the "sufferings and difficulties" of all homosexual people.[64] In this light, the *Letter* deplores *every* type of violent speech or action aimed against homosexual persons and indicates that such violence

"deserves condemnation."[65] The *Letter* notes that "irrational and violent reactions increase" when homosexual activity is condoned or protected civilly.

4. No support can be given by the church's pastors to "any organizations which seek to undermine the teaching of the church, which are ambiguous about it, or which neglect it entirely."[66] This teaching does not preclude the church's pastors from sponsoring gatherings and religious devotions (e.g., the celebration of the eucharist) for homosexual people. It does preclude, however, the possibility of supporting such gatherings for *organizations/groups* which uphold and articulate a non-supportive and condemnatory attitude toward the church regarding the teaching on homosexuality and homosexual activity. It is critical, then, to pastorally distinguish non-support for organizations which undermine the teaching of the church, and upholding at the same time necessary support for the human dignity of every homosexual person.[67]

F. Some Considerations Concerning the Catholic Response to Legislative Proposals on the Non-Discrimination of Homosexual Persons

These *Considerations* were sent to all U.S. bishops on June 25, 1992 from the Congregation for the Doctrine of the Faith. On July 23, 1992, the Vatican's press office offered an explanation of this document: "For some time, the Congregation for the Doctrine of the Faith has been concerned with the question of legislative proposals advanced in various parts of the world to deal with the issue of the non-discrimination of homosexual persons. A study of this question culminated in the preparation of a set of observations which could be of assistance to those concerned with formulating the Catholic response to such legislative proposals."

This clarification goes on to say that the observations "were not intended to be an official public instruction on the matter from the Congregation but a background resource offering discreet assistance to those who may be confronted with the task of evaluating draft legislation regarding non-discrimination on the basis of sexual orientation." It notes further that since the observations had become public, a "slight revision of the text was undertaken and a second version prepared." Consequently, even though this document does not represent official Catholic teaching, I am including it here because of the wide-spread responses it did receive.

The document's Foreword gives precise focus to the Congregation's concern: "Recently, legislation has been proposed in various places which would make discrimination on the basis of sexual orientation illegal."[68] It is critical to note that the *fundamental* caution raised in these observations is that "Such initiatives...may in fact have a negative impact on the family and society."[69] This concern is repeated several times: the nature and rights of the family are placed "in jeopardy" when homosexual activity is seen to be equivalent to or as acceptable as "the sexual expression of conjugal love";[70] bishops should keep as their "utmost concern" the defense and promotion of the family;[71] and provisions of proposed measures must be evaluated carefully: "How would they affect adoption or foster care? Would they protect homosexual acts, public or private? Do they confer equivalent family status on homosexual unions, e.g., in respect to public housing or by entitling the homosexual partner to the privileges of employment which might include such things as 'family' participation in the health benefits given to employees."[72]

This emphasis comes to its conclusion in the final paragraph of the document: "The Church has the responsibility to promote family life and the public morality of the entire civil society on the basis of fundamental moral values, not simply to protect herself from the application of harmful laws."[73]

On June 22, 1992, Archbishop Daniel E. Pilarczyk, President of the N.C.C.B., issued a letter which also endorses this primary focus: "The Congregation's concern is that proposals to safeguard the legitimate rights of homosexual persons not have the effect of creating a new class of legally protected *behavior*, i.e., homosexual behavior, which, in time, could occupy the same position as non-discrimination against *people* because of their race, religion, gender, or ethnic background. The document rightly warns against legislation designated more to legitimate homosexual behavior than to secure basic civil rights and against proposals which tend to promote an equivalence between legal marriage and homosexual lifestyles." The document's interest seems primarily aimed at protecting and upholding the centrality of family life.[74] Discrimination and homosexuality are thus evaluated in *relationship* to the family in society.

Since this document is not intended to be an official instruction from the Congregation, certain standard features in Roman curial documents are lacking: (a) the document bears no letterhead of the Congregation; (b) it does not *per se* indicate what type of document it is: e.g., a decree, an instruction, a letter; (c) it does not bear the signature of the Prefect of the Congregation, nor of the Secretary (nor any signature at all); and (d) it does not indicate papal approbation. Archbishop Pilarczyk's comment is thus helpful as to how these observations are to be used: "Bishops will continue to evaluate local legislation with these considerations clearly in mind. However, as the considerations note, it would be impossible to foresee and respond to every eventuality in respect to legislative proposals in this area..." The counsel given in the Congregation's 1986 *Letter* also explains: "...(T)hey (bishops) should decide for their own dioceses the extent to which an intervention on their part is indicated. In addition, should they consider it helpful, further coordinated action at the level of their National Bishops' Conference may be envisioned....In a particular way, we would ask the Bishops to support, with the means at their disposal, the development of appropriate forms of pastoral care for homosexual persons."[75]

What conclusions can be drawn from this document?

1. While the *Considerations* uphold the possibility of discrimination in certain specified areas (consignment of children to adoption or foster care; employment of teachers or coaches; and military recruitment[76]), discrimination is "obligatory" only in the case of "objectively disordered external conduct" or of "culpable behavior."[77] Number 12 concludes with a critically important phrase that helps exegete possible discrimination: "in order to protect the common good." In other words, this document suggests that discrimination is "sometimes" (the document's word) licit when external conduct is harmful to the common good. Since the Foreword states that it is "impossible to anticipate every eventuality" and thus is this document concerned with identifying "principles and distinctions of a general nature," it is clear that church authorities are being asked to exercise discrimination *only* in those cases where the common good is being harmed.

2. The *Considerations* state that "there is no right to homosexuality" and refer to number 10 of the C.D.F.'s *Letter* in this regard. It is critical to note the *Letter* states that it is "homosexual activity" that is

the "behavior to which no one has any conceivable right...." Archbishop Pilarczyk's commentary is helpful: the legitimate rights of homosexual persons need to be safeguarded, while not creating a "new class of legally protected *behavior*...."[78]

3. Archbishop Pilarczyk's final words of comment are important:

> I believe that the bishops of the various local Churches in the United States will continue to look for ways in which those people who have a homosexual orientation will not suffer unjust discrimination in law or reality because of their orientation. In our teaching, pastoral care, and public advocacy, bishops will, of course, continue to strive to be faithful to Church teaching on homosexuality, to uphold the values of marriage and family life, to defend the basic human dignity and human rights of all and to condemn violence, hatred and bigotry directed against any person.

G. Catechism of the Catholic Church

The new *Catechism of the Catholic Church* was solemnly promulgated by Pope John Paul II on December 7, 1992. Homosexuality is dealt with in paragraphs 2357–2369, entitled "Chastity and Homosexuality," appearing in Section II, "The Vocation to Chastity," of Article 6, "The Sixth Commandment," in Book Three, "The Life of Faith."[79] The official English translation of the French text is as follows:

> Homosexuality refers to relations between men or between women who experience an exclusive or predominant sexual attraction toward persons of the same sex. It has taken a great variety of forms through the centuries and in different cultures. Its psychological genesis remains largely unexplained. Basing itself on Sacred Scripture, which presents homosexual acts as acts of grave depravity,[80] tradition has always declared that "homosexual acts are intrinsically disordered."[81] They are contrary to the natural law. They close the sexual act to the gift of life. They do not proceed from a genuine affective and sexual complementarity. Under no circumstances could they be approved.

The number of men and women who have deep-seated homosexual tendencies is not negligible. They do not choose their homosexual condition; for most of them it is a trial. They must be accepted with respect, compassion and sensitivity. Every sign of unjust discrimination in their regard should be avoided. These persons are called to fulfill God's will in their lives and, if they are Christians, to unite to the sacrifice on the Lord's Cross the difficulties they may encounter from their condition.

Homosexual persons are called to chastity. By the virtues of self-mastery that teach them inner freedom, at times by the support of disinterested friendship, by prayer and sacramental grace, they can and should gradually and resolutely approach Christian perfection.

The *Catechism* names the homosexual orientation as a "condition" and describes it by reference to "basic tendencies."
What conclusions can be drawn?

1. The disapproval of homosexual activity is based on two grounds: deprivation of finality: "They (homosexual acts) close the sexual act to the gift of life"; and "they do not proceed from a genuine affective and sexual complementarity."
2. There is the recognition that persons do not choose their homosexual orientation and no attempt is made to explain why certain people sustain a homosexual orientation. It is significant to note that the *Catechism* mentions that the number of persons with a homosexual orientation is "not negligible."
3. It is of great importance that the *Catechism* also condemns every form of unjust discrimination against homosexual persons.

Conclusion

The twentieth century has seen a rich development in official Catholic teaching regarding human sexuality and marriage.[82] In a century characterized at face value by growth in the breakdown of marriage and family life and the commercialization of human sexuality, the Catholic Church has patiently affirmed and reaffirmed the dignity of human sexuality, the sacred character of marriage, and the inviolability of family life. In fact, the church has consistently attempted to speak clearly about *values* related to human sexuality. *Educational Guidance in Human Love* comments:

> In the teaching of John Paul II, the positive consideration of *values*, which one ought to discover and appreciate, precedes the *norm* which one must not violate. This norm, nevertheless, interprets and formulates the values for which people must strive.[83] In documents such as *Gaudium et Spes* (1965), *Humanae Vitae* (1968) and *Familiaris Consortio* (1981) there has been development and refinement of the Church's teachings on human sexuality which stress the priority of conjugal love as the context or ground for affirming the unequivocal inseparability of the procreative and unitive dimensions of the conjugal act and, by extension, of any meaningful act of sexual intercourse - which the Church sees as necessarily occurring within marriage.

James Pollock comments,

> Although the Church's official teaching regarding human sexuality comes in for considerable attack from diverse quarters, these documents will reward careful readers with a sense of the extraordinary efforts the Church has made to revitalize and to formulate its teaching.[84]

Chapter 5

SPIRITUALITY AND OTHER PASTORAL CONCERNS

Spirituality

In *Another Kind of Love: Homosexuality and Spirituality*, Richard Woods writes that "Living with homosexuality means…living with a difference."[1] This "difference" has been detailed by John Fortunato in *Embracing the Exile* as he describes the homosexual person's "sense of being on the fringes, cut off, banished."[2] This "difference" and "loneliness" and "hiding" (Fortunato's terms) has been accurately described in *Coming Out Within: Stages of Spiritual Awakening for Lesbians and Gay Men.*[3] The authors describe serious "losses" in the lives of homosexual men and women, losses which often lead to feelings of isolation, depression and self-loathing. What are these losses?

1. *FAMILY.* Homosexual persons are usually accepted within their families of origin as long as they maintain a heterosexual image. This situation changes drastically for many gay men and lesbian women when they disclose their orientation. Many parents give to their children two choices: either "please yourself and lose me" or "lose yourself and please me." In addition, many homosexual persons lose the family-of-dreams: i.e., the normative heterosexual marriage with children which most people try to match with an almost unconscious blueprint or model.

2. *WORK.* Some homosexual people become so broken that they are no longer able to imagine that anything they plan will materialize. Many fail to realize their potential due to prejudicial treatment in their work environment. In addition, many gay and lesbian people fear exposure and thus remain underemployed relative to their true talents and skills. Some homosexual people sustain an inability to focus on vocational plans because so much energy is given to issues related to their sexual orientation. Some homosexual persons indeed achieve work-satisfaction and accomplishment, but at the price of pretense. Lifelong disillusionment sets in.

3. *HEALTH and SAFETY.* Violent assaults on gay men and lesbian women have been increasing. Nationally, the number of anti-gay incidents reported in 1992 increased 4% to 1,898, but one year later the total of such incidents almost tripled.[4] HIV infection and AIDS have dramatically claimed the lives of thousands of homosexual people.

4. *RELIGION.* A number of homosexual persons do not feel that their basic human goodness is affirmed by their religion and thus they feel thrust into a struggle between a personal sense of "rightness" and a perceived sense of "sinfulness." A number of homosexual people feel alienated from religion and from a sense of belonging to a religious community.

5. *COMMUNITY.* Many homosexual people feel a pervasive sense of not belonging, something akin to James Baldwin's comment, "It is a great shock at the age of 5 or 6 to find that in a world of Gary Coopers you are the Indian."

Joseph Campbell has pointed out that shaping stories or myths helps us to understand our passage from birth to death, to find out who we are, to touch the transcendent, and to discover "the rapture of being alive." In many cases, as evidenced above, the messages conveyed to homosexual persons and the losses they experience make them feel left-handed in a right-handed world; and this leads to the inability to reconcile one's inner world with the outside world.

In the midst of such a profound sense of alienation, it is critical to uphold the value and dignity of every human person. The affirmation of Genesis 1:27 is critical—that every person is created in the image and likeness of God. In this first chapter of Genesis the human person, unlike other creatures, is defined on the basis of a relationship with God.[5] This truth establishes the dignity and radical equality of all human beings. This essential truth of being in the divine image is linked with being male and female; both are persons to an equal degree in the likeness of a personal God. They are given a blessing which also relates them to God: they are to be fruitful and multiply, i.e., as spouses, to pass on the divine image to their children by procreation. They are to have dominion over all the earth (Genesis 1:28). Like God, man and woman are rational beings, superior to the rest of creation of which they are made the stewards.

The second chapter of Genesis contributes a more subjective definition of the human being. "Adam" is depicted as coming to self-awareness, and, in dialogue with God, exercising self-determination. Human subjectivity, which is constituted through self-knowledge, is revealed in "Adam's" discovery of his dissimilarity from the animal world and his consequent solitude. This solitude signifies the specific subjectivity of the person, even apart from reference to sex and the search for a companion. This portrait of the human person is completed when God gives "Adam" a command regarding the tree of the knowledge of good and evil. "Adam," who was self-aware, is faced with the moment of choice and self-determination. Moreover, "Adam" is a person in relationship with God, one whose choice regarding good and evil affects his situation with respect to a "covenant" partnership. The human person, as the subject of this covenant, is revealed to have a unique capacity for God. In this account of human subjectivity one discovers the truth that every individual is made in the image of God, insofar as he or she is a rational and free creature capable of knowing God and loving God.

The homosexual person in his or her experience of "difference" ideally needs to develop a spirituality which recognizes one's "unique capacity for God." No one is created unlike the image of God. In his catechetical addresses from his Wednesday audiences published as *Original Unity of Man and Woman, Blessed are the Pure of Heart and The Theology of Marriage and Celibacy*,[6] Pope John Paul II teaches that in his original solitude "Adam" is searching for a life's companion. The circle of solitude is broken when God creates a woman from Adam's rib. The metaphor of the "rib" points to the homogeneity of being in the same somatic structure. In the biblical language the essential identity in human nature of the two is also reflected in the words for man and woman: "She shall be called woman (*'Issah'*) because she was taken out of man (*'Is'*)" (Genesis 2:23). This essential identity in human nature is disclosed also when the man recognizes her as "flesh of his flesh and bone of his bone." His response is a cry of joy in the discovery of one who is another "I," i.e., another personal subject, in a common humanity. She is a second "self," a "helper" fit for him.

In the language of myth the biblical account expresses the truth that humankind exists in two different "incarnations." There are two "ways of being a body" in the same humanity which, in their physical difference, have an exact correspondence (another way of speaking of complementarity) to each other.

In the creation of the woman, the original solitude is overcome. Solitude, in its second aspect, creates the expectation of communion. "Adam" looks for a companion, another personal subject. The woman, who like the man is distinct from the animal world, exists as a subject. In their "double solitude" the man and the woman have the capacity for existing in a special reciprocity and mutuality, a *communion of persons*. According to John Paul II, it is in communion, more than in solitude, that the human person becomes the image of God.

God's creation of humankind as male and female discloses the vocation to personhood as an *invitation to relationship*. Genesis presents the partnership of man and woman as the first primary form of the communion of persons. The "unity of the two" depicted in the second creation account is marriage, a unity which is realized through the body, through two becoming "one flesh" (Genesis 2:24). From the beginning, there is an "incarnate" communion of persons in which each of the two, who are made for each other, enrich the other.

In her article "Personhood, Sexuality and Complementarity In The Teaching of Pope John Paul II," Sara Butler explains:

> When Pope John Paul speaks of the "nuptial meaning" of the body, he refers to the capacity for intimacy and self-donation which is inscribed in the body-person. A person makes "a sincere gift of self" in and through the body. This is most clearly disclosed in the "one flesh" of married love, where the mutual relationship of persons is the object of personal choice. The man and the woman cling to each other (Genesis 2:24). As male and female they are a "gift" for one another in their reciprocal complementarity and mutuality. Through the "language" of the body they overcome their existential solitude in a communion of persons. In making the gift of self to each other they fulfill and discover themselves in a way that corresponds to their vocation as persons.[7]

What has all of this to do with spirituality and homosexuality? With the introduction of the notion of person in *Gaudium et Spes* (the *Pastoral Constitution on the Church in the Modern World*), as "achieving self by the gift of self," the notion of person as "gift" and hence as relation, has universally and constantly been offered as the core concept in all the papal pronouncements and magisterial offerings in the last 26 years since Vatican II; and particularly in the last 13 years in the pontificate of John Paul II.[8] In other words, relation to God and to all others is something I first am (*esse*), rather than something I first do or achieve (*agere*). Consequently, we are not isolated individuals whose only responsibility is to "look after number one." In the words of Bishop Walter Kasper, the "existence" of the human person is "possible only in co-existence with other persons. The human person is possible only in the plural; it can exist only in reciprocal acknowledgement, and it finds its fulfillment only in the communion of love. Persons thus exist only in mutual giving and receiving."[9]

The church places marriage and the family in the context of the nature of the human person who, in the words of Vatican II, "can fully discover his true self only in a sincere giving of himself" (*Gaudium et Spes*, n 24). Thus, John Paul II stated in his 1981 Apostolic Exhortation *Familiaris Consortio* that "sexuality...is realized in a truly human way only if it is an integral part of the love by which a man and a woman commit themselves totally to one another until death. The total physical self-giving would be a lie if it were not the sign and fruit of a total personal self-giving, in which the whole person, including the temporal dimension, is present: if the person were to withhold something or reserve the possibility of deciding otherwise in the future, by this very fact he or she would not be giving totally."

It is thus of great importance—critically for the homosexual person who experiences "distance" and "isolation"—that one develops a profound sense of spirituality by recognizing first of all the unconditional love of God who gives to each person his or her individual human dignity. Only after we have experienced love and acceptance from another person can we begin to believe in the possibility that God loves us. Only then can we learn to love ourselves. And we can then, in turn, share that love with others—a critical factor in developing ourselves-as-relational. In developing such a spirituality, these questions are critical:

1. How do I claim an identity, not just in psychological terms but in faith-terms as well?

2. Is my sexuality a blessing or a curse, a help or a hindrance?
3. How do I develop myself *in relation* to others?

Since one's homosexual orientation is not sinful, one needs to believe this fact in one's heart. For a gay man and a lesbian woman to claim his or her own inherent goodness, takes immense conviction. Becoming free of the voices of doubt takes a great deal of work.

Because of the homosexual person's experience of alienation, he or she is in a better position to relate to other oppressed and marginalized people and groups. Jesus himself in the gospels had a special regard for and sensitivity to those who are marginalized. Because of their struggle to overcome a negative self-image and negative social-image, homosexual people can be stronger as individuals. Because of their experience of rejection, they can be much more aware of their dependence on the love of God.

Jesus is the Lord who loves all of us. As beloved, we all enter into a personal, intimate relationship with the Son of God who loves us and desires only to draw us to himself. Out of that relationship we are sustained, and we are called to relate to other people with the same degree of tenderness that Jesus relates to us: "When I was thirsty, when I was hungry, when I was naked..."[10] As the homosexual person attempts to realize in his or her life ever more deeply this love of God and this need to relate to others, perhaps the observation of Carl Jung will become more clear and evident that homosexual persons can make a special contribution to the spiritual development of humanity: "They are endowed with a wealth of religious feelings which help them to bring the *ecclesia spiritualis* into reality, and a spiritual receptivity which makes them responsive to revelation."[11] In Exodus 20:1–2, God speaks the first commandment, "I am the Lord your God, who brought you out of the land of Egypt, out of the house of bondage. You shall have no other gods before me." Our morality and spirituality need to keep this covenant-relationship in mind that we have no other god besides the Lord because he is the one who has delivered us from Egypt; the Lord is the one who delivers us from all of the "exiles" and "differences" of our lives.

Rudolf Otto captures this same point in *The Idea of the Holy*[12] when he speaks of the importance of "creature conscience": the awareness of one's own nothingness against that which is supreme in the creator. It is more than a feeling; it is living in this awareness. Out of the depths of one's goodness and human dignity, even experienced at times in loneliness and isolation, the homosexual person can allow his or her life to mirror forth the person of Jesus—a Jesus who was so powerfully aware of the reality of God in his life that through images and stories he was able to reveal that depth experience perfectly:

> It was love to which Jesus' heart was devoted unreservedly, in depth and to the ultimate consequences. His God was named "Love," creative, forgiving and loyal Love. To him, this was the "You" which he addressed as *Abba*.[13]

We always find Jesus in relationship with his Father, fully in touch with the world in which he lived and in which he proclaimed the primordial word. In the gospels, we find Jesus reaching out to others. He taught them that the place to find beauty is in their very world. More often than not, we find Jesus celebrating life at table. He showed how near to God he was in this table fellowship. Jesus sat down to eat with those who were not aware of the reality of the Father's love. Jesus continues this fellowship with all of us, especially those who feel the depths of poverty, loneliness and distance.

Consequently, the homosexual person—as every person—is called into relationship and connectedness with others. While total complementarity can be achieved only in the man-woman relationship of marriage, every person has a spiritual quest to be in partnership with others, thus fulfilling the *imago Dei* (image of God). This quest is doubtlessly painstaking and difficult for the gay man and lesbian woman who are called by the church to live this complementarity in chastity. It is not mere rhetoric to claim, then, that a homosexual person is challenged to a high degree of spirituality.

Homosexual Youth

Despite an unprecedented public awareness of adult homosexuality and its relevance to a variety of individual and public health issues, disproportionately little attention has been focused on the antecedents of homosexuality in childhood and adolescence.[14] We have noted elsewhere that many authors suggest that a self-identification as homosexual occurs only in one's early twenties.[15] Daniel Levinson's research also endorses the point that many people today require most of the decade of their twenties to come to a sense of their sexual identity.[16] Granting this research, it would be false and harmful to assume that the homosexual adult springs from the heterosexual child at the age of 18 or 20 years. Not only does this perspective preclude understanding the origins of development of sexual orientation, but it potentially damages the lives of millions of persons who experience the sudden upheaval of sexual and social identities as they reach the age of majority.

Male and female homosexual adolescents share the common dilemmas of membership in sexual minority groups. Before the work of Kinsey three other studies focused on homosexual behavior among American men and two of these exclusively involved male adolescents. Unfortunately, there is a paucity of written information about lesbian adolescents and the cultural differences between male and female homosexual people. In a study of 291 junior and senior high school boys, Ramsey[17] found that 30% had a homosexual experience of orgasm, and Finger[18] reported that 27% of a college class of 111 admitted to "at least one overt homosexual episode involving orgasm."

In 1948, Kinsey and his colleagues noted that homosexual behavior occurred in nearly one male in three during the late teenage years and then diminished slightly in frequency during the third decade of life. This decline was attributed to conformity to societal norms of heterosexual behavior and marriage. There were no further attempts to survey adolescent homosexuality until Sorenson's work, published in 1973.[19] He found that 17% of boys and 6% of girls between the ages of 16 and 19 years reported at least one homosexual experience.[20]

There is a popular paradigm, whose origins are obscure, that homosexuality is a "normal" phase in adolescent sexual development and that it is discarded, rather than integrated into sexual identity, as a person reaches adulthood. As we have noted, however, for both heterosexual and homosexual persons, sexual behavior during adolescence may be congruent or incongruent with the direction of their adult sexual expression. However, there is clearly a large body of both experimental and descriptive data indicating that the foundations for adult homosexuality and heterosexuality are laid in early childhood (and perhaps beforehand) and adolescence. Despite numerous methodological difficulties in various studies that have been done on gay identification and adolescence, the weight of evidence from case descriptions and prospective and retrospective studies indicate that (1) homosexual activity occurs with some frequency among adolescents; (2) genital sexual behavior is not an absolute predictor of sexual orientation; (3) there is a subset of adolescents who clearly identify themselves as homosexual persons; and (4) for many homosexual adolescents and adults, the roots of their sexual orientation extend to early childhood as reflected in their childhood memories and/or behavior.

Counseling Youth

It is both reasonable and judicious to avoid applying potentially stigmatizing labels to children and adolescents. It is wrong, for example, to encourage a teenager to "come out of the closet" simply because the teenager feels himself or herself to be homosexual. It seems wise to adopt a "wait and see" approach to a teenager's homosexuality, while providing appropriate support and counselling. A great deal of data suggests that adolescents who are struggling with the issue of homosexuality and who are not receiving appropriate counseling and support from family and community are in jeopardy of serious emotional, social, and physical difficulty. The potential cost of such problems for the individual adolescent is illness, dysfunction, or even suicide.

Research shows that gay and lesbian adolescents suffer a great deal of psychological and emotional turmoil over issues associated with the acceptance or non-acceptance of their sexual orientation.[21] This turmoil, often carried out by the young person in silence, is partially the result of society's non-acceptance or oppression of gay and lesbian persons. The adolescent internalizes this discrimination. In the isolation that follows a realization that one is a gay man or lesbian woman, the young person may consider suicide, substance abuse, or other risky behaviors. Further, young persons who tell family and friends that they may be a gay man or lesbian woman can face ostracism from the only support systems they know.

One of the first issues upon which a teenager may focus is whom to tell about the evolving understanding of his or her sexuality. It is often the teenager's teacher or school counselor in whom the gay or lesbian teen confides. What are some general criteria that a teacher, counselor or parent should adopt in listening to a teenager's discussion of his or her possible homosexuality?

In general, it is important to create a "safe space" for the teenager by assuring him or her that what is shared with you is respected. Such questions as these are helpful: How can *I* be of help to you? How/when did you come to this awareness? How has the growing awareness been—easy, difficult? Have you discussed this with anyone else, and how did they respond?

Suggest that the teenager do some reading on the topic of homosexuality. Reading is a safe way for the young person to learn about the feelings he or she may be experiencing. Offer necessary information regarding HIV and other sexually transmitted diseases, as well as abuse of drugs and alcohol.

If the adolescent is sharing his or her self-identity questions as homosexual with a school counselor, the supportive environment that the counselor hopefully creates may lead the young person to assume that others will respond similarly. The personal safety of the young person is paramount. Caution the teenager that he or she has a lifetime to discuss orientation matters. Remind him or her that others may not be as receptive as you have been. Peer support will be an important adjunct to any encouragement a counselor or parent might provide. If a teenager has many questions about issues of sexuality and is experiencing periods of depression or confusion, it is sometimes better to wait before telling family and friends. Unless the teenager is comfortable with his or her growing awareness, dealing with the concerns of others may prove a liability. Encourage the teenager to continue to talk with you and ideally to talk to his or her parents. It is of maximum help if the teenager struggling with this self-identity question can find support in a loving and understanding parent.

The timing of talking with one's family is critical. It is important to explore with a teenager his or her general relationship with his/her family. Are there stresses at home such as divorce, issues with a sibling, a new home, a new school, or job changes, that may make it more difficult for the student at this time? If the student is financially dependent upon parents (which is likely), and if the parents do not receive the news well, will the young person be ostracized from the family home? It is believed by many researchers that the largest number of young persons living on the street are there because their homosexuality was not accepted by their parents.[22]

If a youth approaches you regarding a possible homosexual

identification, the first thing to recall is that he or she likes and trusts you—or the teenager would not be speaking with you in the first place. What type of responses are important?

1. Be yourself; and thank the person for trusting you.
2. Be conscious about the fear involved in this self-disclosure.
3. Youth often have stereotypes and misinformation about homosexuality and these will need to be clarified.
4. Use the same vocabulary as the teenager: e.g., homosexual; gay/lesbian; bisexual. If the youth is uneasy in this regard, simply use the term "same sex feelings."
5. Ask *yourself* some questions: e.g., How knowledgeable am I? How comfortable am I with this subject?
6. Ask the youth about his or her support systems: e.g., friends; a role model; a family member; parents.
7. Be sensitive about the family's role and be especially aware of cultural issues that may be present.
8. Is the youth romantically involved with someone and what does this mean?
9. Speak clearly about sexually transmitted diseases and HIV/AIDS.
10. Assess for danger: e.g., suicidal thoughts/attempts; substance abuse; isolation; lack of nourishment.

In Is It A Choice?[23] Eric Marcus writes:

The statistics on suicide sadly confirm how unhappy many people are about being gay or lesbian—especially while they're first dealing with their feelings of attraction for the same sex....(S)ome studies say that 40% of all homosexuals make attempts on their lives when they're young....And one-third of teenage suicides involve gay and lesbian teens.

In the "Report of the Secretary's Task Force on Youth Suicide" released by the Department of Health and Human Services (DHHS) in 1989, the government reported that gay and lesbian youth are two to three times more likely to commit suicide than heterosexual youths. Consequently, the members of the task force called for an "end [to] discrimination against youths on the basis of such characteristics as disability, sexual orientation, and financial status."[24] The members of the task force were trying to initiate positive steps to reduce suicide attempts among gay and lesbian youth.[25]

In a study in June of 1990 reported in *Pediatrics*, researchers from the University of Minnesota and the University of Washington found that 30% of homosexual and bisexual male youths aged 14 to 21 attempted suicide. Half of these youths attempted suicide more than once. This study, although using a relatively small sample size, demonstrated that the attempted suicide rate among homosexual males is two or three times higher than the rate among heterosexual males in the same age group.

Paul Gibson, a clinical social worker who was involved in the 1989 DHHS report, notes:

> While the problems faced by lesbian, gay and bisexual youth may seem overwhelming, they are also one of the easiest groups of young people to help. Once they gain a positive understanding of their sexual orientation, acceptance from others, and support in dealing with the conflicts they face from others, many of their problems are greatly diminished. Most importantly, this includes suicidal feelings and behavior once they recognize they have a life that is worth living.

Outing

The Congregation for the Doctrine of the Faith's *Declaration on Certain Questions Concerning Sexual Ethics* (1975) and the *Letter to the Bishops on the Pastoral Care of Homosexual Persons* (1986) affirm that no person should be discriminated against because of his or her sexual orientation. The *Letter* specifically states that "It is deplorable that homosexual persons have been and are the object of violent malice in speech or in action. Such treatment deserves condemnation from the Church's pastors wherever it occurs."[26] The United States Catholic Conference's document *Human Sexuality*[27] affirms:

> We call on all Christians and citizens of good will to confront their own fears about homosexuality and to curb the humor and discrimination that offend homosexual persons.

We understand that having a homosexual orientation brings
with it enough anxiety, pain and issues related to self-
acceptance without society adding additional prejudicial
treatment....(W)e affirm that homosexual men and women
"must certainly be treated with understanding" and sustained in Christian hope.

Clearly, church teaching affirms that homosexual people should
not suffer prejudice against their basic human rights. Since the church
upholds a position of non-discrimination and equality for all citizens,
is forcing certain closeted homosexual persons out of their private
lives a form of public discrimination?

The AIDS Coalition to Unleash Power (ACT-UP) specifically
proposes a tactic of revealing the names of homosexual clergy, religious and political figures who hide their sexual orientation and habits
but who attack homosexual persons who do not. ACT-UP has coined
the term "Outing" for the tactic of revealing the closeted homosexuality
of politicians and religious people who oppose gay interests.

Advocates of "Outing" are concerned about three critical religious areas which they presume to be accurate:

1. Members of the hierarchy who refuse to acknowledge the
   numbers of homosexual people within the clergy.
2. Official church documents which undermine the possibility of
   homosexual people realizing the "giftedness" of their homosexuality.
3. Homosexual priests who evidence "In their private lives, clan-
   destine [homosexual] behavior...."

In light of the church's teachings regarding non-discrimination,
the tactic of "Outing" would seem to represent violence to a person's
right to privacy. Outing is a form of intimidation, a kind of public
relations blackmail. Justice is not attained by destroying another's
individual dignity. Forcing a person into the "passage" of public disclosure is an act of violence against human dignity.

Confrontational tactics as proposed in "Outing" do violence to
human dignity and seem to be a threat against the need to continue to
uphold nondiscrimination for persons in light of their sexual orientation. The problem with "Outing" is that it claims an unjustifiable right

to sacrifice the lives of others.[28] At the same time, of course, all homosexual people must be self-critical about possible ways they might be openly and unjustly oppressing gay men and lesbian women.

Sexual Addiction

Sexual addiction is certainly not a phenomenon that touches solely the lives of homosexual people. To make such an assertion is totally erroneous, false and misleading. Like any other individual, some homosexual people are influenced by addictive behavior in their sexuality. Eric Marcus puts it this way:

> If you believe what some people say about gay men, you would think that all gay men have had a thousand or more sexual partners by the time they're thirty. Some very sexually active men—straight and gay—have had a thousand or more sexual partners by time they're thirty....Most gay men who have lots of different sexual partners aren't doing it because of the desire to challenge society's general condemnation of promiscuity. They're doing it for a simple reason: They want to.[29]

Because this problem does exist in the homosexual community, some word should be said here regarding the general problem of *sexual addiction*. A number of books deal well with the question of sexual addiction[30] but perhaps Patrick Carnes' *Out of the Shadows*[31] describes most succinctly this whole question and problem. Carnes explains that a common definition of alcoholism or drug dependency is that a person has a pathological relationship with a mood-altering chemical.[32] The alcoholic's relationship with alcohol becomes more important than family, friends and work. The relationship progresses to the point where alcohol is necessary to feel normal. To feel "normal" for the alcoholic is also to feel isolated and lonely since the primary relationship he or she depends upon to feel adequate is with a chemical, not other people.

A sexual addiction is parallel. The addict substitutes a sick relationship to an event or process for a healthy relationship with others. The addict's relationship with a mood-altering "experience" becomes central to his or her life.

As Carnes describes, for a sexual addict an addictive experience progresses through a four-step cycle which intensifies with each repetition:

1. *Preoccupation*—the trance or mood wherein the addict's mind is completely engrossed with thoughts of sex. This mental state creates an obsessive search for sexual stimulation.
2. *Ritualization*—the addict's own special routines which lead up to the sexual behavior. The ritual intensifies the preoccupation, adding arousal and excitement.
3. *Compulsive Sexual Behavior*—the actual sexual act, which is the end-goal of the preoccupation and ritualization. Sexual addicts are unable to control or stop this behavior.
4. *Despair*—the feeling of utter hopelessness addicts have about their behavior and their powerlessness. This despair then leads back into the first stage of preoccupation, thus creating a cycle difficult to break.

Sexual addicts are hostages of their own preoccupation. Every passerby, every relationship, and every introduction to someone passes through the sexually obsessive filter. More than merely noticing sexually attractive people, there is a quality of desperation which interferes with work, relaxation, and even sleep. People become objects to be scrutinized. A walk through a crowded downtown area is translated into a veritable shopping list of "possibilities."

Carnes suggests the following formula as a guideline: Signs of compulsive sexuality are when the behavior can be described as follows:

1. It is a *Secret*. Anything that cannot pass public scrutiny will create the shame of a double life.
2. It is *Abusive* to self or others. Anything that is exploitive or harmful to others or degrades oneself will activate the addictive system.
3. It is used to avoid (or is a source of) painful *Feelings*. If sexuality is used to alter moods or results in painful mood shifts, it is clearly part of the addictive process.
4. It is *Empty* of a caring, committed relationship. Fundamental to the whole concept of addiction and recovery is the healthy dimension of human relationships. The addict runs a great risk of being sexual outside of a committed relationship.[33]

Experts believe that most sexual addiction is rooted in dysfunctional early childhood experiences within the family. Dr. Paul McHugh, Chief Psychiatrist at The John Hopkins Medical School, contends that a high percentage of sexual addicts were sexually abused as children. In a sense, he observes, they are trying to re-create the childhood situation, hoping somehow to repair it (Freud called the phenomenon the "repetition compulsion").[34] Recognizing this childhood abuse is an important part of recovery. Carnes writes, "For the addict, part of the therapy is to discover the role of the previous generation in the addiction."

Sexual addiction, like other addictions, often involves a co-addict—a loved one or friend who becomes so involved in the life of the addict that he or she truly starts to participate in the same impaired mental process of the addict. Family members, as co-addicts, become part of the problem. Because they feel their own failing so deeply (inadequacy), they feel responsible for other people's actions (grandiosity). The co-addict has low self-esteem and attempts unsuccessfully to control the addict's behavior. Both need treatment if their relationship is to survive.

Sexual addiction is emerging from out of the shadows as a disease that is recognized, discussed, and treated, and from which there is "recovery" and/or "control." The introduction of daylight on this subject is an encouraging sign of the growing health of our society.[35]

Same-Sex Marriages

In "The Politics of Homosexuality,"[36] Andrew Sullivan indicates that a critical measure for full equality for the gay and lesbian community is equal access to marriage. Sullivan writes:

> If the military ban deals with the heart of what it is to be a citizen, the marriage ban deals with the core of what it is to be a member of civil society. Marriage is not simply a private contract; it is a social and public recognition of a private commitment. As such it is the highest public recognition of our personal integrity. Denying it to gay people is the most public affront possible to their civil equality.[37]

What reasons do gay and lesbian people give for society supporting same-sex marriages? Simply put, the main reason is framed in the context of civil equality. Sullivan remarks:

> The vast majority of us—gay and straights—are brought up to understand that the apex of emotional life is found in the marital bond. It may not be something we achieve, or even ultimately desire, but its very existence premises the core of our emotional development. It is the architectonic institution that frames our emotional life. The marriages of others are a moment for celebration and self-affirmation; they are the way in which our families and friends reinforce us as human beings. Our parents consider our emotional lives to be more important than our professional ones, because they care about us at our core, not at our periphery. And it is not hard to see why the marriage of an offspring is often regarded as the high point of any parent's life.[38]

In other words, through same-sex marriages, gay and lesbian people are seeking a level of relationship that would give them in society an anchor, an endpoint, a way of integrating themselves fully into the network of family and friends.

In *Is It A Choice?*, Eric Marcus asks the same question: Why are gay people fighting for the legal right to get married? He replies in virtually the same way as Sullivan: "(T)hey want the same legal protections and financial benefits granted to heterosexual married couples."[39] Marcus outlines the "legal protections and benefits of marriage" that are present in most states: Married couples have the legal right to be on each other's insurance and pension plans; they get special tax exemptions and deductions, and are eligible for Social Security survivor's benefits; they may inherit property and may have automatic rights of survivorship that avoid inheritance tax; and marriage laws offer legal protection in the event a relationship comes to an end, providing for an orderly distribution of property. In the case of death or medical emergency, a spouse is the legal "next of kin," which means that he or she can make all decisions regarding medical care and funeral arrangements. In addition, the next of kin is granted automatic visitation rights.

Marcus specifically points out that for gay and lesbian couples who are raising children, the fact that they cannot marry means that only one of the two parents can have legal custody of the child. (Only very rarely are the two unmarried people allowed to adopt the same child.) In the event the couple separates or the legal parent dies, the nonadoptive parent faces a legal nightmare if he or she wishes to retain custody of the child or even secure visitation rights.[40]

Brooklyn Law School Professor Nan D. Hunter puts it this way:

> The fundamental inequity is that...virtually any straight couple has the option to marry and thus establish a next-of-kin relationship that the state will enforce. No lesbian or gay couple can. Under the law, two women or two men are forever strangers, regardless of the relationship.[41]

The Hawaii State Supreme Court ruled in a split decision in May of 1993 that state laws banning same-sex "marriages" are unconstitutional because they discriminate on the basis of sex. The court said the state must justify the ban for it to remain in effect. If it fails to do so, Hawaii could be the first state to officially recognize what are now called homosexual or same-sex marriages.[42]

How are we as members of the church to respond to this question of same-sex marriages?

Two of the basic meanings for the existence of the two human sexes are companionship and procreation. *Both* are inherently linked in marriage. This link elevates procreation to be more than just a biological function. Human beings do not anonymously meet and mate and move on. For humans,"procreation" *de facto* begins prior to the union of egg and sperm, with the establishment of a loving, complementary community of two persons with the ability and desire to conceive and welcome a child. We name this status a marriage. After conception, procreation continues with the contribution by both mother and father to their child of the love and attention, education and guidance every developing human being needs and to which each is entitled. This bearing and raising of children is so serious that the church views marriage as a sacrament and teaches that sexual relations are only moral in the context of a marriage. It is so serious that the secular state licenses marriage, and deems it necessary to attach legal consequences, benefits and responsibilities.

Consequently, the church's opposition to same sex marriages is based on more than the procreative dimension of marriage. The church also understands the *unity* of marriage as a complementarity/union whose essence involves a relationship which transcends sexual differences. Gay and lesbian marriages contradict both the procreative and the unitive dimension of marriage.

To allow a man to "marry" a man or a woman to "marry" a woman is to deny the inherent procreative nature of marriage and therefore change its very definition. It not only changes the definition, it essentially voids it. This point is made by the U. S. Bishops' Committee for Pro-Life Activities in its statement on the 25th Anniversary of *Humanae Vitae*: "Sexuality…is not merely a matter of biology, nor is it simply a source of personal pleasure. Rather, it concerns, as Pope John Paul II reminds us in the apostolic exhortation, *Familiaris Consortio*, the innermost being of the human person as such. It is realized in a truly human way only if it is an integral part of the love by which a man and woman commit themselves totally to one another until death" (n 11). The law cannot require a married couple to have children any more than it can force them to love each other or stay together for life. But, at the very least, the law can require that a marriage be modeled in accord with its inherent procreative nature which means, of course, a male and a female.

The potential for children justifies additional civil requirements, namely, that a couple be old enough and not closely related. If one eliminates procreation from the basic definition of marriage, on what legal basis could one stop three people from getting married, or a mother and a son, etc.? The most basic and ideal building block of society and our communities is the biological family—mother, father and children. A healthy society needs children conceived and nurtured in loving family environments in order to become productive and contributing adults. The benefits given by the state to married couples endorse this basic premise. These are not privileges and rights for couples so much as they are endorsement and support *for families.* The marriage license exists, then, for the benefit of a union that presumes children and, therefore, for society's healthy and productive future. Simply put, the license is primarily for the sake of the children, not the couple.

Since its inception, our society has provided to married couples and families certain benefits that are not available to nonmarried individuals (e.g., tax incentives, health care rights, pension and survivor benefits).[43] At the root of this traditional societal and governmental concern for marriage and the family has been the belief that marriage constitutes the most beneficial environment for raising the next generation of citizens. Society has thus perceived itself to have a vested interest in supporting strong, stable, committed marital relationships so that children will have a stable and nurturing environment in which to be raised.

It is particularly important to recognize this point: The benefits accorded to families by government and society are not primarily rendered to individuals who are married (though they do extend to married couples without children and to couples whose children are grown). Even so, benefits are rendered to establish a nurturing environment for children. Any discussion of same-sex partnerships/marriage that misses this point will become mired in confusion, for it is impossible to justify special benefits to married couples if these benefits are seen first and foremost as benefits to the spouses themselves.

The same-sex relationships—domestic partnerships—idea rests upon a sociological fact and a value judgment. The sociological fact is that there is a great diversity of living arrangements in our society today. The value judgment is that individuals in all or at least some of these living arrangements have an equal right to the benefits that government and society presently give to married couples.

Statistics indicate that of the nation's 91 million households, 2.6 million are inhabited by unmarried adults of the opposite sex. Some 1.6 million households involve unmarried adults of the same sex. These figures include a disparate array of personal arrangements: young male-female couples living together before getting married, elderly friends who decide to share a house, platonic roommates, and romantic gay or straight lovers. As these statistics demonstrate, substantial numbers of Americans live in non-traditional households. Those who favor "domestic partnerships" say that government should recognize this diversity and distribute benefits without regard to whether it is a traditional marriage, a committed partnership without benefit of marriage, or merely a temporary arrangement of convenience.

While it is true that domestic partnership proponents frequently speak of giving benefits only to truly committed couples, the *majority* of legislative proposals advanced would have the legal effect of providing such benefits without any requirements for a long-term committed relationship.

We should not overlook the fact that some changes are needed in civil law to address inequities created by the increased diversity of American family life: e.g., it is unjust for people who are living together not to have the right to visit their partner in the hospital as would "family," or to receive bereavement leave from work upon the death of their partner. However, domestic partnership and/or same-sex relationship may be damaging to society and is objectionable to the church because it further weakens the institution of marriage and encourages heterosexual couples to forego the marital commitment.

Chapter 6

Discrimination and Homophobia

Discrimination

A well-respected priest who works in a large American archdiocese with gay and lesbian persons wrote to me:

Homosexual people have an active role in the Christian Community. As a group of men and women who are inclined sexually to what is beyond moral norms of the church and for which there is no legitimate expression, their lives are often marked by anxiety and pain, issues of self-acceptance and constant fear of discovery. What is rarely appreciated are the untold injustices suffered daily by homosexuals to their very personhood. Such injustices are not a response to sexual acting out. Simply being homosexual or being perceived as such can be the occasion for all kinds of discrimination. Some Catholics have sent a clear and consistent message to homosexual Catholics of either indifference or covert hostility. Such an attitude is so ingrained in the life of ordinary Catholics that it is often taken for granted. An environment of indifference and hostility shames homosexual people. When homosexual people internalize the shame, they may act it out in ways that are self-destructing and alienating. Shame can lead homosexual men and women far beyond the required chaste life. They can easily be convinced to change their orientation. They may attempt to enter into unwise and impossible heterosexual marriage instead of attempting to build chaste and intimate relationships with men and women. They may seek a "cure" instead of a healing. They may reduce the totality of Christian life to chastity alone, neglecting the other Christian virtues. Whenever expectations exceed the boundaries of grace and possibility, one is left with despair. Despair leads to promiscuity, any number of addictions, and even to suicide. I have seen it all—enough to break my heart open.

How are we as members of the church to respond to this type of scenario? We must first seek to repair any damage we caused by confronting our own fears about homosexuality. The church follows a middle course between being harsh or permissive. The church thus avoids identifying itself with the political extremes either to the right or the left and is especially cautious of contaminating its clear teaching with influences from political pressure groups. The church tries to offer to homosexual people what it tries to offer every member of the church—a loving and hospitable environment. Hospitality involves drawing so close to homosexual persons that one knows and experiences the pain and wounds of this orientation as if they were one's own.

It is precisely this kind of solidarity that gives birth to whatever change and conversion the Lord wills. It is in such an atmosphere that a homosexual person is able to make decisions and choices that are more and more in conformity with the gospel and the teachings of the church. It is this kind of indiscriminate mercy that is at the heart of our faith and is the goal for any legitimate ministry in the church. Such ministry normally has little to boast about because conversion is usually a very slow process in our Catholic tradition and being successful is not the focus of such an approach. The only concern is being a faithful witness to God's relentless love by the gift of hospitable presence. Such ministry lives with high hopes for the homosexual person. The difference between expectations and hopes is that hopefulness gives great space for the tender mercies of our God to accomplish God's work.

Jonathan Rauch has written a provocative article "Beyond Oppression."[1] He writes:

Homosexual [people] are objects of scorn for teenagers....
They grow up in confusion and bewilderment as children, and often pass into denial as young adults and sometimes remain frightened even into old age....There is also AIDS and the stigma attached to it, though AIDS is not uniquely a problem of gay people. And there is the violence.[2]

Rauch argues that the "oppression model" regarding homosexual people should be "junked" because the insistence that homosexual people are oppressed is very damaging in the end, because it implies that to be a homosexual person is to suffer. What does he suggest as the "right model"? Not that of an oppressed people seeking redemption through political action; rather, that of an ostracized people seeking redemption through personal action.

In September of 1992, *Newsweek* also addressed the question of gay and lesbian people and discrimination. *Newsweek* explained:

> Homosexuals have little legal recourse against even blatant bias. There is no federal law protecting gays and lesbians from losing their jobs, being evicted from their homes or being denied a bank loan because of sexual preference. For 15 years gay groups have lobbied unsuccessfully to amend the 1964 civil rights act—which bans bias based on race, ethnicity, gender and religion—to include sexual orientation. Only 6 states and about 110 municipalities have statutes barring discrimination against gays. The resulting patchwork of state and local laws has produced a situation notable chiefly for its confusion and inconsistency.[3]

John Coleman, S.J. forthrightly addresses the question of discrimination in this manner:

> I have long held that a classic Catholic case can and should be made for support of civil liberties for homosexual people grounded on their human dignity as persons and that this case *need not*, in principle, in any way compromise the affirmation made in the CDF letter that "It is only in the marital relationship that the use of the sexual faculty can be morally good. A person engaging in homosexual behavior therefore acts immorally" (n 7).[4]

Cardinal Joseph Bernardin has also addressed this point in a very careful position on gay rights legislation: "In the case of gay rights legislation I seek to balance two values: (1) the fact that no person should be discriminated against because of his or her sexual orientation; (2) the normativeness of heterosexual marital intimacy as the proper context for intimate genital encounters."[5]

Both John Coleman and Cardinal Bernardin are arguing that no logic demands that acceptance of the teaching in the CDF letter include a program to deny civil liberty to homosexual citizens. Catholic logic might argue for the very opposite. Catholics who view homosexual behavior as a moral error cannot deny that homosexual persons continue to have and deserve all their basic human rights. Coleman argues that, "It has been my understanding of the *Declaration on Religious Freedom* that Catholic teaching should support these rights—not necessarily laws which recognize homosexuality as such as a social alternative (e.g., domestic partner laws), but certainly all ordinary civil liberties against discrimination in housing, employment, job opportunities, and so on."[6]

In other words, laws which discriminate against homosexual people perpetrate a great moral evil that must be resisted on traditional Catholic grounds. As Coleman points out, John Courtney Murray argued in *We Hold These Truths* that laws against contraception would involve a greater evil of state intrusiveness into bedrooms. A similar logic applies to the private acts of consenting homosexual adults. Coleman concludes,

> It is clear, to me at least, that a classic and traditional case can be made for Catholic support for civil liberties for homosexual people....For this reason, I think the U.S. Catholic bishops were much closer to the mark when they taught that, "Homosexuals, like everyone else, should not suffer from prejudice against their basic human rights. They have a right to respect, friendship and justice. They should have an active role in the Christian community."[7]

In his book *Is It A Choice?*, Eric Marcus helps delineate the various ways gay and lesbian people feel discrimination. They have, e.g., been fired from their jobs, evicted from their homes, and denied custody of their children. Until recently, gay and lesbian persons were routinely discharged from the military.[8]

University of California research psychologist, Dr. Gregory M. Herek, author of *Hate Crimes: Confronting Violence Against Lesbians and Gay Men*, states that for most people who are biased against gay people, homosexual persons "stand as a proxy for all that is evil....(S)uch people see hating gay men and lesbian [women] as a litmus test for being a moral person." Young people in particular are often motivated by a desire to be "part of the crowd" or to gain the approval of their peers or family and thus may engage in anti-gay activity. Another explanation for what motivates people who are anti-gay is fear of their own homosexual feelings. According to Dr. Herek, "Although the explanation probably is used more often than is appropriate, it does apply to some men who will attack gays as a way of denying unacceptable aspects of their own personalities."[9]

Why is it that we find such a concern about discrimination toward homosexual people? Educator Ann Northrop explains:

> Homosexual [people] are taught from preconsciousness to be ashamed of themselves and to hate themselves and to think that they are disgusting, aberrant, immoral human beings. So the achievement of any kind of self-esteem in a lesbian or gay person is an incredible victory against almost insurmountable odds in the society we live in. Those of us who have achieved any small measure of self-esteem celebrate and take pride in the extent to which we've been able to achieve it. When you've been given the exact opposite all your life, there is a great need to achieve a sense of pride.[10]

In order to properly appreciate this entire question of discrimination, it is critical to understand its contextualization. Andrew Sullivan has outlined carefully the various ways people view gay-straight relations:[11]

1. The conservative politics of sexuality: Its fundamental assertion is that homosexuality as such does not properly exist. Homosexual behavior is aberrant activity either on the part of heterosexual people whose intent is to subvert traditional society, or by people who are prey to psychological, emotional or sexual dysfunction. In this viewpoint, the existence of homosexual people is a grave problem.

2. In a radical politics, homosexuality is viewed very similar to the first point but here homosexuality is also seen as a cultural construction, a binary social conceit forced upon the sexually amorphous: i.e., the rest of us. Here, homosexuality is seen as definitely a choice:

the choice to be a "queer," the choice to subvert oppressive institutions, the choice to be an activist.

3. A moderate politics of homosexuality: Unlike the conservatives (model one) and the radicals (model two), the moderates do believe that a small number of people are inherently homosexual: but they also believe that others are susceptible to persuasion in that direction and should be dissuaded. This politic is not intolerant, but opposes the presence of openly gay teachers in schools; they have gay friends but hope their child isn't homosexual; they are in favor of ending the military ban but would seek to do so either by reimposing the closet (ending discrimination in return for gay people never mentioning their sexuality) or by finding some other kind of solution, such as simply ending the witch hunts. If they support sodomy laws, they prefer to see them unenforced.

4. A liberal politics of homosexuality: Like the moderates (model three), the liberals accept that homosexuality exists, that it is involuntary for a proportionate group, that for a few more it is an option and that it need not be discouraged. Viewing the issue primarily through the prism of the civil rights movement, the liberals seek to extend to homosexual persons the same protections they have granted to other minorities. The prime instrument for this is the regulation of private activities by heterosexual people, primarily in employment and housing, to guarantee non-discrimination against homosexual people. Sexual orientation is simply added to the end of a list of minority conditions, in formulaic civil rights legislation. This strategy is based on two assumptions: that sexuality is equivalent to race in terms of discrimination; and that the full equality of homosexual people can be accomplished by designating gay people as victims.[12]

5. Another politic begins with the view that for a small minority of people, homosexuality is an involuntary condition that can neither be denied nor permanently repressed. This viewpoint adheres to an understanding that there is a limit to what politics can achieve and trains its focus not on the behavior of private heterosexual citizens but on the actions of the public. While it eschews the use of law to legislate culture, it strongly believes that law can affect culture indirectly.

This politic affirms a simple and limited criterion: that all *public* discrimination against homosexual people be ended and that every right and responsibility that heterosexual people enjoy by virtue of the state be extended to those who grow up differently. And that is all: no cures or re-education; no wrenching civil litigation; no political imposition of tolerance; merely a political attempt to enshrine formal civil equality, in the hope that eventually, the private sphere will reflect this public civility. This politic banishes the paradigm of victimology and replaces it with one of integrity.

These five optics should assist us in properly contextualizing our personal viewpoints regarding acceptance/discrimination relative to homosexual persons. In light of these categories, the treatment of discrimination in the *Encyclopedia of Homosexuality* is helpful.[13] According to the *Encyclopedia*, discrimination refers to treatment that disadvantages persons by virtue of their perceived membership in a group. Historically, a pattern of ostracism and general intolerance drove homosexual men and women to desperate measures of concealment and deception in order to avoid the economic and social penalties which a hostile environment sought to inflict upon them. Until the 1940s the right of employers, landlords and the like to discriminate on the grounds of racial or ethnic origin went unchallenged. Then a movement began to declare such forms of exclusion illegal that led to the enactment of many state laws forbidding such practices, and ultimately to the Civil Rights Act of 1964.

However, discrimination based upon the sexual orientation of a person was upheld by the courts as a right to eliminate "immoral" persons from the work force or from housing. The judiciary consistently echoed the cultural norms of the heterosexual majority as binding upon the whole of society. Early attempts to include homosexual people within the protections afforded cultural, religious, and racial minorities met uniformly with failure. Only gradually did groups concerned with civil liberties come to believe that discrimination against homosexual persons violated their civil rights. The struggle to include "sexual orientation" in the protected list of anti-discrimination laws began in the 1970s and has led in the United States to the passage of some 50 municipal ordinances with such guarantees.[14]

Homosexual teachers and counselors often face dismissal on the basis of substantive rules that disqualify such employees for "moral turpitude" or "immoral or unprofessional conduct." Because popular belief often misidentifies the homosexual person with a child molester, school teachers face a particularly invidious type of discrimination.

Oregon Citizens Alliance (OCA) produced Ballot Measure 9 which would invalidate the phrase "sexual orientation" in any statute where it now appears. It also requires educators to set curriculum standards equating homosexuality with pedophilia, sadism and masochism.

More recently, a few courts have held that an employee's private life should not be of concern to an employer unless it could be shown to affect the employee's ability to perform his or her duties. In practice, the criterion has often been the employee's visibility: if his or her sexual activity is covert and unknown to the community, the school officials can overlook it, but if it becomes publicly known, they feel obliged to "protect the reputation of the institution." Such is also the logic of court decisions that uphold the right of an employer to dismiss a gay activist whose political overtness has made him or her notorious.

From the late 1960s onward, laws and guidelines were enacted that called for "affirmative action" to increase the numbers of women and ethnic minorities in fields from which they had traditionally been excluded or limited to low-level, menial positions. These have even included actual quotas that an employer needed to meet to comply with the law. None of these programs has contained any measure to increase the number of homosexual people in any firm or industry. (I have treated this subject in more detail in the chapter on Church Documentation, specifically regarding the C.D.F. letter on Discrimination).

Discrimination in housing is another barrier that homosexual people face, particularly when trying to rent apartments. Single homosexual persons who "pass" as heterosexual people are not likely to encounter difficulty; moreover, gay people are recognized by many landlords as likely to improve property. When two prospective tenants of the same sex apply, however, they may be denied at the whim of the owner or, in the case of large corporate landlords, as the result of company policy. The argument is voiced that their presence will have a "morally corrupting influence" on the children of families living in the same building or in the general area.

The campaign for anti-discrimination ordinances parallel to those protecting other minorities will indeed be a major part of gay movement activity in the decades ahead. Such ordinances are understood to be the only positive guarantees of the fundamental liberties that homosexual people need to become full-fledged members of modern society.

As members of the Roman Catholic Church, we will continue to face the problems of discrimination and these principles, culled from recent documents, can be used as guidelines:

1. *To Live in Christ Jesus* affirms that homosexuals "should not suffer from prejudice against their basic human rights" (n 52).
2. The church disavows all forms of "unjust discrimination." (*Considerations Concerning Non-Discrimination of Homosexual Persons*, n 10).
3. Sexual orientation does not constitute a quality comparable to race, ethnic background and sex; consequently, homosexual orientation itself cannot be the ground for legislative entitlements. (*Considerations*, nn 10 and 14).
4. Discrimination is not unjust when homosexual activity is judged to be harmful or manipulative. (*Considerations*, nn 11 and 14).
5. Every person deserves respect in word, action and law (*Letter to the Bishops*, n 10). These rights can be legitimately limited only when there is "objectively disordered external behavior" and there is need "to protect the common good" (*Consideration*, n 13).
6. Homosexuality itself cannot be considered "as a positive source of human rights, for example, in respect to so-called affirmative action or preferential treatment..." (*Considerations*, n 13).
7. It is wrong to confer "equivalent family status on homosexual unions" (*Considerations*, n 15).

A final word should be added about certain false, erroneous "myths" that foster discrimination against homosexual people:[15]

1. Gay and lesbian people sustain certain common traits: e.g., certain "gay" names, voices, mannerisms and demeanors.
2. Homosexuality is caused by sinfulness. For example, Patrick Buchanan has written, "The poor homosexuals—they have declared war upon nature, and now nature is exacting an

awful retribution (i.e., AIDS)." In other words, to be homosexual is an arrogant and sinful act of volition.[16]

3. Homosexuality is caused by mental illness. In this point of view, the "depravity" of homosexuality involves genes or twisted parenting. Homosexuality is a pathological problem and persons with this "illness" need medical and psychological treatment. In this viewpoint, homosexual people are often viewed as degenerate and "odd."[17]

4. Homosexuality is caused by an ingrained fear or dislike of the opposite sex.

5. Homosexuality is caused by recruitment: i.e., homosexuality-through-seduction.

6. All homosexual people are sexual addicts. Hostile heterosexual people are particularly fond of the analogy to bestiality— probably because this calls to mind a picture which is inhuman and vulgar, certainly at the hinterland of sexual abnormality.

7. Homosexual people are unproductive and untrustworthy members of society. Because of this myth, homosexual people are distrusted as a class because they are believed to act only as a self-interested group, one that sticks together and favors its own whenever possible. *Homohatred* is frequently validated by "the myth of the powerful homosexual, first cousin to the myth of the powerful Jew."

Homophobia

Ho'mo-pho'bi-a—a noun meaning: irrational fear or hatred of homosexual people. Homophobia generally refers to "the dread of being in close quarters with homosexual [people]."[18] However, since its inception the term homophobia has been transformed in usage and precision and is now used to refer to a range of affective and behavioral components. These components include a rational fear, hatred (homohatred), hostility, and/or assault as well as a low grade discomfort and/or amiable indifference.[19]

From the ever-expanding findings of research in this area, we have learned that homophobia has been highly correlated with the male gender, authoritarianism, low educational levels, lack of life experience with and/or exposure to homosexual individuals, and a lack of formal academic education in the area of human sexuality.[20] Research has found that formal academic training at the college level in the area of human sexuality decreased the degree of homophobia in individuals. Individuals with lower education levels tend to be more prejudiced toward homosexual people.[21]

Those who believe that homosexuality is learned, and therefore something that the individual might have control over, tend to be more homophobic.[22] A major portion of the variance in negative attitudes toward homosexual people, according to research, can best be explained by an individual's adherence to the belief in the controllability of homosexuality.

In a provocative article entitled "Gay Godfathers,"[23] the authors rightfully assert: "We have an obligation to the world not to perpetuate its homophobia." How might this happen? We need to *internalize* the belief that all gay men and lesbian women, like all human persons, deserve love and respect; that gay men and lesbian women, like all human persons, are to be cherished, and sustain a significant place in the human and church community.

We want our children to grow up free. Homophobia, like any prejudice, twists and cramps with fear and hatred the lives of those who hold it. Unaddressed, it keeps children from growing into whole adults. One child-development expert thus writes that the three magic words of child rearing are, "Example, Example, Example." The authors write, "We think about that a lot. We try to avoid stereotypes of how men and women act. Often this is inconvenient. We take turns driving the car, doing laundry, accompanying our daughter to pre-school picnics, playing ball with kids. We admit when we are struggling with a task or an issue. We try to let them know that being an adult does not mean we have gone on 'automatic pilot,' that things are still difficult and yet worth struggling over...."

In addition, homophobia may encourage promiscuity. Especially young people afraid of being gay/lesbian, or having other people think they are, might engage in multiple sexual encounters to prove to themselves and to others that they are "straight." Responsible parents talk about homosexuality. They tell their children that such promiscuity proves only the frightened immaturity of the person involved.

Language is also a critical element. Even the youngest children pick up derogatory antigay or antilesbian terms. The key here is consciousness-raising. Let children imagine what it would feel like to be slurred and slandered. Children are sensitive to name-calling, and they will understand this well. They face considerable homophobic pressure in their lives from other kids, teachers and the media.

What are some significant responses to the problem of homophobia?

1. Care should be taken to identify homophobia as a *prejudice*, comparable to racism and anti-Semitism, rather than an irrational fear similar to claustrophobia or agoraphobia.

2. We need to help ourselves and others to situate our homophobic attitudes and behaviors. A psychodynamic explanation proposes that homophobic individuals themselves fall into one of these categories: (a) they have unconscious homosexual desires which, because of societal attitudes, cause them great anxiety and thus their homophobia serves as a psychological defense by disguising those desires; (b) they are ignorant about homosexuality and thus assume many of the myths mentioned above; and (c) they are persons who lack virtually any personal contact with homosexual men and women and also assume many of the myths already discussed. Homophobia consequently serves different social and psychological functions for different persons. For some it is a strategy for psychological defense; for others it is a way of making sense of past interactions with gay people; for others, expressing homophobic sentiments provides a means for gaining social approval or for affirming a particular self-concept through expressing values important to that self.

3. Lesbian women and gay men themselves are not immune from homophobia, since they are socialized into a culture where hostility toward homosexuality is the norm. Homophobia among gay people is termed "internalized homophobia" and is understood to involve a rejection of one's own homosexual orientation. This phenomenon is analogous to the self-contempt felt by members of stigmatized ethnic groups. Such persons need to be assisted to become ego-syntonic with their homosexuality.[24]

A good example of "internalized homophobia" is found in John Reid's *The Best Little Boy in the World*:

One ingenious defense was to remain as ignorant as possible on the subject of homosexuality. The less I knew, I reasoned, the less chance that I would start looking like one or acting like one. Those people I saw on the streets with their pocketbooks and their swish...they disgusted me...so I never read anything about homosexuality. No one would ever catch me at the "Ho" drawer of the New York Public Library Card Catalog.[25]

Internalized homophobia can also be a problem for some homosexual people. It is a form of post-traumatic stress, with such symptoms as hypervigilance (an acute awareness of potential danger), anxiety, mistrust, and withdrawal, developed in response to putdowns, discrimination and assaults.

This is a summary of tasks that can facilitate a healing process for homosexual people suffering from internalized homophobia:

- Acknowledge how you may have been abused
- Identify post-traumatic effects
- Recognize self-destructive behavior
- Get support for recovery
- Work through feelings
- Counter shame and negative messages
- Combat homophobia
- Learn how to nurture yourself

4. As members of the church, we must condemn all forms of violence either in attitude, language or behavior. The 1986 *Letter of the Congregation for the Doctrine of the Faith* asserts, "It is deplorable that homosexual persons have been and are the object of violent malice in speech or in action. Such treatment deserves condemnation from the Church's pastors wherever it occurs."[26] The U.S.C.C. document *Human Sexuality* affirms this same point:

We call on all Christians and citizens of good will to confront their own fears about homosexuality and to curb the humor and discrimination that offend homosexual persons. We understand that having a homosexual orientation brings with it enough anxiety, pain and issues related to self-acceptance without society adding additional prejudicial treatment....(W)e affirm that homosexual men and women "must certainly be treated with understanding" and sustained in Christian hope.

5. As a church, we must sponsor workshops to help sensitize families, students, parents, employees, and religious and community leaders to the problems connected with homophobia: i.e., homophobia is a form of oppression and is pervasive throughout our society; we must accept responsibility for it within ourselves and realize that homophobia hurts all people: a true sense of community, where all people are valued and supported, is a goal worth working toward.[27]

6. When possible, each diocese should promote programs which authentically support homosexual persons and uphold the church's teachings and appoint priests and religious who will demonstrate viable pastoral care to people with a homosexual orientation (*Letter to the Bishops*, nn 13–17). The *Letter* also encourages Bishops to "promote appropriate catechetical programs based on the truth about human sexuality in its relationship to the family as taught by the church. Such programs should provide a good context within which to deal with the question of homosexuality" (n 17).

Homosexuality and the Military

Randy Shilts begins his book *Conduct Unbecoming: Gays and Lesbians in the U.S. Military* by stating:

The history of homosexuality in the United States armed forces has been a struggle between two intransigent facts— the persistent presence of gays within the military and the equally persistent hostility toward them. All the drama and controversy surrounding the demand for acceptance by lesbians and gay men in uniform represents the culmination of this conflict, one that dates back to the founding of the Republic....

In the past decade, the cost of investigations and the dollars spent replacing gay personnel easily amount to hundreds of millions. The human costs are incalculable. Careers are destroyed; lives are ruined. Under the pressure of a purge, and in the swell of rumors that often precedes one, despairing men and women sometimes commit suicide.[28]

The issue of homosexuality has clearly arrived at the forefront of our political consciousness. "The nation is embroiled in debate over the acceptance of openly gay soldiers in the U.S. military," wrote Chandler Burr in the March 1993 edition of *The Atlantic*, in an article that explores the relationship between homosexuality and biology. During the first weeks of debate over the proposal to lift the ban on gay men in the military, President Clinton drew a clear distinction between "conduct and status," a phrase picked up and expanded by Maine Democrat and Senate Majority Leader George J. Mitchell, who spoke of "the distinction between disciplinary action taken on the basis of conduct as opposed to disciplinary action taken on the basis of status." Similarly, an editorial in *America* endorsed the distinction "between conduct and status so that homosexual persons who refrain from advocacy and observe the behavioral code can serve in the military without fear of discrimination...," reasoning that "this is about all that can be asked of any workable compromise."

This "compromise" became real on Monday July 19, 1993 when President Clinton decreed a policy that allows homosexual people to serve in the armed forces as long as they do not engage in homosexual acts—or tell their comrades that they are gay men or lesbian women. Clinton's policy essentially allows gay men and lesbian women to serve in the military as long as they keep their sexual orientation to themselves. The policy discourages the military from conducting investigations on the mere suspicion that an individual is homosexual. But it would still give unit commanders broad latitude, allowing them to determine whether "credible information" exists that an individual is engaging in homosexual conduct, which is defined as "a homosexual act, a statement by the service member that demonstrates a propensity or intent to engage in homosexual acts, or a homosexual marriage or attempted marriage." Military commanders will not initiate inquiries or investigations "solely" to determine someone's sexual orientation. However, commanders may order investigations if there is "credible information" that a member of the armed forces has engaged in homosexual conduct.[29]

In March of 1994 five men and one woman brought a suit against the Clinton policy, claiming that it is unconstitutional. A federal district judge in New York barred the government from investigating or discharging these six gay service-members while this lawsuit is pending. U. S. District Judge Eugene H. Nickerson wrote, "The message to those with such an orientation appears to be not to avoid private homosexual acts but to stay in the closet and to hide their orientation."

What motivates opposition to homosexual people in the military?[30] "Many people fear that social approval of homosexuality will lead to other forms of "unnatural" vices, including an increase in violence, not to mention other forms of sexual misconduct. Others predict that acceptance of homosexual persons in the military will open the door wider to a larger gay rights agenda, which ultimately aims at winning full social approval, and not merely tolerance, for homosexuality. Those in favor of lifting the ban, however, think the violence done to homosexual people and suspected homosexual people has already harmed society, not merely the homosexual persons involved.

The military's traditional policies are based on the premise that homosexuality is a pathological condition, hence, "Homosexuality is incompatible with military service" (Defense Department Directive 1332.14). No overt act is required to effect the ban on homosexual people in the military.

As Shilts has pointed out, over the past decade, homosexual persons have been discharged from the armed services at the rate of about 1,500 a year. Rarely do the expulsions involve any of the acts so commonly cited as a threat by those who oppose homosexual people in the military: e.g., harassment of straight colleagues, fondling or staring in the showers, or nocturnal visits to unsuspecting bunk mates.

Official discrimination against homosexual people began during World War II and became consolidated as policy during the 1950s, reaching its height during the 1980s. During World War II, a study of the unfit soldier classified homosexual people with eneuretics, as presumably both were guilty of incontinence. Toward the end of the war, a systematic effort was made to detect and exclude gay men and lesbian women from the American armed forces. According to the General Accounting Office, chasing suspected homosexual people out of the military service costs the Pentagon about $27 million each year—an arguably inadequate measure, since it does not reflect the human cost of ruined careers, disrupted lives, and widespread fears of gay-bashing.

The intolerance of the American military mounted in the wake of Senator Joseph McCarthy's charges that the Truman administration was "harboring sex perverts in government," followed by the report of a 17-member subcommittee that found homosexual people to be security risks. Even the armed forces of America's allies in NATO, many of which had no penal laws against homosexual behavior, were pressured to adopt them. Procedures used to obtain confessions from suspected homosexual people often violated the rights guaranteed a defendant in a criminal case in civilian life, yet the courts have been loath to deny the armed services the option of discharging individuals whose homosexuality has come to light, even if no criminal behavior while on duty could be imputed to them. The well-known case of Keith Meinhold is a recent example.

The ban has not, however, been uniformly applied. In 1945, during the height of the final European offensive against the Third Reich, Secretary of War Henry Stimson ordered a review of all gay discharges in the previous two years, with an eye toward reinducting gay men who had not committed any in-service homosexual acts. Orders went out to "salvage" homosexual men for the service whenever possible. Similar examples could be cited during the Vietnam war and Operation Desert Storm.

The argument that homosexual people will unilaterally subvert discipline and good order in the military is very hard to justify given the actual history of the U.S. armed forces. According to Allan Berube, author of *Coming Out Under Fire*, 100,000 to 200,000 of the two million members of the U. S. armed forces are gay, lesbian, or bisexual persons. The question then is not, "What happens if we let gays in the military," because Berube writes, "At least 99% stay and serve."

In light of President Clinton's new policy, even if the military can manage the compromised-transition well, that does not necessarily mean the controversy will fade.[31] There is a deeper source of discontent: "They want us to move faster than the country," said a former General. Sodomy laws based on religious prescriptions are still on the books in 24 states. The District of Columbia recently moved to drop its sodomy law, but Congress, which has final say, blocked a similar attempt in 1981. The Supreme Court, too, was disinclined to undo a taboo that it says dates to biblical times. In its 1986 decision Bowers vs. Hardwick, the Court upheld Georgia's sodomy law.

Some soldiers are so upset by the prospect of including gay men in the ranks that they are willing to break the rules by assaulting fellow soldiers. Their explanation is that they fear attack or unwanted sexual advances (sexual harassment). It is likely, too, that some soldiers fear their own reactions and the prospect that they might respond sexually. Psychologist Ken Corbett has written that, "Hatred of gay men is based on fear of the self, not of an alien other." The Department of Defense regulations adopted in 1982 allow a heterosexual to have homosexual sex and to be exonerated—so long as he or she states that the incidence was a lapse. Gay and lesbian soldiers, by contrast, have been discharged just for identifying themselves as such.

In *Coming Out Under Fire*, Allan Berube traces the start of a gay rights movement in America to the military itself. He argues that the relative openness of gay and lesbian relationships in the military in World War II eventually led to those veterans settling in port cities like San Francisco and New York where, for the first time, they established identifiable subcultures.

In an open letter to his soldiers printed in the Marine magazine *Leatherneck* in May of 1993, General Carl E. Mundy, Jr., the Marine Corps Commandant, advised: "We are made up not of individuals who seek self-identity, but of selfless men and women who place country and corps ahead of self....(W)hatever their privately held preferences or belief may be." He urged tolerance: "We treat all Marines with firmness, fairness and dignity."

Treating one another with dignity is certainly at the heart of this difficult but important question. It lies at the heart of President Clinton's basic case for lifting the military's ban on gay and lesbian people: "The principle behind this for me is that Americans who are willing to conform to the requirements of conduct within the military services in my judgment should be able to serve in the military, and that people should be disqualified from serving in the military based on something they do, not based on who they are. This is the elemental principle."[32]

In December of 1993 The Pentagon announced its new policy on homosexual people in the military (see description below)—scheduled to take effect on February 5, 1994. The new Pentagon rules ban sexual acts between members of the same sex—including kissing, holding hands or otherwise "touching a person or allowing such a person to touch you for the purpose of satisfying sexual desires."

The policy [dubbed "Don't ask, Don't tell, Don't pursue] bars the Pentagon from asking service members if they are homosexual. But gay men and lesbian women still can be discharged if they declare their sexual orientation, and the regulations give local unit commanders wide flexibility in deciding whether to bring proceedings against those who are found out. This policy is interestingly quite distinct from the Catholic position already explained which counsels understanding and compassion toward people with a homosexual orientation.

A NEW POLICY ON GAYS

Here are the basic elements of the new policy:

Compatibility
- The military will drop its earlier policy declaring homosexuality incompatible with military service, and instead will discharge only those personnel who have engaged in "homosexual conduct."
- The definition of such conduct is a broad one that includes anyone who has committed a homosexual act, who marries or attempts to marry a person of the same sex or who declares that he or she is gay or lesbian.
- Service personnel who admit they are gay, lesbian or bisexual would be allowed to continue in the military only if they can "demonstrate" that they neither engage in homosexual acts nor have "a propensity or intent to do so."

"Don't Ask"
- Recruits or new officer candidates no longer will be asked about their sexual orientation before they are allowed to join the military—unless authorities receive "independent evidence" that they have engaged in homosexual conduct in the past.

Investigations
- The services no longer will launch criminal investigations "solely to determine a service member's sexual orientation," and "normally" will not investigate sexual miscon-

duct when the sex act occurs in private between consenting adults.

- But they will be able to initiate investigations in cases involving "aggravating circumstances," ranging from force, coercion and intimidation and sex with people under 16 to abuse of position or rank and "conduct that raises a security concern."

- Any evidence of homosexual conduct will be turned over to unit commanders for fact-finding investigations. The administration served notice that it wanted most such cases to be handled administratively rather than by court-martial, as sometimes was the case before.

Security Clearances

- Authorities granting security clearances no longer will conduct investigations solely to determine a soldier's sexual orientation, and homosexuality in itself no longer will be grounds for denying a clearance to a service member.

- But investigators may push for more information in cases in which a person's sexual orientation raises the possibility that it may become a "security concern"—as in the case of a person who is concealing his sexual orientation, who might easily be subject to blackmail.

Notification

- Military authorities will take steps to keep all personnel apprised of the new policy, both when they first join the service and in periodic training sessions. They also will seek to train commanders and senior enlisted personnel in how to handle such cases.

- Under the new regulations, anyone expelled from the armed forces for engaging in homosexual conduct is still likely to be given an honorable discharge. But the discharge would be "other than honorable" if the case involved force, a minor or a subordinate.

Chapter 7

HIV/AIDS AND THE HOMOSEXUAL COMMUNITY

In *Is It A Choice?*, Eric Marcus discusses the interrelationship of HIV/AIDS and the homosexual community:

> AIDS is caused by HIV, a virus, not someone's sexual orientation, and it is spread in a number of ways, not just by one kind of sexual act....AIDS is a human disease, and in most parts of the world it's a predominantly heterosexual disease. In the United States, where AIDS first spread among gay men in major urban areas, the majority of those already infected with HIV (as of the early 1990s) were gay men. But with each passing day, gay men make up a smaller and smaller percentage of total AIDS cases in the United States as the disease continues to spread....Lesbians get AIDS just like everybody else, although female-to- female transmission of HIV through sex is rare....The most immediate and tragic impact of AIDS on gay people has been the death of the tens of thousands of gay men. But the epidemic has had other effects as well, from increased discrimination against gay people and unprecedented media attention, to the mobilization of more gay men and lesbians on a single issue than at any time in the history of the struggle for gay and lesbian equal rights. Many of these men and women had never before been involved in any organization that had anything to do with gay people.[1]

William Henry has argued that the AIDS epidemic has made gay men and lesbian women a community even as it has consumed their lives.[2] Henry writes that many gay men and lesbian women become infuriated by talk of "innocent" victims of HIV/AIDS, with the implication that gay victims are all guilty and deserve their fate. This anger becomes enlarged when ostensibly sympathetic people voice concern but fail to grasp the depth of the emotional exhaustion, isolation and

145

sense of loss. For example, many gay men live with a constant sense of doom, an anguishing irrational certainty that this virus will some day, somehow, come to get them, too.

At the same time that HIV/AIDS has coalesced an emerging gay and lesbian community, the disease has also divided it. The most obvious chasm is between those who are already infected with the disease, or at least the virus that brings it on, and those who test negative for it. The greatest concern of many, if not most, HIV-positive men is to ensure that someone will be around to ease them through their final illness, whenever it comes. The greatest concern of many HIV-negative men is to avoid becoming the caregiver, with all the soul-depleting effort it implies. Psychologists and social workers who specialize in treating gay communities see the condition of survivor guilt with growing frequency. "We gay men are living under a pile of corpses that we can't bury emotionally," writes Franklin Abbott, a psychotherapist who practices in Atlanta. In extreme cases, he maintains, when "A lover has died, a patient may feel unworthy to be still alive." Almost every other dichotomy among homosexual people has been profoundly influenced by the split between those who are infected and those who are not. AIDS divides older homosexual people, the generation most addressed because it was active during the years before people realized the impact of HIV/AIDS, from the teens and younger homosexual community.

One result of this chasm between those infected with HIV and those not infected has been a surge in unsafe sex among uninfected men unable to cope with their feelings. This problem has led to some advocacy for more support and community services for uninfected men—although certain gay groups condemn these efforts as supportive of "viral apartheid."

What is AIDS?[3] Acquired Immune Deficiency Syndrome is a medical condition that produces a radical suppression of the human immune system, permitting the body to be ravaged by a variety of opportunistic diseases. It is believed to be caused by the Human Immunodeficiency Virus (HIV), which can exist in the body indefinitely before symptoms emerge. In advanced industrial countries, and in Latin America, AIDS occurs mainly among gay men and intravenous (IV) drug users; in Africa it is found primarily among heterosexual people; and in the United States a growing number of heterosexual people are infected with HIV/AIDS.

The first (retrospectively identified) case of HIV infection has been described in a British sailor in the 1950s. The first U.S. case (also retrospectively identified) occurred in a St. Louis teenager in 1969. However, HIV did not affect a sufficient number of persons to lead to the widespread recognition of a new disease until 1981. In that year, clusters of gay men from Los Angeles, San Francisco and New York who had unusual tumors (such as Kaposi's sarcoma) and infections (such as *Pneumocystis carinii* pneumonia) led investigators to appreciate that a new disease entity was occurring in the human community, one that we have now come to know as AIDS. In 1983 the AIDS virus itself (HIV) was discovered, in 1985 an antibody test to detect the presence of HIV infection was developed, and in 1987 the FDA licensed zidovudine (AZT or ZDV) as the first anti-HIV drug.

The as-yet-unnamed syndrome first came to the attention of the medical community through a report released in June 1981 by the Centers for Disease Control, a Federal Agency, concerning five California cases. Because the first cases studied were in homosexual men, the syndrome became associated with homosexuality itself. In fact, one of the first suggestions for a name was GRID (Gay-Related Immunodeficiency). Although this was shortly changed to AIDS, a ceaseless flow of media reports about gay men affected by the disease served to fix the connection in the public mind.

It is critical to keep in mind, then, that although certain groups have been identified as having an increased risk of exposure to HIV—including homosexual and bisexual men—the virus can infect anyone. Although various groups (e.g., hemophiliacs; individuals who have received blood or blood products between 1978 and 1985; those who use intravenous drugs; sexual partners of infected persons; immigrants from certain central African countries; children of infected mothers) have a relatively high incidence of HIV infection, the *critical* factor is not the group to which one belongs, but the behavior in which one engages. Thus it is more accurate to speak of "high risk activity" than of "high risk groups." *All* individuals need to avoid high risk activity.

For the first few years the number of cases in the United States doubled annually, and about half as many of those already infected died. Not only was the disease spreading very quickly but it was highly lethal. While it appears that the earlier idea that it is invariably fatal is mistaken, it is a very difficult disease for a patient to cope with, and even with the most determined and successful strategy no cure is effected—the disease is simply kept at bay. At first the American cases were largely confined to New York City and its environs, the San Francisco Bay Area, greater Los Angeles, and Miami. Although AIDS subsequently was found in nearly every state, this pattern of concentration in these metropolises on the two coasts has continued. Foreign physicians found AIDS in Canada, Europe, and Latin America, though the incidences are generally lower than in the United States.[4] By 1988 over 65,000 AIDS cases had appeared in the United States, 64% of the reported total world-wide.

HIV cannot be transmitted by any form of casual contact, but must go from blood to blood or from semen to blood. Blood-to-blood transmission occurs when intravenous drug users share narcotics needles, or occasionally through accidental needle-sticks among health-care givers. It may also occur when a surgeon will nick him or herself with a scalpel, which may cut through gloves. Sexual transmission occurs when a seminal discharge of an infected person passes into the bloodstream of another. The sexual contact that is most at risk is anal penetration; oral and vaginal contacts are likely to transmit HIV only if there is a lesion in the affected part of one or both partners.

Taken together these data point out that one can become infected with the AIDS virus only by consciously making a decision to engage in high risk, intimate activity such as sexual intercourse or drug use. There is no risk of acquiring the virus simply from living together, from being in the same workplace, from coughing or sneezing, from shaking hands or using public toilets, or from nonsexual physical contact. Neither is there evidence to support the suggestions that mosquitoes or other insects could transmit HIV between human beings.

Because of these facts, the CDC places no restrictions on the activity of HIV-infected students, employees, including food handlers, beauticians, cosmetologists, or teachers, with the sole exception that persons with wet sores need to be appropriately restricted if such sores cannot be adequately bandaged. Preschool children (who are at risk of acquiring routine childhood infections from their peers), children with uncontrolled biting behavior, and those with bloody diarrhea need to be educated in special circumstances. Infected health care workers who perform invasive procedures such as surgery are currently being handled on a case-by-case basis.

The majority of persons infected with HIV show no symptoms, and it remains uncertain how many will develop AIDS itself. The emergence of the condition is signaled by night sweats, loss of weight, and other signs of physical distress. The patient will usually develop kaposi's sarcoma—a previously rare type of cancer producing numerous lesions on the outside or inside of the body—a pneumocystis carinii (PCP), a form of pneumonia that is devastating to the patient. PCP usually requires hospitalization with intensive care and the administering of a variety of drugs.[5]

Gay self-help groups specifically concerned with HIV have emerged in the United States, involving many people who in the previous decade had turned a deaf ear to the call for movement-work. By the end of the 1980s there were several hundred of these organizations in North America and many others in Europe. Other groups were formed of people with AIDS (PWAs, the term preferred by those who have the disease). Gay and lesbian lawyers mobilized to meet a host of legal problems triggered by the spread of the epidemic. This manifold response contrasted with the apathy of the IV-drug user community, which remained unorganized, without media of its own, and therefore almost entirely dependant on public health advocates and facilities.

The church enters into this tragic story with the gospel of faith and hope. This ecclesial conversation is of extreme significance, especially when noting the alarming statement of Dr. Halfan Mahler, head of the World Health Organization, in a statement made six years into the AIDS epidemic:

> I don't know of any greater killer than AIDS, not to speak of its physiological, social and economic maiming.... Everything is getting worse and worse in AIDS and all of us have been underestimating it....[5]

There are three epidemics associated with the AIDS crisis:

The *first* is the public health epidemic that has been caused by the spread of HIV.

The *second* is the epidemic of HIV/hysteria and discrimination caused by ignorance about HIV/AIDS and prejudice toward many people with HIV/AIDS.[6]

The *third* is the selective silence epidemic which fails to clearly face the direct link between sexual promiscuity, intravenous drug use, and the development of the HIV virus. To be silent about this "link" is dishonest and certainly a form of discrimination. This "third epidemic" has been named by some as A.R.C.: AIDS Resentment Complex. This resentment complex speaks of HIV/AIDS as if it were not a serious and tragic problem.

In his April 1989 visit to Africa, Pope John Paul II indicated clearly the complexity of these various "epidemics." Naming AIDS as "very emblematic of our times," the pope remarked, "It is itself a health problem, but one cannot hide its moral aspects."[7]

These epidemics engage all of us in a variety of cognitive, emotional and spiritual responses. Because of the nature of these epidemics, it is important to resist labelling the person with HIV/AIDS as a *victim* of this disease. An ancient religious usage, the term victim referred to a living creature that was sacrificed. A victim was thus a disposable commodity. By definition, then, a victim has little hope. We should reject labelling the person with HIV/AIDS as a victim, as such an assertion can too easily negate their right to be treated as persons. The person with HIV/AIDS retains full possession of his or her human rights and dignity and equally has a responsibility to control his or her life.[8] Currently, the preference of those suffering with AIDS is to use the acronym PWA (Persons With AIDS).

In 1987, the Administrative Board of the United States Catholic Conference of Bishops issued *The Many Faces of AIDS: A Gospel Response.*[9] The Introduction of this document asserts the need to confront the "significant event" which the "ominous presence of the disease known as AIDS" presents in our society. This document encourages Roman Catholic believers to view PWAs as a positive challenge to live out our faith in everyday terms:

> For Christians…stories of persons with AIDS must not become occasions for stereotyping or prejudice, for anger or recrimination, for rejection or isolation, for injustice or condemnation. They provide us with an opportunity to walk with those who are suffering, to be compassionate toward those whom we might otherwise fear, to bring strength and courage to those who face the prospect of dying as well as to their loved ones.[10]

Compassion

On September 17, 1987, Pope John Paul II visited Mission Dolores Basilica in San Francisco. In his talk there to the gathered group of elderly, infirmed and ill, the Pope said:

> ...(A)s I come to your city on this pastoral visit, I think of all that St. Francis means....(T)here is something about this man...that continues in our day to inspire people of vastly different cultures and religions.... St. Francis was a man of peace and gentleness, a poet and lover of beauty. He was a man of poverty and simplicity....Above all, Francis was a man of prayer whose whole life was shaped by the *love of Jesus Christ*....I come in the spirit of this Saint whose *whole life proclaims the goodness and mercy of God*....(T)he love of God is so great that it goes *beyond the limits of human language*, beyond the grasp of artistic expression, beyond human understanding. And yet it is *concretely embodied in God's Son, Jesus Christ*, and in His Body, the Church....God loves you all, without distinction, without limit. He loves those of you who are elderly, who feel the burden of the years, he loves those of you who are sick, those who are suffering from AIDS and from AIDS-related complex. He loves the relatives and friends of the sick and those who care for them. He loves us all with an unconditional and everlasting love.[11]

Called to Compassion and Responsibility: A Response to the HIV/AIDS Crisis is the 1989 document of the U. S. Conference of Catholic Bishops.[12] *Called to Compassion* teaches that we might ordinarily think of compassion as commiseration: feeling the suffering of another person. Compassion, however, is an experience of intimacy. With compassion, we enter into all of the passions of another, both delight and sorrow, joy and anger. In this light, the Vatican Council's *Pastoral Constitution on the Church in the Modern World* is a call to enter into the suffering and the joys of another person and thus to be of authentic service. By empathy, compassion gives us a capacity to participate in another's inner world, without being engulfed by or fused with that person.[13]

Compassion for the sick, for the wounded, for those contaminated by disease and evil, is a true mark in the ministry of Jesus. Jesus touches lepers (Matthew 8:3; Mark 1:41; Luke 5:13); He shares a meal with people who are officially impure (Matthew 26:6, 9:10, 11:11; Mark 2:15–16; Luke 5:30); and disregards the recriminations of those who have made themselves the judges of the adulteress woman (John 8:1–11). With compassion, Jesus broke through the barriers raised by sickness or moral failing in order to encounter the wounded person and thus be present to his or her suffering.

Compassion and tenderness are deeply interwoven. John Paul II wrote in *Love and Responsibility*:

> Tenderness...springs from awareness of the inner state of another person (and indirectly of that person's external situation, which conditions his inner state) and whoever feels it actively seeks to communicate his feeling of involvement with the other person and his situation. This closeness is the result of an emotional commitment....That sentiment enables us to feel closer to another "I"....

The Introduction to The NAMES Quilt presents a good summary regarding compassion:

> AIDS has come upon us with cruel abandon. It has forced us to confront and deal with the frailty of our being and the reality of death. It has forced us into realizing that we must cherish every moment of...life....The Quilt gives us our most direct feelings back: our feelings of belonging, our sense of the precariousness of life, why it is worth clinging to, how it can be lived, how tragically it can be lost, how beautifully...it can be relinquished and how vibrantly it can be remembered.[14]

HIV/AIDS and Homosexuality

Since HIV/AIDS have been experienced in great measure in the homosexual communities, it is important to reiterate the church's theology of sexuality in terms of the specific question of homosexuality. This reiteration certainly calls us to a life of chastity and a change of heart.

The 1986 document from the Congregation for the Doctrine of

the Faith *Letter to the Bishops of the Catholic Church on the Pastoral Care of Homosexual Persons* clearly reaffirms the church's moral evaluation of homosexual acts, as well as a moral evaluation of homosexuality itself (I have dealt with this point in detail in the chapter on church teaching). While this document clearly points out that "...The particular inclination of the homosexual person is not a sin...," it is clear that "...Homosexual activity is [not] a morally acceptable option."[15]

HIV/AIDS certainly has had a significant impact on the homosexual community. While reaffirming the church's teaching on the immorality of homosexual activity, it is also important here to recall the words of Cardinal Joseph Bernardin:

> Unfortunately, in our efforts to teach the wrongness of homosexual acts, at times all that has been heard is the sound of condemnation and rejection. What is missed, then, what is not heard, is the Church's teaching that people with a homosexual orientation, like everyone else, are created in God's image and possess a human dignity which must be respected and protected. With vigor and clarity we must proclaim the love of Christ and His Church for every individual so that this message can be heard by members of the homosexual community and the broader community.[16]

Who Has HIV/AIDS?

America's AIDS epidemic has entered what scientists call the "mature" phase, an agonizing long-term presence with a slowly shifting profile. The virus is no longer spreading explosively among gay men and drug users as it did in the late 1970s and the early 1980s, infecting huge numbers before most realized what was happening. Largely because of that early sweep, Federal experts believe, perhaps one million living Americans carry HIV, an awesome personal and social tragedy that will play itself out over two decades or more. So far, 200,000 people have developed outright AIDS, according to the current definition of the disease, and more than 125,000 of them have died.

Now, perhaps 50,000 more people become infected with the virus each year, according to very rough estimates by the Centers for

Disease Control. To describe who these people are is to describe the prevention challenge. Compared with the population as a whole, the newly infected are much more likely to be people of color, much more likely to be residents of inner cities, much more likely to be economically disadvantaged.

They include teenage boys discovering their homosexuality, not believing that even a single unprotected encounter may hold deadly risk. They include new recruits to the underworld of intravenous drug addicts, too desperate or self-destructive to faithfully use sterile needles. They include female crack addicts who trade their bodies for drugs. Increasingly they include homeless men and women, who may shoot drugs, prostitute themselves or both.

To a very minor degree they include men who receive the virus from one of a multiplicity of heterosexual partners. Far more often than before they include women, Black or Hispanic, who are infected by a husband, boyfriend or casual sex partner. And they include babies: some 1,500 to 2,000 born with the virus each year. And, last of all, there are a very restricted number who caught the AIDS virus through a blood transfusion before the blood supply was being carefully monitored.

Federal scientists who chart the epidemic have been quite consistent in their statements: AIDS is a sexually transmitted disease, and heterosexual intercourse with an infected partner carries risk. The chance of transmission is lower in vaginal than anal intercourse, studies have shown, and the virus passes much more easily from man to woman than the other way.

For many who are likely to spread HIV in the years ahead, society cannot keep its end of the bargain. All too often, poor people who test positive get a session of counseling and a list of phone numbers of overburdened public clinics. Many never get the expensive immune tests and drugs that can prolong their lives. In New York City clinics, there can be a one to four month waiting list just for an initial appointment. Then it takes all day at the clinic, so if you have a job you have to take the day off. Many poor people with HIV infections do not qualify for Medicaid, the Federal-State Insurance Program, until—in a horrible catch-22—they are declared "disabled" because they develop outright AIDS. Hence they may miss the irretrievable chance to stave off the disease as long as possible.

The epidemic was first recognized in the United States in 1981. By 1988, at a time when women accounted for just 9% of all U.S. cases, AIDS had become the nation's eighth leading cause of death among women aged 25–44, and in New Jersey it was the leading cause of death in this age group, exceeding causes two and three combined (unintentional injuries and heart disease).[17] By 1990 AIDS had become the leading cause of death among young Black women in New York State, and in 1991, with women representing at least 11% of all cases, AIDS became the fifth leading cause of death among all young women in this country. Between 1988 and 1989, when AIDS cases increased by 18% among men, they jumped by 29% in women.[18]

Among young men aged 25 to 44, by 1988 AIDS had become the third leading cause of death, and by 1989 had arisen to the number two position. In 1990 AIDS was the leading cause of death among young men in Los Angeles, San Francisco, and New York City.[19] While there are currently believed to be one million HIV-infected persons in the U. S., this number rises to ten million in the world at large, with 30% of infections occurring in women. The vast majority of these are in Africa where up to 40% of women of childbearing age in certain urban areas are infected, and where one million children have already become AIDS orphans. By the year 2015, some seventy million persons are expected to be infected in Africa, accounting for 17% of the continent's population. African life expectancy will be reduced by nineteen years, and AIDS will account for nearly 80% of the deaths of women in childbearing years, leaving some sixteen million children orphaned.

The Use of Prophylactics[20]

The *Many Faces of AIDS* (1987) in its section on "The Prevention of AIDS" (paragraphs 18–20) speaks about the use of prophylactics.

> We recognize that public educational programs addressed to a wide audience will reflect the fact that some people will not act as they can and should; that they will not refrain from the type of sexual or drug-abuse behavior that can transmit AIDS. In such situations, educational efforts, if grounded in the broader moral vision outlined above, could include accurate information about prophylactic devices

and other practices proposed by some medical experts as potential means of preventing AIDS. We are not promoting the use of prophylactics, but merely providing information that is part of the factual picture. Such a factual presentation should indicate that abstinence outside of marriage and fidelity within marriage as well as the avoidance of intravenous drug abuse are the only morally correct and medically sure ways to prevent the spread of AIDS. So-called safe sex practices are at best only partially effective.

This section ultimately refers to "the teaching of classical theologians" and footnotes St. Augustine and St. Thomas.[21]

A great deal of debate surrounded this statement.[22]

Called to Compassion (1989) also treats the question of prophylactics and counsels in part:

The use of prophylactics to prevent the spread of HIV is technically unreliable. Moreover, advocating this approach means in effect promoting behavior which is morally unacceptable. Campaigns advocating "safe/safer" sex rest on false assumptions about sexuality and intercourse.[23]

The *difference* in the two approaches to the question of prophylactics is quite significant. *The Many Faces of AIDS* in weighing the consequences of becoming infected by a life-threatening virus, judges that prophylactics are the lesser of two evils. Jon D. Fuller comments, "It has essentially made a proportionalist argument based on the relative weight it gives to two bad outcomes: HIV infection vs. condom use. This method weighs evils and finds it ethically appropriate to support the lesser one in order to avoid the greater."[24]

Called to Compassion rejects condom education for several reasons: This approach *in effect* promotes behavior which is morally unacceptable (the "safe/safer" campaigns); it does not recognize adequately the failure rate of prophylactics and the high risk that an infected person who relies on them will eventually transmit the infection; and condom education *de facto* does not promote appropriate attitudes regarding human sexuality, integrity and dignity.

It is important to note that *both* of these documents indicate that the "safe/safer sex" approach to preventing HIV/AIDS compromises human sexuality and leads to promiscuous sexual behavior. Both documents affirm that any person who is at risk of having been exposed to HIV or has been tested as positive for the virus must always act in a morally responsible way: i.e., should not act in such a way as to bring harm to another: this means not sharing needles used intravenously, and not engaging in sexual intercourse—either heterosexual or homosexual.[25]

A Call to Conversion

Effective ministry to and with persons suffering from HIV/AIDS must be grounded in a deep faith-perspective, a profound sense of prayer, and a willingness to manifest the authentic compassion of Christ. God is a loving and compassionate God. God is not a vengeful God. The "A" of AIDS indicates that this disease is *acquired*. While it is true that the HIV virus can be a result of immoral human behavior, it might also be acquired in totally "innocent" ways: e.g., a child from an infected mother or a transfusion from contaminated blood. To say, then, that God is punishing people with AIDS is like saying that God is a vindictive, capricious God who, at whim, strikes down some people with the disease and spares others. The 1983 document of the National Conference of Catholic Bishops, *Pastoral Care of the Sick: Rights of Anointing and Viaticum* is instructive to this point:

> Although closely linked with the human condition, sickness cannot as a general rule be regarded as a punishment inflicted on each individual for personal sins (See John 9:3).[26]

Any suggestion that God is capable of vengeance or of any willful desire to make his creatures suffer is misguided. It is a false caricature of God to say that God is vengeful. In the New Testament, Jesus reveals a God who is a compassionate and forgiving Father, the suffering being special objects of God's merciful love. Jesus nowhere connects human misfortune with either sin or divine anger. On the contrary, when his disciples suggest such a connection, Jesus explicitly repudiates it (John 9:1–3).[27]

HIV/AIDS is surely a disease which causes suffering. However, Christian faith looks upon suffering as a liberating and grace-filled experience. Suffering and death, joined to the suffering and death of Jesus, the Lord of Life, represents not dissolution but growth, not punishment but fulfillment, not sadness but joy. Suffering is not a moral evil nor without supernatural and human benefits. Great good can come out of suffering, when this is joined to the suffering of Jesus. John Paul II addressed this point well in a 1980 address in Belem:

> I know very well, that under the weight of illness, we are all exposed to the temptation of losing heart. One often wonders sadly, why have I fallen ill? What wrong have I done to deserve it? A look at Jesus Christ in His earthly life and a look of faith, in the light of Jesus Christ, at our own situation, changes our way of thinking. Christ, the innocent Son of God, knew suffering in His own flesh....He was disfigured, no longer having a human appearance (Is. 53:2)....The Gospel and the whole of the New Testament tell us that, accepted and lived in this way, the cross became redemptive....Your life is no different. Illness is truly a cross, ...an ordeal that God permits in a person's life, within the unfathomable mystery of a plan that escapes our ability to understand. But it must not be regarded as a blind fatality.[28]

Suffering need not be a wasteland but can be a vital time in one's life, the period of reconciling one's self to life and to death and for attaining interior peace. John Paul II has explained:

> Suffering has a special value in the eyes of the Church. It is something good, before which the Church bows down in reverence with all the depth of her faith in the redemption....[29]

The suffering caused by HIV/AIDS calls upon the entire Christian and human community to respond with compassion, love and support. Our fundamental task is to assist the suffering and the dying. Our ministry must be to assist the suffering in their transfiguration and to adopt a pastoral pedagogy which consists not in condemning those who suffer for the causes of their sickness; or to imply fault; or to say that God has caused them to be sick. People might well be culpable in some ways for their behaviors. However, our Christian faith does not lead us to conclude that God is punishing such people for their behavior. To approach HIV/AIDS in such a way would be a radical departure from our traditional understanding of the meaning of suffering.

Both pastoral and medical experience give ample evidence that persons with HIV/AIDS are exposed to some of the most profound human feelings: e.g., anger; moments of despair; great optimism about a new treatment or drug; profound disappointment when it does not prove viable. HIV/AIDS has placed the human community in a unique encounter with suffering and death, and thus have we been brought face to face with two of the primary mysteries which color and shape all of our experience.

Every human death is a reflection of the death of Christ. It is the entrusting of the spirit to him who created us for immortality.[30] When faced with death, the Christian is rooted in sereneness because of the certainty of Jesus' promise: "In my Father's house are many rooms....I go to prepare a place for you" (John 14:2). John Paul II's words are important here:

> ...(W)e know that Christ was able to make of death an act of *offering*, an act of *love*, an act of *ransom*, and of *liberation* from sin and from death itself. By accepting death in a Christian way we conquer death forever....Life on earth is not a journey towards death, but a journey towards life and light, towards the Lord. Death, beginning with that of sin, can and must be overcome.[31]

What Dr. Elisabeth Kübler-Ross calls the "acceptance" of death is not a resigning of oneself to death. Rather it is acceptance for the first time that one's life includes death. Life and death are not opposites, and "accepting" life is at the same time accepting death. For many people, HIV/AIDS means death and thus the Christian faith which places death in the context of life and of life everlasting is vital, important and deeply consoling.[32]

Christian Hope

In the midst of suffering and death, Christian hope is critical and essential. Gregory the Great has spoken magnificently to this point:

> "Even if he kills me I shall hope in him (Job 13:15)." The virtue of patience is never to the fore in times of happiness.

The truly patient person is the one who is exhausted by adversity, yet is not deflected from the rightness of his hope....He [Jesus] has promised us the resurrection when He revealed himself....So our redeemer accepted death so that we should not fear to die. He revealed the resurrection so that we may be sure that we can rise again.[33]

Persons with HIV/AIDS and their families and loved ones have a need for prayer and spiritual support that is sensitive to their specialized situation. Prayer with and for the PWA is an authentically needed and spiritual quest. The spiritual dimension of human existence is concerned with the issues of meaning, hope, freedom, self-identity and self-worth, love, one's image of God, and forgiveness and reconciliation: "What medicine and therapy do for the body, prayer does for the soul."[34]

Pope Paul VI's *On Christian Joy* calls us to this degree of Christian hope and joy:

It is indeed in the midst of their distress that our fellow men need to know joy, to hear its song. We sympathize profoundly with those over whom...sufferings of every sort cast a veil of sadness. We are thinking in particular of those who are without means, without help, without friendship—those who see their human hopes annihilated.[35]

Paul VI offered to us as a modern symbol of hope and joy the person of St. Thérèse of Lisieux, a young woman who suffered greatly and who courageously abandoned herself into the hands of God to whom she entrusted her littleness. Christian hope and joy, then, deepen our awareness of being exiles but guard us from the temptation to desert our place of combat.

The *Pastoral Care of the Sick: Rites of Anointing and Viaticum* presents a significant conclusion to this discussion:

Suffering and illness have always been among the greatest problems that trouble the human spirit. Christians feel and experience pain as do all other people; yet their faith helps them to grasp more deeply the mystery of suffering and to bear their pain with greater courage. From Christ's words they know that sickness has meaning and value for their own salvation and for the salvation of the world. They also know that Christ, who during His life often visited and healed the sick, loves them in their illness....

If one member suffers in the body of Christ, which is the Church, all the members suffer with that member (1 Corinthians 12:26). For this reason, kindness shown toward the sick and works of charity and mutual help for the relief of every kind of human want are held in special honor.[36]

These words of Pope John Paul II, though spoken in another context, clearly apply to the crisis of HIV/AIDS:

Do not turn away from the handicapped and the dying. Do not push them to the margins of society....Let us treasure them, and recognize with gratitude the debt we owe them. We begin by imagining we are giving to them; we end by realizing that they have enriched us.[37]

Chapter 8

HOMOSEXUALITY:
PASTORAL, PERSONAL AND PROFESSIONAL
REFLECTIONS

I have ended this book on a note of hope, a note that needs enlargement so as to embrace all homosexual men and women with compassion, care and understanding.

There is no question that such a challenge is most difficult when faced with certain facts:

1. Church teaching which views the homosexual orientation as disordered, while also naming this orientation as not sinful or chosen. We have noted that it is unfortunate that in our efforts to explain and uphold the wrongness of homosexual activity, we do not sufficiently stress that homosexual people are created in God's image and likeness and possess a human dignity that demands respect.
2. Church teaching which upholds the norm of chastity for all gay men and lesbian women—a norm which is often met with unbelief and even ridicule.
3. A society which harbors a good deal of homophobic prejudices, evidenced in misunderstanding, anger, hatred and violence.
4. A small portion of the homosexual community which receives media attention focused on the outlandish elements of the gay and lesbian experience.

These and so many other factors make the pastoral journey very difficult and at times disturbing and discouraging.

We must not lose hope, however, but maintain a clear course of moral and pastoral guidance. We must not lose sight of important benchmarks mentioned throughout the course of this work:

1. We are a church of sinners called by Christ to integrity and fullness of life. We are not perfect. We are all bound under the princi-

ple of gradualism, a principle which calls us slowly but deliberately to greater holiness and human authenticity.

2. Homosexual women and men deserve our respect, friendship, compassion and understanding. Dioceses and parishes must promote these factors through sound instruction and healthy example. There are many fine and superb gay men and lesbian women working to further the gospel message. We need to acknowledge and respect this fact.

3. We must consistently evaluate our language and attitudes toward homosexual people. I have tried to demonstrate that "homosexual" is an adjective and describes only part of who a person is. We must make efforts to model this belief in our vocabulary and teaching by referring to homosexual people and to gay men and lesbian women. Language helps support respect and respect fosters understanding and compassion.

4. No one's sexuality is immune from sin. And not all forms of sexual attraction should lead to genital sexual experience. The biblical prohibition against incest, for example, helps make the family a safe place where parents and children, sisters and brothers, can trust each other. Similarly, the prohibition against adultery helps nurture trust within marriages.[1]

The scriptures confront us with the challenge to maintain responsible boundaries. We have seen that human sexuality calls for companionship and friendship. We have also seen that the Church consistently holds up marriage as the only responsible forum for sexual activity.

This tension is a very difficult one for gay and lesbian persons and thus we must bring to this tension every bit of pastoral sensitivity and spiritual counseling that our Catholic tradition offers. We must never compromise the moral teachings of the Church. Such compromises only damage the church and ultimately hurt individual Catholics who try to live good lives within the parameters of the Catholic community.

We must recall the teaching in the 1986 *Letter to the Bishops* that "Everyone living on the face of the earth has personal problems and difficulties, but challenges to growth, strengths, talents and gifts as well."[2] Consequently, we are called to assist homosexual persons at all levels: personal support in order to avoid shame; spiritual nourishment through the sacraments; friendship and care; hope and freedom from unjust discrimination.

5. We must take seriously the advise given in the U.S.C.C. document *Human Sexuality*:[3]

> ...(H)omosexuality cannot and ought not to be skirted or ignored. The topic "must be faced in all objectivity...when the case presents itself." First and foremost, we support modeling and teaching respect for every human person, regardless of sexual orientation. Second, a parent or teacher must also present clearly and delicately the unambiguous moral norms of the Christian tradition regarding homosexual genital activity, appropriately geared to the age level and maturity of the learner. Finally, parents and other educators must remain open to the possibility that a particular person, whether adolescent or adult, may be struggling to accept his or her own homosexual orientation. The distinction between *being* homosexual and *doing* homosexual genital actions, while not always clear and convincing, is a helpful and important one when dealing with the complex issue of homosexuality particularly in the educational and pastoral arena.

Notes

Introduction

1. James P. Hanigan subtitles his book *Homosexuality* precisely as "The Test Case for Christian Sexual Ethics," New York: Paulist Press, 1988.

2. James D. Whitehead and Evelyn Eaton Whitehead, "The Shape of Compassion: Reflections on Catholics and Homosexuality," *Spirituality Today* 39 (1987), 126–136.

3. Lisa Sowle Cahill, *Between the Sexes*, Philadelphia: Fortress Press, 1985, 152.

4. John Paul II, *Veritatis Splendor*, Origins 23 (1993), 297–334.

5. I am most indebted to Paul D. Duke and his unpublished paper "Homosexuality and the Church" for providing an important context in which to address this and other important questions. See Duke's *Irony in the Fourth Gospel*, Atlanta: John Knox Press, 1992.

6. Congregation for the Doctrine of the Faith, *Letter to the Bishops of the Catholic Church on the Pastoral Care of Homosexual Persons* 1986, n 16.

7. See "Sex Survey Surprise," *The New York Times*, April 17, 1993, 14; and F. Barringer, "Sex Survey of American Men Finds 1% Are Gay," *The New York Times*, April 15, 1993, 1 and 9.

8. Eric Marcus, *Is It A Choice?*, San Francisco: Harper, 1993, 24.

9. In current usage the term "life-style" refers to the ensemble of choices that an individual may make in employment, leisure activities, dress, and self-presentation that serve to link him or her with a larger group in society (e.g., the hippie, jet set, and yuppie life styles). The element of choice is central: although an individual may have been raised in one life-style, he or she may elect to join another. See Warren Johansson, "Lifestyle" in *Encyclopedia of Homosexuality*, ed., Wayne R. Dynes, New York/London: Garland Publishing, Inc., vol.1, 1990, 736–739.

10. James B. Nelson, *Embodiment*, Minneapolis: Augsburg Publishing House, 1978, 188–199.

11. Karl L. Barth, *Church Dogmatics*, III/4, Edinburgh: T. and T. Clark, 1961, 166.

12. See William Muehl, "Some Words of Caution" and William Muehl and William Johnson, "Issues Raised by Homosexuality," *Y.B.S. Reflection* 72 (1975), 4.

13. Helmut Thielicke, *The Ethics of Sex*, New York: Association Press, 1966, 282–283.

14. Friends Home Service Committee, *Towards A Quaker View Of Sex*, London: Friends House, 1963, 45.

15. See John F. Harvey, "Homosexuality" in *New Catholic Encyclopedia*, VII (1967), 117–119.

16. Bruce Bawer, *A Place at the Table*, New York, Poseidon Press, 1993, 48–49.

17. This approach is exampled in John J. McNeill, "The Christian Male Homosexual," *Homiletic and Pastoral Review LXX* (1970), 747–758 and 828–836.

18. National Conference of Catholic Bishops, *Human Sexuality*, Washington, D.C.: U.S.C.C. Office for Publishing and Promotion Services, 1990, 19.

19. National Conference of Catholic Bishops, *Principles to Guide Confessors in Questions of Homosexuality*, 1978, 9.

20. *Ibid.*, 11.

21. Ronald Lawler, Joseph Boyle and William E. May, *Catholic Sexual Ethics*, Huntington: *Our Sunday Visitor, Inc.*, 1985, 202–203.

22. Thomas Merton, *Conjectures of a Guilty Bystander*, New York: Doubleday, 1966, 140.

Chapter 1

1. "A Ministry to Lesbian and Gay Catholic Persons," *Homosexuality and the Magisterium*, ed., John Gallagher, Maryland: New Ways Ministry, 1986, 36–41; citation at 39.

2. See also *Sharing the Light of Faith: National Catechetical Directory for Catholics in the United States*, National Conference of Catholic Bishops, 1977, n 191; *Educational Guidance in Human Love*, Congregation for Catholic Education, 1983, n 4; and *Human Sexuality: A Catholic Perspective for Education and Lifelong Learning*, United States Catholic Conference, 1990, 54.

3. Karol Wojtyla, "Antropologia Encykliki '*Humanae Vitae*,'" *Analecta Cracoviensia* 10 (1978), 13.   ·

4. Cited in Arno Karlen, *Sexuality and Homosexuality*, New York: W. W. Norton, Co., Inc., 1981, 255.

5. Congregation for the Doctrine of the Faith, *Letter to the Bishops of the Catholic Church on the Pastoral Care of Homosexual Persons*, October 1, 1986, printed in the U.S.A. by the Daughters of St. Paul under the title On the *Pastoral Care of Homosexual Persons*, 1986.

6. *Ibid.*, n 1.

7. James P. Hanigan, *Homosexuality: The Test Case for Christian Sexual Ethics*, New York: Paulist Press, 1988.

8. John E. Fortunato, *Embracing the Exile*, New York: The Seabury Press, 1982, 17.

9. Sigmund Freud, "Letter to an American Mother" (1935), reprinted in Ronald Bayer, *Homosexuality and American Psychiatry*, Princeton: Princeton University Press, 1987, 27.

10. Sigmund Freud, quoted in *Die Zeit*, Vienna, October 27, 1903, 5. In 1930 Freud signed an appeal to the German Reichstag to repeal that part of the German penal code that since 1871 had made homosexual relations a crime. This petition stated, in part: "Homosexuality has been present throughout history and among all peoples....Their sexual orientation is just as inherent to them as that of heterosexuals. The state has no valid interest in attempting to motivate heterosexual intercourse or marriage on the part of homosexuals for this would perforce lead to unhappiness for their partners, and it is quite likely that homosexuality would reappear in one of the ensuing generations....This law represents an extreme violation of human rights, because it denies homosexuals their very sexuality even though the interests of third parties are not encroached upon....Homosexuals have the same civil duties to fulfill as everyone else." Cited in Richard A. Isay, *Being Homosexual,* New York: Avon Books, 1989, 135–136.

11. Isadore Rubin, "Homosexuality," Siecus: Discussion Guide, No. 2, New York: 1965, 1.

12. Judd Marmon, ed., *Sexual Inversion*, New York: Basic Books, 1965, 4.

13. John C. Dwyer, *Human Sexuality: A Christian View*, Kansas City: Sheed and Ward, 1987, 64.

14. William F. Kraft, "Homosexuality and Religious Life," *Review for Religious* 40 (1981), 371.

15. George A. Kanoti and Anthony R. Kosnik, *Encyclopedia of Bioethics*, New York: The Free Press, vol. 2, 1978, 671. See also *Encyclopedia of Homosexuality*, ed., Wayne R. Dynes, Hamden: Garland Publishing, 1992.

16. This "distinction" is a highly debated one among psychologists. Some schools of thought maintain that it is impossible for any person to have a profound sense of his or her own sexual orientation without having had some genital experience. This would be applicable to both the heterosexual and homosexual orientation. Still others claim that "actual sexual fulfillment of this desire" is not absolutely necessary for a self-awareness of one's sexual orientation. From the Church's viewpoint, it is more reasonable and correct to assert that genital activity is not necessary for orientation-awareness, lest the impression and counsel be given that sexual activity must precede awareness of one's orientation.

17. Eric Marcus, *Is It A Choice?* San Francisco: Harper, 1993, 6.

18. This distinction between homosexual and gay/lesbian is not meant to indicate that a homosexual person who has not publicly identified his or her homosexuality cannot be ego-syntonic. The ego-syntonic homosexual is the one who recognizes that in developing into an adult, it is best to grow into someone who will be as comfortable in the company of heterosexuals as in the company of homosexuals, who is honest about his or her sexual orientation, but knows that it is only one aspect of the totality of one's being, and who understands that discovering of oneself as homosexual is only a part of discovering oneself. The point of the distinction is to indicate that gay/lesbian more often than not refers to the homosexual who is *publicly* known to be homosexual. While some indicate that the word *gay* has its origins in the usage given to the 17th century troubadours, the actual origin of this term remains somewhat obscure. On the other hand, most writers accept the fact that the word *lesbian* derives from the tradition that the poet, Sappho of Lesbos, was homosexual.

19. See Bruce Bawer, *A Place at the Table*, New York: Poseidon Press, 1993.

20. *Ibid.*, 38.

21. We will follow here the treatment of this subject by Stephen B. Levine, "The Origins of Sexual Identity: A Clinician's View" in *Sexuality and Medicine* ed., Earl E. Shelp, Dordrecht: D. Reidel Publishing Co., vol. I, 1987, 39–54. See also Gerald D. Coleman, *Human Sexuality: An All-Embracing Gift*, New York: Alba Press, 1992, 60–68.

22. Simone de Beauvoir, *The Second Sex*, New York: W. B. Key, 1953, 41.

23. Stephen B. Levine, *op.cit.*, 42.

24. We will follow here the thought of John Money, "The Development of Sexual Orientation" in *The Harvard Medical School Mental Health Letter* 4 (1988), 4–6.

25. Vincent J. Genovesi, *In Pursuit of Love: Catholic Morality and Human Sexuality*, Delaware: Michael Glazier, Inc., 1987, 141.

26. See, e.g., Lillanna Kopp, "A Problem of Manipulated Data," and Robert Nugent, "Sexual Orientation in Vatican Thinking" in *The Vatican and Homosexuality*, New York: Crossroad, 1988, 40–47; and 48–58.

27. National Conference of Catholic Bishops, *Principles to Guide Confessors in Questions of Homosexuality*, Washington, D.C.: United States Catholic Conference, 1973, 11.

28. Eric Marcus, *Is It A Choice?*, op.cit., 1.

29. James P. Hanigan, *Homosexuality: The Test Case for Christian Sexual Ethics*, New York: Paulist Press, 1988, 20–21. See also George M. Regan, *New Trends in Moral Theology*, New York/Paramus: Newman Press, 1971, 163–171.

30. See Vincent J. Genovesi, *op.cit.*, 252.

31. See James J. Gill, "Homosexuality Today," *Human Development* 3 (1980), 16–25.

32. See, e.g., M. Saghir and E. Robbins, *Male and Female Homosexuality*, Baltimore: Williams and Wilkins, Co., 1973; and

Michael E. Cavanaugh, "Homosexuality" in *Make Your Tomorrows Better*. We will rely here on Cavanaugh's treatment.

33. This point is emphasized by Alan P. Bell and Martin S. Weinberg in *Homosexualities*, New York: Simon and Schuster, 1978.

34. Alfred Kinsey, Wardell Pomeroy and Clyde Martin, *Sexual Behavior in the Human Male*, Philadelphia: Saunders, 1948; and *Sexual Behavior in the Human Female*, Philadelphia: Saunders, 1953. See also James Hanigan, *op.cit.*, 24 (We will follow Hanigan's interpretation).

35. Sharon MacIsaac, *Freud and Original Sin*, New York: Paulist Press, 1974, 80–81, gives a clear explanation of what Freud meant by this claim and the rationale for it.

36. Bell and Weinberg, *op.cit.*, 329. In "Assessment of Sexual Orientation," *Journal of Homosexuality* 14 (1987), 9–24, Eli Coleman also concludes by stating, "The labels homosexual, bisexual and heterosexual seem meaningless when one understands the complexity of sexual orientation. The words 'homosexual' and 'heterosexual' seem the most limiting. If labels are used, the phrases 'predominantly homosexual' or 'predominantly heterosexual' are probably more accurate..." (p 23).

37. *Diagnostic and Statistical Manual*, 3rd ed., Washington, D.C.: American Psychiatric Association, 1980, 281.

38. *Ibid.*, 282.

39. See John F. Harvey, "Changes in Nomenclature and Their Probable Effect" in J. R. Cavanaugh, *Counselling the Homosexual*, Huntington: Our Sunday Visitor Press, 1977, 30–36; citation at 32.

40. James D. Whitehead and Evelyn Eaton Whitehead, "Three Passages of Maturity" in *A Challenge to Love*, ed., Robert Nugent, New York: Crossroad, 1983, 174–188.

41. *Ibid.*, 175.

42. Douglas C. Kimmel, "Adult Development and Aging: A Perspective," *Journal of Social Issues* 34 (1978), 113–130.

43. Cited in "Three Passages of Maturity," *op.cit.*, 179.

44. *Ibid.*, 181.

45. *Ibid.*, 185.

46. See Xavier John Seubert, "The Sacramentality of Metaphors: Reflections on Homosexuality," *Cross Currents* 18 (1991), 52–68.

47. N.C.C.B., *Human Sexuality*, 1990, 54.

48. We should not assume that "coming out" is automatically the right thing to do or the salutary thing to do. It is important to repeat that a person can be at peace with his or her homosexuality without the "coming out" step.

49. Amity Pierce Buxton, *The Other Side of the Closet: The Coming-Out Crisis for Straight Spouses*, Santa Monica: IBS Press, 1991, 49.

50. See Robert T. Francoeur, *Becoming a Sexual Person*, New York: John Wiley and Sons, 1982, 513–516; and Michael R. Peterson, "Psychological Aspects of Human Sexual Behaviors" in *Human Sexuality and Personhood*, St. Louis: Pope John XXIII Medical-Moral Research and Education Center, 1981, 86–110; and James P. Hanigan, *op.cit.*, 30.

51. Judd Marmor, "Homosexuality," *Encyclopedia Americana*, vols. 14, 1990, 334. In the 1987 edition of the *New Catholic Encyclopedia*, John F. Harvey states that 4% of males are exclusively homosexual in behavior and 1% of females are exclusively homosexual in behavior.

52. J. Gordon Melton, *The Churches Speak Out: Homosexuality*, Detroit: Gale Research, Inc., 1991, 30.

53. See *Sex In America*, Robert T. Michael, John H. Gagnon, Edward O. Laumann and Gina Kolata, Boston: Little, Brown and Co., 1994, chapter 9.

54. See Paul Robinson, "The Way We Do the Things We Do," *New York Times Book Review*, 99 (1994), 21–22; and Philip Elmer-Dewitt, "Now the Truth About Americans and Sex," *Time*, October 17, 1994, 63–70; and Michael Marriott, "Not Frenzied, But Fulfilled," *Newsweek* 124 (1994), 70–71.

55. Dr. John Haas has written, e.g., that "the act associated with homosexuality…is that of sodomy." Such assertions, of course, relegate homosexuality to *one* particular form of genital behavior and indeed a behavior that can be practiced by heterosexuals. See John M. Haas, "Dangers of Sodomy," *Ethics and Medics* 18 (1993), 1–3; citation at 1.

56. See Wayne R. Dynes, "Language and Linguistics" in *Encyclopedia of Homosexuality*, ed., Wayne R. Dynes, New York/London: Garland Publishing, Inc., 1990, vol. 1, 674–676. We will follow Dynes' treatment of this subject.

57. G.S. Simes, "Slang Terms for Homosexuals in English" in *Encyclopedia of Homosexuality*, op.cit., vol. 2, 1200–1204.

58. M. Goodlich, *The Unmentionable Vice: Homosexuality in the Later Medieval Period*, Santa Barbara: ABC-CLIO, 1979, 18.

59. Some gay and lesbian people have chosen the word "queer" for themselves because they feel it is more inclusive than gay and lesbian; and they feel that by "reclaiming" a word that has been used by those who hate gay people, they have stripped it of its original hurtful intent and transformed it into something positive. Queer Nation was organized in New York City in 1990 by several members of ACT-UP who wanted to focus their energy specifically on gay and lesbian right issues. One of its group founders has said, "We wanted to do direct action, to get out on the streets, to scream and yell, to stage very visible protests against antigay violence and discrimination."

60. *Letter to the Bishops, op. cit.,* n. 10.

Chapter 2

1. Eric Marcus, *Is It A Choice?*, San Francisco: Harper, 1993, 9.

2. For a fuller discussion of this subject, see William Dudley, ed., *Homosexuality: Opposing Viewpoints*, San Diego: Greenhaven Press, 1993, chapter 1.

3. Morton Hunt, *Gay: What Teenagers Should Know About Homosexuality and the AIDS Crisis*, New York: Farrar, Straus and Giroux, 1987, 84.

4. Judith A. Reisman and Edward W. Eichel, *Kinsey, Sex, and Fraud: The Indoctrination of a People*, Lafayette: Huntington House Publishers, 1990, 62–63.

5. See Patricia Hersch, "The Causes of Homosexuality Are Unimportant" in *Homosexuality: Opposing Viewpoints, op.cit.,* 56–57.

6. The Preface to Chapter One in *Homosexuality: Opposing Viewpoints, op.cit.,* points out that "The question of causation has important political implications for gays and lesbians. Some hope that if

homosexuality is proven to be inherent in a person's physical makeup, prejudice and discrimination will decrease....Others are not so sure whether evidence demonstrating physical causes of homosexuality would have such a favorable impact on society's attitudes toward homosexuals. Science writer Denise Grade writes in *Discover* that some homosexuals 'fear that the brain difference will be viewed as a defect, fueling homophobia—a pretext to screen fetuses and abort homosexual ones, or inject them with 'corrective' hormones, or even to press for brain-cell transplants to 'cure' homosexuality.'" Consequently, the "cause" of homosexuality is of more than scientific interest—it is an issue that has social repercussions as well.

7. One early medical text, e.g., stated confidently that male homosexuals could not whistle and favored the color green. See "Straight Talk About Gays," *U.S. News and World Report* 115 (1993), 41–52; and Arno Karlen, *Sexuality and Homosexuality*, New York: W. W. Norton Co., Inc., 1971.

8. Eric Marcus, "They're Not Telling the Truth," *Newsweek* 71 (1992), 41.

9. See J. DeCecco, "Homosexuality's Brief Recovery: From Sickness to Health and Back Again," *The Journal of Sex Research* 23 (1987), 106–129; and W. Ricketts, "Biological Research On Homosexuality: Ansell's Cow or Occam's Razor?" *Journal of Homosexuality* 9 (1984), 65–93. We will rely here on the rather good analysis of the origins of homosexuality found in the *Minority Report of the Special Committee on Human Sexuality* that was prepared for the 203rd General Assembly of the Presbyterian Church in the United States in 1991.

10. See J. Carrier, "Homosexual Behavior in Cross-Cultural Perspective" in J. Marmor, ed., *Homosexual Behavior: A Modern Appraisal*, New York: Basic Books, 1980, 100–122. See also B. Risman and P. Schwartz, "Sociological Research on Male and Female Homosexuality," *Annual Review of Sociology* 14 (1988), 125–147.

11. D. Greenberg, *The Construction of Homosexuality*, Chicago: University of Chicago Press, 1988.

12. The Minority Report of the Presbyterian Church points out on page 23 (footnote 5): "A number of factors plague all of the research into the causes of homosexuality. Perhaps the biggest problem is the

diversity of persons to whom this description is applied. Persons describing themselves as homosexual range from the male who cannot remember a time when he was not 'different' and attracted to other men, to the female who embraces lesbianism as an adult after years of abusive relationships with men. Almost all of the existing research deals with very heterogeneous groups of people. Another major problem has been that almost all of the research has been with male homosexuals (gays); very little in comparison has been done with lesbians."

13. For example, F. Kallman, "Comparative Twin Study on the Generic Aspects of Male Homosexuality," *Journal of Nervous and Mental Disease* 115 (1952), 137–159.

14. For example, R. Green in "The Imputability of (Homo)sexual Orientation: Behavioral Science in Vocations for a Constitutional (Legal) Analysis," *The Journal of Psychiatry and Law* 16 (1988), 537–575 concludes that the closer the genetic link between persons, the greater the likelihood of similar sexual orientation. However, B. Eckert, T. Bouchard, J. Bohlen and L. Heston in "Homosexuality in Monozygotic Twins Reared Apart," *British Journal of Psychiatry* 148 (1986), 421-425 produced evidence suggesting that there is no genetic factor operative in lesbianism, even though genetics have some mixed role in male homosexuality.

15. See Marcia Barinaga, "Is Homosexuality Biological?" *Science* 253 (1991), 956–957 and Barinaga, "Differences in Brain Structure May Cause Homosexuality" *in Homosexuality: Opposing Viewpoints, op.cit.,* 17–22. We will follow here Barinaga's treatment.

16. The scientific research of Michael Bailey of Northwestern University and Richard Pillard of the Boston University School of Medicine has likewise demonstrated that male sexual orientation is substantially genetic.

17. Barinaga, "Differences in Brain Structure May Cause Homosexuality," *op.cit.,* 18.

18. *Ibid.*

19. See "Homosexuality and Cognition," *Briefings* 539 (1992), 30.

20. Cited in Barinaga, *Science, op. cit.,* 956.

21. See "Sex on the Brain," *Science* 257 (1992), 25–26.

22. Richard C. Pillard, "Does Homosexuality Have a Biological Basis?" *Research News* 33 (1992), 5–7; citation at 5–6.

23. The study of identical twins raised apart is an especially powerful experimental design, because it separates the influence of an identical genetic endowment from that of a closely similar environment. Identical twins raised separately are rare; rarer still are cases in which one twin or both are homosexual. Nevertheless, Thomas Bouchard has identified two such cases in the Minnesota Twin Study: a pair of male twins in which both were gay, and another in which one was gay and the other heterosexual with some incidental homosexual contacts. Although this sample is far too small to prove anything, Bouchard's finding suggests at least some support for the conclusion that about half of male identical twins are concordant for homosexuality.

24. John Money believes that "…According to currently available evidence, the sex chromosomes do not directly determine or program psychosexual status as heterosexual, bisexual, or homosexual." Money has argued that even though there is genetic influence for some, there is no "sexual orientation gene." Sexual orientation is probably indirectly influenced by other factors that are controlled by a person's genes and these factors may predispose some people to homosexuality. See J. Money, "Genetic and Chromosomal Aspects of Homosexual Etiology" in J. Marmor, ed., *Homosexual Behavior: A Modern Reappraisal*, New York: Basic Books, 59–74. See also Simon LeVay, "Are Gay Men Born That Way?" *Time* 138 (1991), 60–61; Barinaga, "Is Homosexuality Biological?" *Science* 253 (1991), 956–957; and Michael Bailey and Richard Pillard, "Are Some People Born Gay?" *New York Times*, December 17, 1991, *op.ed.* and "Gay Men in Twin Study," *ibid.*

25. Quoted in E. Marcus, *op.cit.*, 10–11. For the study itself, see Dean H. Hamer, Stella Hu, Victoria L. Magnuson, Nan Hu, Angela M. L. Pattatucci, "A Linkage Between DNA Markers on the X Chromosome and Male Sexual Orientation," *Science* 261 (1993), 321–327. See also Gerry E. Bishop, "Research Points Toward a 'Gay' Gene," *The Wall Street Journal*, 12 July 1993, B1 and 5; and William A. Henry III, "Born Gay?" *Time* 142 (1993), 36–39.

26. See Robert Pool, "Evidence for Homosexuality Gene," *Science* 261 (1993), 291–292. For a critique of this research, see Ruth

Hubbard, "The Search For Sexual Identity: False Genetic Markers," *The New York Times*, August 2, 1993, A11.

27. Chandler Burr, "Homosexuality and Biology," *The Atlantic Monthly* 271 (1993), 47–65; citation at 65.

28. See L. Ellis and A. Ames, "Meurohormonao Functioning and Sexual Orientation: A Theory of Homosexuality-Heterosexuality," *Psychological Bulletin* 101 (1987), 233–258.

29. For example, R. Green, *op.cit.*

30. See J. Lindesay, "Laterality Shift in Homosexual Men," *Neuropsychologia* 25 (1987), 965–969; and M. Annett, "Comments on Lindesay: Laterality Shift in Homosexual Men," *Neuropsychologia* 26 (1988), 341–343.

31. See R. Green, *op.cit..* However, the findings of D. Swaab and M. Hofmann in "Sexual Differentiation of the Human Hypothalamus: Ontogeny of the Sexually Dimorphic Nucleus of the Preoppic Area," *Developmental Brain Research* 44 (1988), 314–318 refuted the notion that the "sexually dimorphic nucleus of the hypothalamus" of male homosexual and heterosexual brains are structurally different.

32. See, e.g., J. Harry, *Gay Children Grown Up: Gender Culture and Gender Deviants*, New York: Praeger Books, 1982.

33. G. Rekers, S. Mead, A. Rosen and S. Brigham in "Family Correlates of Male Childhood Gender Disturbance," *The Journal of Genetic Psychology* 142 (1983), 31–42 report that "Significantly fewer male role models were found in the family backgrounds of the severely gender-disturbed boys" (p. 31), and that there were more emotional problems in the families of the most disturbed boys.

34. Cited in L. Ellis and A. Ames, *op.cit.* and R. Green, *op.cit.*

35. The Minority Report of the Presbyterian Church, footnote 22 on page 26 cites John Money as explicitly concluding, "...(T)here is no human evidence that prenatal hormonalization alone, independently of postnatal history, inexorably preordains ...[homosexuality]. Rather, neonatal antecedents may facilitate a homosexual...orientation, provided the postnatal determinants in the social and communicational history are also facilitative." In "Sin, Sickness, or Status? Homosexual Gender Identity and Psychoneuroendocrinology," *American Psychologists* 42 (1987), 384–399. This footnote in the Minority

Report concludes, "In other words, prenatal influences may provide a 'push' in the direction of homosexuality, but there is no conclusive evidence that this push is powerful enough to be considered determinative, and there is no evidence that this push is present for all homosexuals."

36. See, e.g., W. Ricketts, *op.cit.*, 71–76 and R. Green, *op.cit.*, 543–545.

37. See, e.g., I. Bieber, H. Dain, P. Vince, N. Drellich, H. Grand, R. Gundlach, M. Kremer, A. Rifin, C. Wilber and T. Bieber, *Homosexuality: A Psychoanalytic Study*, New York: Basic Books, 1962. Different theorists emphasize either the boy-mother or boy-father relationship and postulate different dynamics at work.

38. See C. Wolff, *Love Between Women*, New York: Harper and Row, 1971.

39. See M. Siegelman, "Kinsey and Others Quote Empirical Input" in L. Diamant, ed., *Male and Female Homosexuality: Psychological Approaches*, Washington: Hemisphere Books, 1987, 33–80.

40. For example, proponents of the prenatal hormone hypothesis would argue that all the research documenting problematic relations between pre-homosexual boys and their fathers, rather than proving that rejecting fathers cause homosexuality, instead reflects the tendencies for fathers to reject their gender-inappropriate sons.

41. For example, A. Bell, M. Weinberg and S. Hammersmith, *Sexual Preference: Its Development in Men and Women*, Bloomington: Indiana University Press, 1981.

42. See, e.g., M. Storms, "A Theory of Erotic Orientation Development," *Psychological Review* 88 (1981), 340–353.

43. Joseph Nicolosi, *Reparative Therapy of Male Homosexuality: A New Clinical Approach*, New Jersey: Jason Aronson, 1991. I believe that Nicolosi has irrevocably damaged his professional reputation by making uncritical and even slanderous comments in public about "facts" he has allegedly learned in therapy. I am very skeptical about Nicolosi's analysis of male homosexuality because of its simplistic explanation of origin. Nicolosi demonstrates a certain blindness to the complexities of this question and thus his theory should be viewed with a good deal of caution.

44. For Nicolosi, "gay" describes a contemporary sociopolitical identity and life-style that the non-gay homosexual does not endorse.

45. Cited in C. W. Griffin, M. J. Wirth and A. G. Wirth, "Parent-Child Relationships Do Not Affect Homosexuality" in *Homosexuality: Opposing Viewpoints, op.cit.,* 38–39.

46. *Ibid.,* 42.

47. For an excellent overview of various theories regarding causes of homosexuality, see John F. Harvey, "Some Recent Theories Concerning the Origins of Homosexuality," *The Homosexual Person,* San Francisco: Ignatius Press, 1987, 37–63. See also John C. Dwyer, "The Causes of Homosexuality," *Human Sexuality: A Christian View,* Kansas City: Sheed and Ward, 1987, 67–69.

48. See C. Socarids, *Homosexuality,* New York: Jason Aronson Publishers, 1978.

49. See H. Adams and E. Sturgis, "Status of Behavioral Reorientation Techniques in the Modification of Homosexuality: A Review," *Psychological Bulletin* 84 (1977), 1171–1188; and W. Masters and B. Johnson, *Homosexuality in Perspective,* Boston: Little, Brown and Co., 1979.

50. See E. Pattison and M. Pattison, "Ex-Gays: Religiously Mediated Change and Homosexuals," *American Journal of Psychiatry* 137 (1980), 1553–1562. See also Gerald D. Coleman, "Turning Gays 'Straight'?" Church 7 (1991), 44–46.

51. R. Green, *op.cit.,* 569.

52. See J. Yamamoto, ed., *The Crisis of Homosexuality,* Wheaton: Christianity Today/Victor Books, 1990.

53. See John H. Hampsch, C.M.S., "Straight Talk About Gays," *S.C.R.C. Vision,* February 1993, 1–6; and 11–12.

54. John F. Harvey, "Sexual Abstinence for the Homosexual Person," *Fellowship of Catholic Scholars Newsletter* 15 (1992), 20–22; citation at 20–21.

Chapter 3

1. Congregation for the Doctrine of the Faith, *Letter to the Bishops of the Catholic Church on the Pastoral Care of Homosexual Persons,* 1 October 1986, nn 6–7.

2. *Ibid.*, n 4.

3. *Ibid.*

4. *Ibid.*

5. *Ibid.*, n 5.

6. *Ibid.*

7. *Ibid.*

8. *Ibid.*, n 6.

9. *Ibid.*

10. *Ibid.*

11. *Ibid.*, n 7.

12. *Ibid.*

13. All biblical translations are from the *Revised Standard Version of the Bible*, New York: American Bible Society, RSV Old Testament, 1980 and RSV New Testament, 1973.

14. Victor Paul Furnish, "Homosexuality" in *The Moral Teaching of Paul*, Nashville: Abingdon Press, 1970, 52–82.

15. *Ibid.*, n 56.

16. *Letter*, *op.cit.*, n 6.

17. Lisa Sowle Cahill, *Women and Sexuality*, New York: Paulist Press, 1992, 20–21.

18. Dan Grippo, "The Vatican Can Cite Scripture for Its Purpose" in *The Vatican and Homosexuality, op.cit.*, 33.

19. John Boswell, *Christianity, Social Tolerance and Homosexuality*, Chicago: The University of Chicago Press, 1980.

20. *Ibid.*, 93.

21. *Ibid.*, 94.

22. *Ibid.*, 95.

23. We will rely heavily on Furnish for this biblical exegesis.

24. See John W. Howe, *Sex: Should We Change the Rules?*, Florida: Creation House, 1991, 33.

25. See, e.g., Grippo, *op.cit.*, 35–37.

26. John Boswell, *op. cit.*, 102.

27. *Ibid.*, 105.

28. See Furnish, *op.cit.*, 65–67.

29. Dio Chrysostom, *Discourse* LXXVII/LXXDIII.36

30. Philo, *On Abraham,* 135–136.

31. Seneca, *Moral Epistles XLVII*, "On Master and Slave," 7.

32. Robin Scroggs, *The New Testament and Homosexuality*, Philadelphia: Fortress Press, 1983, 99-122.

33. *A Greek-English Lexicon of the New Testament and Other Early Christian Literature*, ed., W.F. Arndt and F.W. Gingrich, 2nd ed., Chicago: University of Chicago Press, 1979, 488.

34. Furnish, *op.cit.*, 69.

35. John Boswell, *op. cit.*, 110.

36. Richard B. Hayes, "Relations Natural and Unnatural: A Response to John Boswell's Exegesis of Romans 1," *Journal of Religious Ethics* 14 (1986), 184–215. See John Boswell, *Christianity, Social Tolerance, and Homosexuality*, Chicago: University of Chicago Press, 1980.

37. Scroggs, *op.cit.*, 113.

38. *Ibid.*, 127.

39. I am grateful to Michael L. Barre, S.S., for his invaluable help with this scriptural section. Fr. Barre is currently the Editor of the *Catholic Biblical Quarterly Monograph Series.*

40. See, e.g., Grippo, *op.cit.*, 38–39; and Tom Horner, *Jonathan Loved David: Homosexuality in Biblical Times*, Philadelphia: Westminister Press, 1978.

41. *Ibid.* See Michael L. Barre's review of this book in the *Catholic Biblical Quarterly* 41 (1979), 463–465.

42. Horner maintains that Paul's "A Thorn in the Flesh" may have been "latent homosexuality."

43. For a good treatment of this subject, see Edward A. Malloy, *Homosexuality and the Christian Way of Life*, Washington, D.C.: University Press of America, 1981, 198–199. We will follow here Malloy's treatment of this subject.

44. D.S. Bailey concludes in *Homosexuality and the Western Christian Tradition* (London: Longman's, Green and Co., 1955) that "The homosexual interpretation of the friendship between David and

Jonathan...rests upon a very precarious basis" (p 56). Horner also explores the possibility of a homosexual relationship between Ruth and Naomi (pp 40–46). Naomi, the long-suffering widow, and Ruth, her widowed daughter-in-law, take a solemn vow never to desert each other. They even wish to be buried together. The problem with this kind of tentative probing is that the characters in the story are not presumed to be historical figures. As a result, there is no way of ascertaining a deeper level of truth beyond what the details of the story allow for.

45. *Ibid.*, 157.

46. John McNeill, *The Church and the Homosexual*, Boston: Beacon Press, 1993, 4th ed., 59–60. McNeil is here quoting Herman van de Spijker.

47. Letha Scanzoni and Virginia Ramey Mollenkott, *Is the Homosexual my Neighbor?*, New York: Harper and Row, 1978, 71–72.

48. See Sandra M. Schneiders, *The Revelatory Text: Interpreting the New Testament as Sacred Scripture*, San Francisco: HarperCollins, 1991.

49. Don Williams, *The Bond that Breaks: Will Homosexuality Split the Church?*, Los Angeles: BIM, 1978, 53.

50. R.A.F. MacKenzie, "Introduction to the Dogmatic Constitution on Divine Revelation" in *The Documents of Vatican II*, ed., W.M. Abbott, New York: America Press, 1966, 108–109.

Chapter 4

1. Louis J. Cameli, "Preaching and Teaching Sexuality: The Dilemmas and Possibilities," *Chicago Studies* 32 (1993), 54–63.

2. We will follow here Cameli's treatment of this subject, 54–57.

3. *Ibid.*, 54.

4. *Ibid.*, 55.

5. *Ibid.*, 56.

6. Lisa Sowle Cahill, *Between the Sexes*, Philadelphia: Fortress Press, 1985, 150–151.

7. *Summa Theologiae* II-II, 154, a 1, 12.

8. *Ibid.*, I, II, Q. 94, art. 3.

9. In his 1984 "Apostolic Exhortation on Reconciliation and Penance," Pope John Paul II revisits this Thomistic teaching: "(S)ome sins are intrinsically grave and mortal by reason of their matter. That is, there exists acts which, *per se* and in themselves, independently of circumstances, are always seriously wrong by reason of their object. These acts, if carried out with sufficient awareness and freedom, are always gravely sinful" (*Origins* 14 (1984), 433–458, n 17).

10. Walter G. Jeffko, "Processive Relationalism and Ethical Absolutes" in *Readings in Moral Theology*, ed., Charles E. Curran and Richard A. McCormick, vol. 1, New York: Paulist Press, 1979, 199–214; citation at 209.

11. Congregation for the Doctrine of the Faith, *Declaration on Certain Questions Concerning Sexual Ethics* (1975), n 59.

11a. John Paul II, *Evangelium Vitae*, Vatican City: Liberia Editrice Vaticana, 1995, 137–138.

12. Patrick J. Boyle, *Parvitas Materae In Sexto in Contemporary Thought*, New York: University Press of America, 1987, 95. See also Eduardus Genicot, *Theologiae Moralis Institutiones*, VIth edition, Vol. 1, Bruxellis: A. Dewit, 1909, 34.

13. Patrick J. Boyle, *Ibid.*, 102 and 105.

14. Thomas Aquinas, *Summa Theologiae*, vol. 20, "Pleasure," trans., Eric D'Arcy, London: Blackfriars, 1975 [1a 2ae, 31–39].

15. The key elements of this text in Latin read: "*Contingit enim in aliquo individuo corrumpi aliquod principiorum naturalium speciei; et sic id quod est contra naturam speciei, fieri per accidens naturale huic individuo; sicut huic aquae calefactae est naturale quod calefaciat. Ita igitur contingit quod id quod est contra naturam hominis, vel quantum ad rationem, vel quantum ad corporis conservationem, fiat huic homini connaturale, propter aliquam corruptionem naturae in eo existentem.*"

16. *Summa Theologiae*, I, II, Q. arts. 3 and 6.

17. National Conference of Catholic Bishops, Bishops' Committee on Pastoral Research and Practices, *Principles To Guide Confessors in Questions of Homosexuality*, Washington, D.C., National Conference of Catholic Bishops, 1973, 3.

18. See James J. Gill, "Homosexuality Today," *Human Development* 3 (1980), 16–25; M. Saghir and E. Robbins, *Male and Female Homosexuality*, Baltimore: Williams and Wilkins Co., 1973; and Alan P. Bell and Martin S. Weinberg, *Homosexualities*, New York: Simon and Schuster, 1978.

19. A. Kinsey, W. Pomeroy and C. Martin, *Sexual Behavior in the Human Male*, Philadelphia: W. B. Saunders, 1948, 639.

20. Principles To Guide Confessors, *op. cit.*, 4.

21. Marc Oraison, *The Homosexual Question*, New York: Harper and Row, 1977, 54.

22. *Principles, op.cit.*, 5. The italics are in the original text.

23. National Conference of Catholic Bishops, *Human Sexuality: A Catholic Perspective for Education and Lifelong Learning*, Washington, D.C.: United States Catholic Conference, 1990, 54.

24. National Conference of Catholic Bishops, *Sharing the Light of Faith: National Catechetical Directory for Catholics in the United States*, Washington, D.C., N.C.C.B., 1977, n 191.

25. Congregation for Catholic Education, *Educational Guidance in Human Love*, Washington, D.C., U.S.C.C., 1983, n 4.

26. *Ibid.*, nn 101–103.

27. *Principles, op.cit.*, 7.

28. *Ibid.*, 8.

29. *Ibid.*, 8–9.

30. *Ibid.*, 10–11.

31. *Ibid.*, 11.

32. *Ibid.*

33. *Ibid.*, 10.

34. *Ibid.*, 11.

35. *Ibid.*

36. For a fuller development of this subject, see *Ministry and Homosexuality in the Archdiocese of San Francisco*, San Francisco, Senate of Priests, 1983, 14–18.

37. See, e.g., John A. McHugh, O.P. and Charles J. Callan, O.P., *Moral Theology: A Complete Course, Based on St. Thomas Aquinas*

and the Best Modern Authorities, vol. I, New York: Joseph F. Wagner, Inc., 1958, 222, n 621.

38. John Paul II, *Apostolic Exhortation on the Family,* 1991, n 9. In n 8 of the closing homily of the 1980 Synod of Bishops, John Paul II made an important distinction between "a pedagogy, which takes into account a certain progression in accepting the plan of God, a doctrine proposed by the church, with all its consequences, in which the precept of living according to the same doctrine is contained; in which case there is not a question of a desire of keeping the law as merely an ideal to be achieved in the future, but rather of the mandate of Christ the Lord that difficulties constantly be overcome. Really, 'the process of gradualness' as it is called, cannot be applied unless someone accepts divine law with a sincere heart and seeks those goods that are protected and promoted by the same law. Thus, the so-called *lex gradualitatis* (law of gradualness) or gradual progress cannot be the same as *gradualitas legis* (the gradualness of the law), as if there were in divine law various levels or forms of precept for various persons and conditions."

39. See Rudolph Schnackenburg, *The Moral Teaching of the New Testament,* New York: Herder and Herder, 1965; and Celaus Spicq, *Théologie Morale du Nouveau Testament,* 2 vols., Paris: Gabalda, 1965.

40. Congregation for the Doctrine of the Faith, *Persona humana,* 1975, n 8.

41. *Ibid.*

42. National Conference of Catholic Bishops, *To Live in Christ Jesus: A Pastoral Reflection On the Moral Life,* 1976, n 7.

43. *Ibid.,* n 52.

44. *Ibid.,* 52.

45. *Principles, op.cit.,* 10.

46. See Gerald D. Coleman, *Human Sexuality: An All-Embracing Gift,* New York: Alba House, 1992, 21–22.

47. Jack Dominian, "Chastity," *The Tablet* 240 (1986), 7601. In light of a good deal of scriptural testimony (e.g., 1 Thessalonians 4:1–8; 1 Corinthians 6:18; and Colossians 3), chastity is a call to act

in accord with who we really are: transformed people who were once in darkness, but now are in the light of the Lord.

48. Congregation for the Doctrine of the *Faith, Letter to the Bishops of the Catholic Church on the Pastoral Care of Homosexual Persons*, 1986, n 3. The final paragraph of the *Letter* indicates that it was "approved" by Pope John Paul II "in an ordinary session" of the Congregation of the Doctrine of the Faith. This means that the *Letter* was approved *in forma communi*. This "form" of approval means that the pope, while not making the document his own (which would be *in forma specifica*), does indicate that the document is legitimate and authentic. But it does remain a document of the Congregation, and not a document of the pope himself. An authentic document of this kind carries significance independent of its intrinsic arguments by reason of the formal authority of the Apostolic See and the Congregation itself. This *Letter* is thus an act of the teaching church and should not simply be regarded as another theological opinion.

49. *Ibid.*

50. John R. Quinn, "Toward an Understanding of the Letter on the Pastoral Care of Homosexual Persons," *America* 156 (1987), 92–95 and 116.

51. On this point, see Lisa Sowle Cahill, *Between the Sexes*, New York: Paulist Press, 1985.

52. *Declaration on Certain Questions Concerning Sexual Ethics*, n 8.

53. *Letter, op.cit.*, n 3.

54. Archbishop John R. Quinn, *op.cit.*, 94. In a letter dated January 28, 1987, Cardinal Joseph Ratzinger wrote to Archbishop Quinn (173/74): "...It had always, naturally, been our hope that the Bishops upon receipt of the *Letter* addressed primarily to them, would welcome it as you have, drawing from it any pertinent guidelines for their local Church situation, and that they would recommend it to their clergy, religious and laity. May I express our gratitude to you then for your careful analysis and our hope that all the faithful entrusted to your care will profit from the clarity and pastoral sensitivity you have shown in this most sensitive matter."

55. P.A. van Gennip, "Pastoral Care of Homosexual Persons: Whose Definitions?" in *The Vatican and Homosexuality, op.cit.*,

66–80. P.A. van Gennip is General Secretary of the Catholic Council for Church and Society, an agency of the Roman Catholic hierarchy of the Netherlands.

56. *Ibid.*, 72–73.

57. Ronald Modras, "Pope John Paul II's Theology of the Body" in *The Vatican and Homosexuality, op.cit.*, 119–126.

58. Karol Wojtyla, "Personalizm Tomistyczny," *Znak* 13 (1961), 664–676; *The Acting Person*, Dordrecht, Holland/Boston: D. Reidel, 1979; and *Love and Responsibility*, New York: Farrar, Straus and Giroux, 1981.

59. Modras, *op. cit.*, 120.

60. *Letter*, n 10.

61. *Ibid.*, n 11.

62. *Ibid.*, n 12.

63. Lisa Sowle Cahill deals with this point explicitly and superbly in *Between the Sexes, op.cit.*

64. *Letter*, n 12.

65. *Ibid.*, n 10.

66. *Ibid.*, n 17.

67. John F. Harvey has posed this question: "If homosexual orientation is an objective disorder…, then are not homosexual Catholics obliged to seek to change their sexual orientation?" He replies: "…I believe that the person is bound to sexual abstinence by the gospel precept of chastity, …but it seems the moral law does not deposit any obligation to take steps to change orientation. However desirable this change is, in our present state of knowledge we can give no guarantee that if one were to follow a certain program and plan of life to change orientation, that it will always happen." See John F. Harvey, "Sexual Abstinence for the Homosexual Person," *Fellowship of Catholic Scholars Newsletter* 15 (1992), 20–22; citation at 20.

68. *Some Considerations Concerning the Catholic Response to Legislative Proposals on the Non-Discrimination of Homosexual Persons*, Foreword. The first version read, "…legislation has been proposed in some American states which would make discrimination on the basis of sexual orientation illegal." *Origins* 11(1992), 175–177.

69. *Ibid.*

70. *Ibid.*, n 6.

71. *Ibid.*, n 9.

72. *Ibid.*, n 15. The first version did not include the words "such things as...."

73. *Ibid.*, n 16. Most importantly, the first version did not contain the words "family life."

74. This same point has been made numerous times in church documents and most notably in the Holy See's 1983 *Charter of the Rights of the Family*. Pope John Paul II reiterated the family's centrality in society in *Familiaris Consortio* (1981) and the concern is sharply expressed in *Educational Guidance in Human Love*, the 1983 document from the Congregation for Catholic Education: "The family has an affective dignity which is suited to making acceptable without trauma the most delicate realities and to integrating them harmoniously in a balanced and rich personality." (n 48)

75. *Letter to the Bishops of the Catholic Church on the Pastoral Care of Homosexual Persons, op.cit.*, n 17.

76. *Considerations*, n 11.

77. *Ibid.*, n 12. This number adds, "Thus it is accepted that the states may restrict the exercise of rights, e.g., in the case of contagious or mentally ill persons, in order to protect the common good." "Culpable behavior" refers to willful behavior: i.e., a person not only knows of the objective evil of an action, but fully assents to carrying out this action.

78. Number 13 of the *Considerations* raises concern about the homosexual orientation "as a positive source of human rights, e.g., in respect to so-called affirmative action, the filling of quotas in hiring practices." From the late 1960s onward, laws and guidelines have been enacted in the U.S. that call for "affirmative action" to increase the numbers of women and ethnic minorities in fields from which they have traditionally been excluded or limited to low-level, menial positions. These have even included actual quotas that an employer needs to meet to comply with the law. However, none of these programs have contained any measure to increase the number of homosexuals in any firm or industry, although there have been consent

decrees which various government agencies have agreed to which include affirmative action policies for gay and lesbian persons. The *Considerations* endorse this posture by claiming that while such qualities as race, ethnic background (n 10), sex and age (n 14) do not constitute a reason for discrimination, homosexuals should not be designated as a special group for affirmative action. Anti-discrimination laws indicate that it is wrong to discriminate in employment and housing against an individual on the grounds of sexual orientation. Affirmative action laws, on the other hand, create a special and privileged group, usually with specific time-tables and targets to meet quotas in employment and housing. It is this latter category which the *Considerations* do not support.

79. The scriptural texts prefatory to Article 6, and so to "Chastity and Homosexuality" are: "Thou shalt not commit adultery" (Exodus 20:14) and Matthew 5:27–28, "You have heard that it was said 'You shall not commit adultery,' but I say to you that everyone who looks at a woman lustfully has already committed adultery with her in his heart."

80. Genesis 19:1–29; Romans 1:24–27; 1 Corinthians 6:10; and 1 Timothy 1:10.

81. *Persona Humana*, n 8.

82. We will follow here closely the presentation of this subject by James R. Pollock in "Teaching in Transition" in *The Vatican and Homosexuality, op.cit.*, 179–188.

83. Congregation for Catholic Education, *Educational Guidance in Human Love, op.cit.*, n 19.

84. James R. Pollock, *op.cit.*, 180.

Chapter 5

1. Richard Woods, *Another Kind of Love: Homosexuality and Spirituality*, Chicago: The Thomas More Press, 1977, 18. In a provocative article "Healing Homophobia: Volunteerism and 'Sacredness' in AIDS," Philip M. Cayal writes, "It is from this position of marginality and fear that gays have created a radical and authentic religious experience....By willfully identifying with PWAs as carepartners, gay/AIDS volunteerism becomes religious activity because it brings the volunteer back to basics, back to the self in a

binding, accepting way." *Journal of Religion and Health* 31 (1992), 113–128; citation at 118.

2. John E. Fortunato, *Embracing the Exile: Healing Journeys for Gay Christians*, New York: The Seabury Press, 1982, 17.

3. Craig O'Neill and Kathleen Ritter, *Coming Out Within: Stages of Spiritual Awakening for Lesbians and Gay Men, San Francisco: Harper*, 1992. See also Kevin Fedarko, "Coming Out in the Country," Time 142 (1993), 35.

4. David Tuller, "Gay Group Says Attacks in U.S. Rose in 1992," *San Francisco Chronicle*, March 12, 1993, A21.

5. See Sara Butler, "Personhood, Sexuality and Complementarity in the Teaching of Pope John Paul II," *Chicago Studies* 32 (1993), 43–53. We will follow here Butler's treatment of this subject.

6. John Paul II, *Original Unity of Man and Woman, Blessed Are the Pure of Heart and The Theology of Marriage and Celibacy*, Boston: St. Paul Edition, 1981, 1983 and 1986.

7. *Ibid.*, 49.

8. See Robert A. Connor, "The Person as Resonating Existential," *American Catholic Philosophical Quarterly* 66 (1992), 39.

9. Bishop Dr. Walter Kasper, *The God of Jesus Christ*, New York: Paulist Press, 1984, 306.

10. See "Claiming Our Identity," *The CMI Journal*, 1993, 44–48.

11. Carl G. Jung, *The Collected Works*, trans., R. F. C. Hall, New York: Pantheon, 1959, 87. Cardinal Joseph Bernardin made this same point in 1984 when he wrote that "Sexuality is also intrinsically relational—it draws people together. This is true, incidently, not only in a narrow genital sense but in a broader sense. Sexuality, broadly conceived, might be understood as a capacity for entering into relationships with others" ("Archdiocese Says Gay Love Acceptable, Sex Acts Not") *Chicago Sun-Times*, July 20, 1980, 5).

12. Rudolf Otto, *The Idea of the Holy*, London: Oxford University, 1957.

13. Herman-Emiel Mertens, *Not the Cross, But the Crucified: An Essay in Soteriology*, Louvain Theological and Pastoral Monographs 11, Leuven: Peeters, 1990, 155.

14. See Gary Remafedi, "Homosexual Youth: A Challenge to Contemporary Society," *Journal of the American Medical Association* 258 (1987), 222–225. We will closely follow here Remafedi's treatment.

15. Douglas C. Kimmel, "Adult Development and Aging: A Gay Perspective," *Journal of Social Issues* 34 (1978), 113–130.

16. Cited in "Three Passages of Maturity" in *A Challenge to Love*, ed., Robert Nugent, New York: Crossroad, 1983, article by James D. Whitehead and Evelyn Eaton Whitehead, 174–188; citation at 179.

17. G.D. Ramsey, "The Sexual Development of Boys," *American Journal of Psychology* 56 (1943), 217–234.

18. F.W. Finger, "Sex Beliefs and Practices Among Male College Students," *Journal of Abnormal Social Psychology* 42 (1947), 57–67.

19. R.C. Sorenson, *Adolescent Sexuality in Contemporary America*, New York: Work Publishing, 1973.

20. Unfortunately, Sorenson reached the conclusion that homosexuality is "generally an adult rather than an adolescent phenomenon in contemporary American society," because only a small percentage of adolescents had reported a homosexual experience in the two months preceding the interview. Unhappily Sorenson's viewpoint has been reflected in a number of books and periodicals to the present time.

21. We will follow here the treatment of this subject by Kevin R. Gogin, NFCC, "Assisting the Gay/Lesbian/Bisexual Student with Coming Out Issues," San Francisco: Support Services for Gay and Lesbian Youth, 1992.

22. See T.H. Sauerman, *Coming Out to Your Parents*, Washington, D.C.: Parents and Friends of Lesbians and Gays (FLAG), 1991.

23. Eric Marcus, *Is It A Choice?*, San Francisco: Harper, 1993, 29 and 33.

24. Scott A. Hunt, "An Unspoken Tragedy: Suicide Among Gay and Lesbian Youth," *Christopher Street* 169 (1992), 28–30.

25. DHHS Secretary Louis Sullivan, under pressure from conservative religious and family groups, later repudiated the report, precluding further government research on the issue of sexuality and youth suicide.

26. Congregation for the Doctrine of the Faith, *Letter to the Bishops of the Catholic Church on the Pastoral Care of Homosexual*

Persons, 1 October 1986, printed in the U.S.A. by the Daughters of Saint Paul under the title On the *Pastoral Care of Homosexual Persons*, 1986, n 10.

27. National Conference of Catholic Bishops, *Human Sexuality*, Washington, D.C.: United States Catholic Conference Inc., 1990, 55–56.

28. See William A. Henry III, "To 'Out' or Not to 'Out'," *Time* 138 (1981), 17.

29. Eric Marcus, *Is It A Choice?, op.cit.*, 154. In his novel *Dancer from the Dance* (New York: A Plume Book, 1978), Andrew Holleran details how a certain homosexual population has been extremely promiscuous, virtually in an addictive fashion.

30. See, e.g., D. Richard Laws, ed., *Relapse, Prevention with Sex Offenders*, New York: The Guilford Press, 1989; Gerald O'Collins, *The Second Journey: Spiritual Awareness and the Mid-Life Crisis*, New York: Paulist Press, 1978; and Janice Keller Phelps and Alan E. Nourse, *The Hidden Addiction And How To Get Free*, Boston: Little, Brown, and Co., 1986.

31. Patrick Carnes, *Out of the Shadows: Understanding Sexual Addiction*, Minneapolis: CompCare Publications, 1983. We will follow Carnes' treatment of sexual addiction in this section. However, for an extremely important critique of Carnes' methodology, especially regarding addiction toward pedophilia and ephebophilia, see John Bancroft, ed., "Annual Review of Sex Research," vol. III, A Publication of The Society for the Scientific Study of Sex, 1992.

32. See M. MacAuliffe and R. MacAuliffe, *The Essentials of Chemical Dependency*, Minneapolis: American Chemical Dependency Society, 1975.

33. The advantage of this SAFE (Secret, Abusive, Feelings, Empty) formula that Carnes has articulated is that it is built on the basic concept of addiction and is in the spirit of the Twelve Steps. It requires a ruthless honesty given that the addict's sanity is at stake. Using a group or sponsor as an ongoing reality check can help keep the addict "safe." At the same time, however, as the "Annual Review of Sex Research" clearly points out, certain types of addiction cannot be handled in a group and need other types of significant therapy: e.g., pedophilia and ephebophilia.

34. Cited in David Gelman, "Was It Illness or Immorality?" *Newsweek*, June 11, 1990, 55.

35. See Barbara Dolan, "Do People Get Hooked On Sex?" *Time*, 4 June 1990, 72; Mark F. Schwartz and William S. Brasted, "Sexual Addiction," *Current Trends* 19 (1985), 103–107; Philip Yancey, "Not Naked Enough," *Christianity Today* 34 (1990), 48; Robert J. Barth and Bill N. Kinder, "The Mislabeling of Sexual Impulsivity," *Journal of Sex and Marital Therapy* 13 (1987), 15-23; Patrick J. Carnes, "Sexual Addiction: Implications for Spiritual Formation," *Studies Informative of Spirituality* 8 (1987), 165–174; Martin P. Levine and Richard R. Troiden, "The Myth of Sexual Compulsivity," *The Journal of Sex Research* 25 (1988), 347–363; Lester Pincu, "Sexual Compulsivity in Gay Men: Controversy and Treatment," *Journal of Counselling and Development* 68 (1989), 63–66; Mark R. Laaser, "Sexual Addiction and Clergy," *Pastoral Psychology* 39 (1991), 213-135; and Ralph H. Earle and Gregory M. Crow, "Sexual Addiction: Understanding and Treating the Phenomenon," *Contemporary Family Therapy: An International Journal* 12 (1990), 89–104.

36. Andrew Sullivan, "The Politics of Homosexuality," *The New Republic*, May 10, 1993, 24–37.

37. *Ibid.*, 37. Legal protection for homosexual couples in European nations varies widely. Five countries outlaw discrimination against gay people: Denmark, France, Netherlands, Norway and Sweden. Everywhere else, discrimination is *de facto* law. DENMARK: civil marriage between same-sex couples is lawful and includes most marriage rights except for child adoption. SWEDEN: cohabiting same-sex couples have most of the legal rights of married heterosexual couples. NETHERLANDS: thirty local authorities allow civil marriage by same-sex couples. Most civil marriages are not recognized under national law. Some corporations and public institutions do recognize the marriages. ITALY: one city, Bologna, has agreed to recognize same-sex partnerships. Rights are basically restricted to same-sex couples having the same eligibility for public housing as married heterosexual couples. BRITAIN: there is no recognition of gay and lesbian relationships in Britain, where discrimination is open. The age of consent for homosexual behavior is 21—the highest in Europe. Lesbian and gay people are banned from membership in the armed forces. Employment tribunals have ruled an employee can be fired for

reason of being a homosexual. Lesbian mothers and gay fathers are often deemed by courts to be unsuitable parents by reason of their homosexuality. FRANCE: age of consent is 15 for homosexuals and heterosexuals. Antidiscrimination laws protect lesbian and gay people in employment and access to goods and service. Homosexuals can openly serve in the armed forces. GERMANY: age of consent is 14 for heterosexuals and lesbians; (former) West Germany, 18 for gay men, (former) East Germany, 14 for gay men—current legal unification may result in a common age of consent of 16. They can serve in the armed forces. Brandenburg state government has a draft constitution that prohibits discrimination on the grounds of sexual orientation. Occasionally, citizens of other countries seeking asylum in fear of their lives on the grounds of homosexual persecution, such as from Iran, are granted resident rights in Germany. See Peter Tatchell, *Europe in the Pink*, London: Gay Men's Press, 1992.

38. *Ibid.*

39. Eric Marcus, *op.cit.*, 83.

40. An August 27, 1992 *Newsweek* poll revealed that while a majority of Americans were willing to support such rights as health insurance and inheritance rights for gay partners, 58% were against legally sanctioned marriages, and 61% were against adoption rights for homosexuals.

41. Cited in William Dudley, ed., *Homosexuality: Opposing Viewpoints*, San Diego: Greenhaven Press, Inc., 1993, 160.

42. See Patrick Downes, "The Folly of Same-Sex 'Marriages,'" *Hawaii Catholic Herald* 56 (1993), 10–11. We will follow here the treatment of this subject by Patrick Downes.

43. See Gerald D. Coleman, S.S., "Living Together and Marriage," *Church* 6 (1990), 45–46.

Chapter 6

1. Jonathan Rauch, "Beyond Oppression," *The New Republic*, May 10, 1993, 18–23.

2. *Ibid.*, 18.

3. Bill Turque, "Gays Under Fire," *Newsweek*, September 14, 1992, 35–40.

4. John Coleman, "Two Unanswered Questions" in *The Vatican and Homosexuality*, New York: Crossroad, 1988, 59–65; citation at 63.

5. Cardinal Joseph Bernardin, "I Too Struggle," *Commonweal*, December 26, 1986, 683.

6. John Coleman, *op.cit.*, 63.

7. *Ibid.*, 64; the quotation is from the National Conference of Catholic Bishops, *To Live In Christ Jesus*, Washington, D.C., November 11, 1976, n 4.

8. Eric Marcus, *Is It A Choice?*, San Francisco: Harper, 1993, 140–141.

9. Cited in Eric Marcus, *ibid.*, 114. It should be noted that major corporations in the U.S., such as Levi Strauss, AT & T, IBM, Disney, and Citicorp have adopted policies opposing discrimination against gay and lesbian people in hiring and promotions.

10. Cited in Eric Marcus, *ibid.*, 181.

11. Andrew Sullivan, "The Politics of Homosexuality," *The New Republic*, May 10, 1993, 24–37. We will follow here Sullivan's analysis.

12. On this point specifically, see Jonathan Rauch, "Beyond Oppression," *op.cit.*

13. Warren Johansson, "Discrimination" in *Encyclopedia of Homosexuality*, vol. 1, ed., Wayne R. Dynes, New York and London: Garland Publishing, Inc., 1990, 320–323.

14. United States federal government has since the 1940s maintained that homosexual conduct is immoral and that homosexuality in itself establishes unfitness for employment. The argument is that homosexual conduct is scandalous and disgraceful and requires punitive policies on the part of the executive. While more recent court decisions have somewhat limited the Civil Service Commission in this area, they leave open the possibility that homosexual conduct might justify dismissal where interference with efficiency could be proved. The military establishment has almost uniformly been successful in defeating suits brought against it by homosexual and lesbian members of the armed forces threatened with discharge and often loss of benefits as well.

15. We will follow here the presentation of this question by Marshall Kirk and Hunter Madsen in *After the Ball*, New York: Doubleday, 1989, part 1.

16. The Aesthetic Realist Movement is an example of this myth: see Sheldon Kranz, ed., *The H Persuasion*, New York: Definition Press, 1971.

17. There has been a long history which has taught that homosexuality is a crazed result of masturbation: i.e., during adolescence, receiving too much sexual pleasure by one's own hand leaves one "liking" one's sexual "apparatus" and also others whose genitalia are like one's own. The well-respected sexologist Krafft-Ebing wrote, e.g., "Very frequently the cause of such temporary aberration (i.e., homosexuality) is masturbation and its results in youthful individuals...." For a more complete treatment of this subject, see Arno Karlen, *Sexuality and Homosexuality*, New York: W. W. Norton and Co., Inc., 1971.

18. W.W. Hudson and W. A. Ricketts, "A Strategy for the Measurement of Homophobia," *Journal of Homosexuality* 5 (1980) 357–372. See also Helen H. Marble, *Homophobia: Attitudes and Behaviors Among Seminarians*, an N.M.A. Thesis for the Department of Psychology at East Carolina University, May 1991. We will follow here Marble's treatment of this subject.

19. See D. Bhugra, "Homophobia: A Review of the Literature," *Sexual and Marital Therapy* 9 (1987), 169–177; M. Forstein, "Homophobia: An Overview," *Psychiatric Annals* 18 (1988), 33–36; and G.M. Herek, "Can Functions Be Measured? A New Perspective on the Functional Approach to Attitudes," *Social Psychology Quarterly* 50 (1987), 285–303. Hudson and Ricketts restricted their definition of homophobia to the affective realm, and they developed an instrument to measure homophobia as an emotional entity. S. Patel in *Homophobia: Personality, Emotional, and Behavioral Correlates*, an M.A. Thesis for East Carolina University in 1989, on the other hand, focused on behavioral elements with the development of a scale that attempts to move in the direction of assessing the behavioral components of homophobia. The simultaneous use of both scales can add depth to our understanding of the homophobic individual.

20. See R.A. Bouton, P.E. Gallagher, P.A. Garlinghouse, T. Leal,

L.D. Rosenstein and R.K. Young, "Scales For Measuring Fear of AIDS and Homophobia," *Journal of Personality Assessment* 51 (1987), 606–614.

21. S.D. Johnson in "Factors Related to Intolerance of AIDS Victims," *Journal for the Scientific Study of Religion* 26 (1987), 105–110 has attempted to demonstrate that fundamentalists tend to be of low education levels.

22. See J.E. Aguero, L. Bloch and D. Byrne, "The Relationships Among Sexual Beliefs, Attitudes, Experience, and Homophobia," *Journal of Homosexuality* 10 (1984), 95–107.

23. Mary Beth Danielson and Leonard Lamberg, "Gay Godfathers: How to Stop Homophobia at Home," *The Other Side*, January-February 1991, 26–28.

24. See Gregory Herek, "Discrimination" in *Encyclopedia of Homosexuality, op.cit.*, 552–555.

25. John Reid, *The Best Little Boy in the World*, New York: Ballantine Books, 1976, 37–38.

26. Congregation for the Doctrine of the Faith, *Letter to the Bishops of the Catholic Church On the Pastoral Care of Homosexual Persons*, October 1986, n 10.

27. See Warren J. Blumenfeld, ed., *Homophobia: How We All Pay the Price*, Boston: Beacon Press, 1992.

28. Randy Shilts, *Conduct Unbecoming: Gays and Lesbians in the U.S. Military*, New York: St. Martin's Press, 1993, 3–4.

29. According to a July 1993 Gallup Poll, 58% of the public supports President Clinton's policy; and majority support for the policy is found among all major subgroups of the population. This general public endorsement represents a major turnabout in public opinion. Those who prefer to completely end the ban on gays in the military support Clinton's compromise policy 57% to 41%.

30. We will follow here the main lines of the article by Gerald D. Coleman, "Homosexuals in the Military: Policy and Morality," *Church* 9 (1993), 20–23. Eric Marcus comments, "When I first began working on *Making History*...I thought, like most other gay people, that the gay rights movement began in June 1969 with a riot that followed a routine police raid at the Stonewall Inn, a gay bar in

New York City's Greenwich Village. Soon after I started my research, I discovered that by the time of the Stonewall riot, there was already a national, active movement of more than forty gay and lesbian organizations. Though the Stonewall riot was not the beginning, it was, without question, a major turning point in the struggle. It dramatically energized the gay and lesbian rights movement and inspired the formation of scores of new gay and lesbian rights groups across the country." *In Is It A Choice?, op.cit.,* 180-181. For a listing of many of these groups, see Eric Marcus, 122–123.

31. See Catherine S. Manegold, "The Odd Place of Homosexuality in the Military," *The New York Times,* April 18, 1993, 1 and 3. We will follow here Manegold's presentation.

32. Gay rights activists first challenged the U. S. military's ban on gay and lesbian people in 1964, when a handful of protestors picketed the Whitehall Induction Center in New York City, demanding that homosexuals be allowed to enlist. In 1975, Sergeant Leonard Matlovich and Ensign Copey Berg, both of whom were being discharged because they were gay, brought the first two lawsuits against the military in a bid to retain their jobs and overturn the military's antigay policy. Many cases have been brought since, including the challenge made by Petty Officer Keefe Meinhold, who was discharged in 1992 after stating on national television that he was a homosexual. His case was decided in January 1993 by a federal judge in California who ruled that the military ban on homosexuals is unconstitutional. The judge, Terry J. Hatter, Jr., permanently enjoined the military services from discharging or denying enlistment to gay people "in the absence of sexual conduct which interferes with the military mission." He then ordered the Navy to reinstate Keefe Meinhold permanently. In his order Judge Hatter wrote: "Gays and lesbians have served and continue to serve in the United States military with honor, pride, dignity, and loyalty. The Department of Defense's justifications for its policy banning gays and lesbians from military service are based on cultural myths and false stereotypes. These justifications are baseless and very similar to the reason offered to keep the military racially segregated in the 1940s." Cited in Marcus, *Is It A Choice?, op.cit.,* 11.

Chapter 7

1. Eric Marcus, *Is It A Choice?*, San Francisco: Harper, 1993, 118–119. The World Health Organization now calculates that HIV will infect up to forty million people—men and women, adults and children, straight and gay—world wide by the year 2000. AIDS is caused by HIV, a virus, which is in the blood, semen, or vaginal fluids of an infected person. HIV can penetrate mucous membranes that line the vagina, mouth, and other parts of the body. So if one woman has the virus, e.g., she carries it in her vaginal fluids. If her sexual partner gets some of these vaginal fluids in her vagina or mouth, it's possible for her to become infected with HIV. See also Philip M. Kayal, "Healing Homophobia: Volunteerism and 'Sacredness' in AIDS," *Journal of Religion and Health* 31 (1992), 113–128.

2. William A. Henry III, "An Identity Forged in Flames," *Time* August 3, 1992, 35–37.

3. We will follow here the presentation of this subject by Ward Houser, "AIDS" in *Encyclopedia of Homosexuality*, vol. 1, ed., Wayne R. Dynes, New York/London: Garland Publishing, Inc., 1990, 29–32. See also Mark Caldwell, "The Long Shot: Why We Don't Have An AIDS Vaccine," *Discover* 14 (1993), 61–69. We will also cite throughout this chapter an excellent paper written but not yet published by Jon Fuller, S.J., M.D., *Clergy and Religious and the AIDS Epidemic* (August 1993).

4. In most countries the American acronym has been used, but French-speaking nations prefer SIDA (*Syndrome d'Immunodeficience Acquise*); SIDA is also the Spanish acronym.

5. *The New York Times*, November 20, 1986, 1. See also Sandra Panem, *AIDS Bureaucracy*, Cambridge: Harvard University Press, 1988; "The Ethical Response to AIDS," *America* 158 (1988), 135–171; and "The Moral Dimension of AIDS," William C. Spohn, *Theological Studies* 49 (1988), 89–109.

6. See *AIDS: What the Church Is Saying and Doing*, Richard Dunphy, Missouri: Liguori Publications, 1988, 4–8.

7. Pope John Paul II, N.C. *News Service*, May 1, 1989, 7. A number of authors have indicated that AIDS has a "twin disease" referred to as AFRAIDS, Acute Fear Regarding AIDS: i.e., AFRAIDS is unwarranted anxiety about transmission of the virus. Some people are para-

lyzed with fear as a result of misconceptions and myths about AIDS and the transmission of the virus, and this fear can lead sometimes to paranoia and isolation.

8. See Walter J. Smith, *AIDS: Living and Dying with Hope*, New York: Paulist Press, 1988, 40.

9. United States Catholic Conference, Administrative Board, "The Many Faces of AIDS: A Gospel Response," *Origins* 17 (1987), 482–489.

10. *Ibid.*, 484.

11. *The Pope Speaks*, September 17, 1987, 401–403.

12. National Conference of Catholic Bishops, *Called to Compassion and Responsibility: A Response to the HIV/AIDS Crisis, Origins* 19 (1989), 422–434.

13. See *A Sense of Sexuality*, Evelyn Eaton Whitehead and James D. Whitehead, New York: Doubleday, 1989, 286–299.

14. Cindy Riskin, Matt Herron and Deborah Zemke, *The Quilt: Stories from the NAMES Project*, New York: Pocketbooks, 1988, 7.

15. Congregation for the Doctrine of the Faith, *Letter to the Bishops of the Catholic Church On the Pastoral Care of Homosexual Persons*, 1986, n 3. See also "Toward an Understanding of the Letter on the Pastoral Care of Homosexual Persons," Archbishop John R. Quinn, *America* 156 (1987), 92–95, 116.

16. Cardinal Joseph Bernardin, "The Church's Response to the AIDS Crisis," *Origins* 16 (1986), 383.

17. Centers for Disease Control, "Mortality Attributable to HIV Infection/AIDS—United States, 1981–1990" in *Morbidity and Mortality Weekly Report* 40 (1991), 41–44.

18. Centers for Disease Control, "AIDS in Women—United States," *Morbidity and Mortality Weekly Report* 39 (1990), 845–846.

19. Jon D. Fuller in "AIDS and the Church: A Stimulus to Our Theologizing," Cambridge: Weston School of Theology, 1991, points out that it is critical to note the differential impact of HIV upon persons of color. A disproportionate share of the burden is being borne by women of color, especially by black women, and by their children. By 1988, among children aged 1-4 in New York and New Jersey, AIDS was the number one cause of death among Hispanic children and

number two among black children. In the last decade in this country we have witnessed more than 100,000 deaths from AIDS; one-third of them occurred during 1990 alone.

20. In this section, we will follow the treatment of this subject in "HIV/AIDS and the Church" in Gerald D. Coleman, *Human Sexuality An All-Embracing Gift*, New York: Alba House, 1992, 369–404.

21. In *The Many Faces of AIDS* this is footnote 7 and refers to Augustine's *De ordine* ii. 4.12; and Thomas Aquinas' *De regimine principium* iv. 14 and *Summa theologiae* I-II. 96.2; 101, 1ad2; II-II, 10.11. Part of the "unofficial translation" of the *Summa* citation is, "Although God is omnipotent and good in the highest degree, nevertheless he permits certain evil things to develop in the universe, which he would be able to prevent except that, if these things were taken away greater goods would be eliminated and even greater evils would follow as a consequence. So also in human governance, those who govern rightly tolerate certain evils lest certain goods be impeded or also lest some greater evil be obtained...." This footnote also makes reference to various classic authors regarding the toleration of the lesser evil (Dugrey and Zalba). Reference is also made to Pope Pius XII's *Ci riesce* of December 6, 1953.

22. See, e.g., "National Federation of Catholic Physicians' Guilds Proposed Position Paper: Statement on Prevention of AIDS by Condoms," *Linacre Quarterly* 55 (1988), 12–15.

23. *Called to Compassion, op.cit.*, IV:3.

24. Jon D. Fuller, *op.cit.*, 10.

25. See Gerald D. Coleman, "Condoms and the Teaching on the Lesser of Two Evils," *Church* 9 (1990), 49–50.

26. National Conference of Catholic Bishops, *Pastoral Care of the Sick: Rites of Anointing and Viaticum, in The Rites of the Catholic Church*, New York: Pueblo Publishing Co., 1983, 593–740; citation at n 2.

27. There is no question that the God of the Old Testament images forth a certain righteous anger that blazes outrightly against the unrepentant and the hard-hearted: e.g., Adam and Eve; Sodom and Gomorrah; and Lot's wife. Psalm 99:8 reflects, "For them you were a God who forgives; yet you punished all their offenses." However, the God of the Old Testament is primarily covenantal who never breaks

off conversation with the People of Israel, despite their multiple infidelities and sinfulness. Moreover, the book of Job teaches that the human person is never fully in a position to completely understand God's ways or motivations. Ecclesiastes 5:1 underlines this point, "Be in no hurry to speak; do not hastily declare yourself before God; for God is in heaven, you on earth." In the New Testament, Jesus reveals a truly forgiving God and proclaims his graciousness, holiness and goodness. God's anger is directed principally toward those who see themselves as righteous. Most importantly, Jesus nowhere connects human misfortune with either sin or divine anger. See Michael McCabe, "AIDS and the God of Wrath," *The Furrow* 38 (1987), 8–14.

28. John Paul II, "The Cross of Suffering," July 8, 1980, cited in James D. Schall, *Sacred in All Its Forms*, 108.

29. John Paul II, *On the Christian Meaning of Human Suffering*, Washington, D.C.: United States Catholic Conference, 1984, nn 1–8.

30. John Paul II, "Every Human Death a Reflection of the Death of Christ," *L'Osservatore Romano* 15 (1985), 3–4.

31. John Paul II, "Death and Eternity," *L'Osservatore Romano* 45 (1988), 5. See also Psalm 27:1–4.

32. Elisabeth Kübler-Ross, AIDS: *The Ultimate Challenge*, New York: Macmillan Co., 1987. In *The Screaming Room* (Avon: Oaktree Publications, 1986), Margaret Peabody provides many insights into the problems of helping someone with HIV/AIDS to die in a dignified manner. See also "Death is Swallowed Up by Life," Hans Urs von Balthasar, *Communio* 14 (1987), 49–54.

33. St. Gregory the Great, *Moral Reflections on Job, Sources Chrétiennes*, 212.

34. Archbishop John Roach, "Further Development of AIDS Ministry," *Origins* 23 (1988), 380.

35. Pope Paul VI, *On Christian Joy*, Washington, D.C.: United States Catholic Conference, 1975, 8.

36. *Pastoral Care of the Sick: Rites of Anointing and Viaticum*, op.cit., nn 1,5,32.

37. These were the words of John Paul II at the anointing of the sick service at Southwark Cathedral, London, on May 28, 1982.

Chapter 8

1. See Craig R. Koester, "The Bible and Sexual Boundaries," *Lutheran Quarterly*, Winter 1993, 375–390.

2. CDF *Letter to the Bishops...On the Pastoral Care of Homosexual Persons, op. cit.*, n 16.

3. N.C.C.B., *Human Sexuality, op. cit.*, 56.

Index